WOMEN'S PHILOSOPHIES OF EDUCATION

THINKING THROUGH OUR MOTHERS

D0218057

Edited by

Connie Titone
The College of New Jersey

Karen E. Maloney
Harvard University

Merrill,
an imprint of Prentice Hall
Upper Saddle River, New Jersey   Columbus, Ohio

Library of Congress Cataloging-in-Publication Data

Women's philosophies of education: thinking through our mothers / by Connie Titone, Karen E. Maloney
     p. cm.
    Includes bibliographical references.
    ISBN 0-13-618042-6
    1. Women—Education—United States—History. 2. Women in education—United States. 3. Women educators—United States—Biography.   I. Titone, Connie. II. Maloney, Karen E.
    LC1752.T46   1999
    371.822—DC21   98-26476
                                             CIP

Editor: Debra A. Stollenwerk
Production Editor: Mary Harlan
Photo Coordinator: Patty Carro/Carol Sykes
Design Coordinator: Diane C. Lorenzo
Text Design and Production Coordination: Custom Editorial Productions, Inc.
Cover Designer: Ceri Fitzgerald
Cover Art: © Stephen R. Schildbach
Production Manager: Pamela D. Bennett
Director of Marketing: Kevin Flanagan
Marketing Manager: Suzanne Stanton
Marketing Coordinator: Krista Groshong

This book was set in Palatino by Custom Editorial Productions, Inc., and was printed and bound by R. R. Donnelley & Sons Company. The cover was printed by Phoenix Color Corp.

 © 1999 by Prentice-Hall, Inc.
Simon & Schuster/A Viacom Company
Upper Saddle River, New Jersey 07458

Photo Credits: All photos are copyrighted by the individuals or companies listed. P. 10: National Portrait Gallery, London, engraving by Marais le jeune; p. 48: University of Puerto Rico; p. 74: Moorland-Spingarn Research Center, Howard University; p. 98: Schlesinger Library/Radcliffe College; p. 150: Thomas Martin; p. 180: Donna Dietrich.

Printed in the United States of America

10 9 8 7 6 5 4 3 2

ISBN: 0-13-618042-6

Prentice-Hall International (UK) Limited, *London*
Prentice-Hall of Australia Pty. Limited, *Sydney*
Prentice-Hall Canada Inc., *Toronto*
Prentice-Hall Hispanoamericana, S. A., *Mexico*
Prentice-Hall of India Private Limited, *New Delhi*
Prentice-Hall of Japan, Inc., *Tokyo*
Simon & Schuster Asia Pte. Ltd., *Singapore*
Editora Prentice-Hall do Brasil, Ltda., *Rio de Janeiro*

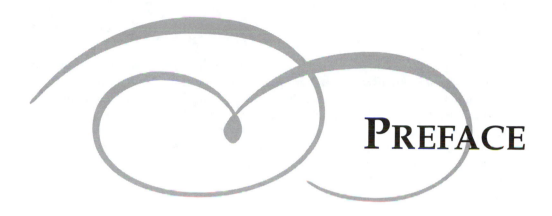

PREFACE

In *Women's Philosophies of Education: Thinking Through Our Mothers*, we present the educational thought of seven women from a variety of times, cultures, and classes, whose ideas have influenced and still influence our thinking on education in the United States. These women are Catharine Macaulay, Ana Roqúe de Duprey, Anna Julia Cooper, Charlotte Perkins Gilman, Mabel McKay, Jane Roland Martin, and bell hooks. They have thought systematically about education and have had important things to say about its purposes, its theories, and its practices. With access to this broader range and depth of information, women and all students of the foundations of education, the philosophy of education, and women's studies will have a more accurate view of the scope of thought on educational questions from and about women in order to form their answers to the essential questions about education.

For most people the word *mother* brings up images of biological and familial parentage, of home and privacy. However, in the case of this book, *mothers* refers to our metaphorical and intellectual mentors, women whose ideas not only came before ours but also can inform our philosophical ideas today. As the tradition of women's ideas about education is more carefully recorded and studied, our complete knowledge of the past may free us from repeating previous ideas or analyses and enable us to move forward in defining today's problems and in articulating their solutions. Moreover, we will receive the benefits that accrue when one generation passes its ideas and beliefs on to the next. This stronger connection to our past helps us realize that we are not working alone to solve problems in education; rather, we are connected to a long and rich tradition of thought. This feeling of connection can give us the courage we need to persevere in our search for answers to education's most pressing problems.

Each of the "intellectual mothers" portrayed in this book lived in a world that she experienced as wrongheaded in very significant ways, and she looked to find explanations for why things were wrong and what could be done to make them right. Each developed her own analysis and solution to the problems based on her experience, background, and the time and place in which she lived. Each sought a deeper sense of being human in order to liberate herself and others from oppressive social restrictions. Because of these facts, each has the potential to contribute to our deep understanding of these same challenges as we face them today.

If we approach contemporary issues in education by "thinking through our mothers,"—by actually using our inheritance—how might it change things? For one thing, it necessarily complicates our responses. But in addition, it adds a richness to our thought that gives us different ways of looking at and being in the world. It gives us a more accurate, more inclusive picture of the world. As we engage with the ideas of these "intellectual mothers," we may even recognize a shift in our own internal paradigm as to how we perceive education and women's place in it. In this way, thinking through our mothers has the potential to broaden and extend our collective educational lineage.

Acknowledgments

This book would not have been written without the groundbreaking work of Jane Roland Martin. We wish to thank and acknowledge her as one of the "intellectual mothers" that we were able to think through during the development of this book. We would also like to thank Maruka, Nicole, Renae, and Jane—who worked long and hard, and under deadline, to present their chapters and give us thoughtful and clear discussions.

We would like to thank Israel Scheffler, who introduced both of us to the world of philosophy of education. He was our first real educator on the topic and his passion for the subject inspired us to delve into this field of study. He also served as primary advisor to each of us on our doctoral work.

Connie thanks The College of New Jersey for the institutional support. And for her encouragement, Karen thanks Joan Casey.

We both would like to thank the following reviewers for their comments and suggestions: Rose Adesiyan, Purdue University–Calumet; Myra Baughman, Pacific Lutheran University; Carlton E. Beck, University of Wisconsin, Milwaukee; Timothy J. Bergen, Jr., University of South Carolina; Mary Ann Clark, Brown University; Clinton Collins, University of Kentucky; Samuel M. Craver, Virginia Commonwealth University; Louise A. Fleming, Ashland University; Jane Hinson, State University of West Georgia; Maike Philipsen, Virginia Commonwealth University; and Dale Titus, Kutztown University of Pennsylvania.

Connie Titone
Karen Maloney

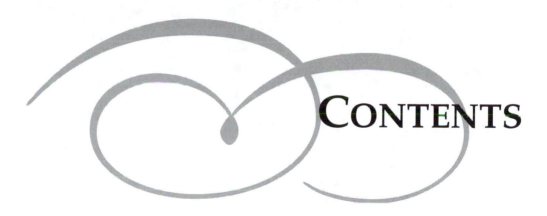

CONTENTS

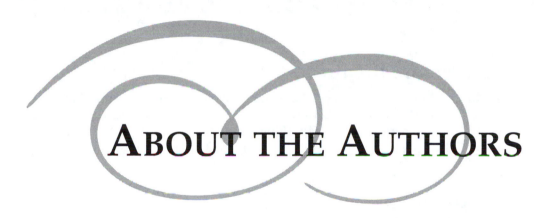

About the Authors

Connie Titone

Connie Titone is Assistant Professor of Educational Administration and Secondary Education at The College of New Jersey. Her research interests include the philosophy of education, both traditional and feminist; multicultural education; and teacher education. Her publications include *Catharine Macaulay's Letters on Education, Teachers College Record,* Winter, 1998, and "Educating the White Teacher as Ally" in *White Reign* (forthcoming).

Karen E. Maloney

Karen E. Maloney is Director of the Harvard Education Publishing Group at Harvard University and General Manager of the *Harvard Educational Review.* She is interested in continuing the work begun in this book of identifying and analyzing the work of women who have developed philosophies of education, particularly across times and cultures. Her other publications include "A Feminist Looks at Education: The Educational Philosophy of Charlotte Perkins Gilman," *Teachers College Record,* Spring 1998.

Maria del Carmen Garcia Padilla

Maria del Carmen Garcia Padilla is Assistant Professor of Philosophy of Education at the University of Puerto Rico. Her research interests include philosophy of education and the preparation of teachers as well as the work on education by nineteenth- and early twentieth-century Latin American women during that period.

Nicole Danielle Pitts

Nicole Danielle Pitts is a tenured English professor at Oakland Community College in Royal Oak, Michigan. Her work outside the classroom has focused on turn-of-the-century African American writers and issues confronting African Americans during that period.

Renae Moore Bredin

Renae Moore Bredin is Assistant Professor of Women's Studies and English at California State University, Fullerton. She has written about the convergences between Native American women's writing and feminism in several journals, and her essay "Theory in the Mirror," is forthcoming in *Other Sisterhoods: Literary Theory and U.S. Women of Color.*

Jane Roland Martin

Jane Roland Martin, Professor of Philosophy Emerita at the University of Massachusetts, Boston, has devoted her career to the study of education. Her most recent books on the subject are *Reclaiming a Conversation* and *Changing the Educational Landscape.*

bell hooks

bell hooks is Distinguished Professor of English at City College in New York. She is the author of numerous books and articles on feminist theory, art and culture, and the politics of race and gender. Her books include *Ain't I A Black Woman: Black Women and Feminism, Talking Back: Thinking Feminist, Thinking Black,* and *Outlaw Culture: Resisting Representations.*

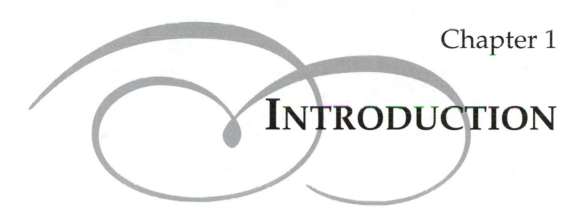

Chapter 1

INTRODUCTION

By Connie Titone and Karen E. Maloney

In *A Room of One's Own*, Virginia Woolf writes about the daunting challenge that faced nineteenth-century women writers: "when they came to set their thoughts on paper . . . they had no tradition behind them, or one so short and partial that it was of little help. For we think back through our mothers if we are women" (Woolf 1929/1981, 76). Until recently, women philosophers of education faced this same challenge. The omission of women as both subjects and objects of educational thought from the canon of philosophy of education, and its effects on our conceptions of education, was first brought to light by Jane Roland Martin (1982, 134). Since then, Martin and others have uncovered and recovered many women who have thought deeply and systematically about education. Most of these women were white, upper-class women—only recently have we begun to discover women from other cultures and classes. This volume continues the work of setting down the tradition and offers a way of making the treatment of philosophy of education multicultural.

Organization of the Chapters

Chapters addressing the work of each woman are guided by several philosophical themes. First, we present each woman's beliefs about human nature and the purpose of life—questions of a metaphysical nature in philosophy. Second, contributors address authors' answers to several normative questions, such as how education "ought" to be, how women "ought" to be educated, and the role that women should play in society.

We also discuss the type of curriculum and pedagogy that emerge from the woman's specific philosophical holdings. In some cases, attention is also given to education outside of the formal classroom in more informal settings such as the family or community. Using the same questions for each chapter enables each writer to capture the essence of these women's philosophies and allows for clearer comparisons among their ideas.

In the cases of those women who lived before the publication of this book, we have included discussion of each woman's life in the context of the time in which she lived. Though this is not customarily done in volumes presenting and analyzing philosophical works, this contextualization is essential for the reader's fuller understanding of each woman's ideas, the significance and uniqueness of those ideas, and the pioneering nature of the author's thought in comparison to more dominant views in the society. In that way, the reader can more easily consider how the lived experience of each woman might have influenced her thought, and how women's positions in their own societies might have enabled them to see dimensions of societal issues and focus on features of societal or educational problems that had not previously been seen. We have also included original materials from Catharine Macaulay, Ana Roqué de Duprey, Charlotte Perkins Gilman, and Anna Julia Cooper at the end of each of those chapters. We encourage the reader to study their words carefully and make their own interpretation of the selections.

Selection Criteria

We employed several criteria in selecting the "intellectual mothers"—Catharine Macaulay, Ana Roqué de Duprey, Anna Julia Cooper, Charlotte Perkins Gilman, Mabel McKay, Jane Roland Martin, and bell hooks—for inclusion in this book. All of these women thought carefully and systematically about education and, more specifically, the education of girls and women. All of these women are pioneers in challenging the paradigms of their day used to think about education and the place of women in education. All of these women have influenced education in the United States—they all spent their lives living and working in this country or its colonies, except for Catharine Macaulay, who was English. She is included because her ideas had a significant impact on U.S. thought about the education of girls and women, particularly in the development of women's academies and colleges. We chose women whose works cover the range of U.S. history, from Catharine Macaulay, who wrote at the time of the American Revolution, to Jane Roland Martin and bell hooks, who are still writing and developing their philosophies of education today.

Though these women lived throughout U.S. history, they represent only a small sample of the diversity of women's experiences and thoughts about education. Their ethnic, racial, class, and historical realities have given them different experiences and perspectives that shaped their own philosophies. Taken altogether, they have the potential to enrich our understanding of women's philosophies of education. This collection is not meant to be comprehensive or exhaustive, nor is it meant to be representative of the cultural groups from which the women come. We hope that we will be able to include the works of additional intellectual mothers in a later volume as other women thinkers on education and their works are uncovered.

Context and Definitions

Since the early 1970s and the impetus of the women's movement, scholars have begun to discover, recover, present, and analyze the ideas of women who have thought systematically about the topics that had been considered part of the public world of politics and business. As these writings were rediscovered, the argument was made to include their thought in the "canon" of their discipline. The "canon" is made up of those texts that comprise a common culture of thought in an area. These are commonly the texts assigned in high school and college courses on a subject. The "canon" can have a prescriptive and limiting use because it prescribes the subjects and the objects about which research and writing in a field can be conducted. If, for example, someone's work is not part of the "canon," he or she may not be acceptable as the subject of a dissertation without first arguing that that person is a legitimate subject of study. In the case of philosophy, according to Richard Rorty (1984, 58), the discipline of philosophy includes study of what are termed "philosophical questions," and there is disagreement within the field as to what questions are philosophical, as well as about the answers to these questions. This process of debating what questions are philosophical, and what answers are philosophical, is the process known as "canon formation."

In the case of *Women's Philosophies of Education: Thinking Through Our Mothers*, we are interested in invigorating both the "canon" of philosophy of education and the philosophical treatment of educational questions by including the philosophical treatment of questions that are relevant to girls' and women's lives and education. This point is very important when studying girls and women because women often bring different answers to the traditional questions of educational philosophy and often ask different questions at the outset. In reading the chapters that follow, it will be clear that this is exactly the case with Macaulay, Roqué, Cooper, Gilman, McKay, Martin, and hooks.

Until the 1970s, when writings by women thinkers in various disciplines began being discovered, presented, and analyzed, no women were part of the canon of philosophy of education. Because of their omission from the canon of recognized discussions and writings about education, it was commonly believed that women had not thought systematically about these issues.

The historical omission of women's thought and writings from the canon of philosophy of education and its effects were first brought to light in 1982 in a groundbreaking article by Jane Roland Martin entitled "Excluding Women from the Educational Realm." As Martin reveals in this article, this exclusion has led to the dominance of male-defined and male-oriented paradigms in the philosophy of education. Martin writes that women are excluded

> both as the subjects and the objects of educational thought from the standard texts and anthologies: as subjects, their philosophical works on education are ignored; as objects, works by men about their education and also their role as educators of the young are largely neglected. (Martin 1982, 134)

One of the reasons why women are excluded as both subjects and objects from philosophy of education lies in how the field has defined "education" as its subject of study and analysis. The field has defined "education" as being fundamentally about the public processes of education—that is, the transmission of the beliefs, skills, and knowledge needed to be successful in the public world of business, politics, the arts, academia, and so forth. This definition excludes from the content of education the educational tasks traditionally associated with the home and with mothers—as Jane Roland Martin writes in her chapter in this book—"the body of knowledge, the network of skills, and the various sets of tasks, duties, and traits that the culture associates with the institutions of home and family." In other words, activities traditionally associated with home and with mothers were not seen as "education" but as "training" or "child-rearing." Part of the project of women philosophers of education beginning with Martin's 1982 article has been to redefine "education" to include women and these other educative processes so that they become bona fide subjects to study. In thus broadening our notion of education, we can develop a richer and more realistic understanding of how various people over time have answered the traditional philosophical questions about education: the nature of teaching and learning, the role of education in society, the nature of knowledge, and so forth. We use this broadened definition throughout the book.

In her 1982 article, Martin documents how the standard texts and anthologies in philosophy of education are silent on many topics of great importance today: the education of girls and women, the role of the home and family in preparing young people to be productive and fulfilled adults in society, and the role of women in society. This book is one attempt to fill some of this void.

Overview

In Chapter 2, Connie Titone analyzes the philosophy of education of Catharine Macaulay, an English historian and insightful author on the topic of the education of young people. In *Letters on Education,* her final work published originally in 1787 and in its revised form in 1790, Macaulay articulated her philosophy of education, which integrated her metaphysical beliefs and her epistemological views with the pedagogy and practice they implied. Her ultimate hope from the educational process was to yield an educated person who had attained the character, morals, and knowledge that she valued in citizens of both genders.

In Chapter 3, Maria del Carmen Garcia Padilla describes and discusses the educational philosophy of Ana Roqué de Duprey, a teacher-educator, feminist, and social reformer in Puerto Rico. Roqué saw education as an essential element in the progress of Puerto Rican society and culture and believed that the education of women was central to this process. Garcia Padilla describes Roqué's efforts in three closely connected endeavors: an effort to educate Puerto Ricans, especially female teachers; a call to women to fulfill their duties; and a struggle in favor of women's right to vote. Roqué believed that Puerto Rico could not develop without the unified efforts of both women and men, and argued that women be educated as well as men so that all Puerto Ricans would be able to use their reason and work hard to fulfill their duties to improve society.

In Chapter 4, Nicole Pitts presents and discusses the philosophy of education of Anna Julia Cooper. Cooper was primarily interested in education as a way of uplifting the Black race after the devastation of slavery. She argued for the right of every person, male and female, Black and White, to an education that is suited to his or her particular talents and abilities, that would enable each of them to develop to the full extent of their potential. She argued that women needed to be educated as well as men so that they could contribute their special talents and traits to the regeneration of the Black race. She believed that women were essential to the progress of the race and that an educated and elevated womanhood was the key to development.

In Chapter 5, Karen E. Maloney describes and analyzes the philosophy of education of Charlotte Perkins Gilman, a prominent social reformer at the turn of the twentieth century. She argues that Gilman developed a philosophy of education based on powerful feminist principles centered around three conceptions of education: education as social nourishment, education as social parentage, and education as social motherhood. She then highlights the radical ramifications of this feminist philosophy of education for the role that women and education should play in society.

In Chapter 6, Renae Bredin presents and analyzes the educational philosophy of Mabel McKay, a Native American weaver, dreamer, Pomo healer, teacher, and leader whose life practically spanned the twentieth century. Bredin explodes our romanticized notions about Native American education while describing the ways in which McKay's pioneering work as a teacher to and for her friend Greg Sarris reasserted traditional tribal practices in the face of continuing internal colonization. Bredin describes these practices as emphasizing the learning process as communal in nature, informal, experiential, sacred, and grounded in oral tradition and storytelling.

In Chapter 7, Jane Roland Martin presents her own philosophy of education. Martin is a contemporary philosopher of education who has developed her own normative philosophy of education based around what she calls the "3 Cs" of care, concern, and connection. Martin's main point is that the family is no longer capable of performing the complex educational tasks that our traditional view of education requires in order to provide all children with the knowledge, skills, attitudes, and values they need to become full and productive members of our culture in the broadest sense of the term. She then explains how school can share some of the family's traditional educational tasks without becoming overburdened.

In Chapter 8, we have reprinted the introduction and first chapter of bell hooks' *Teaching to Transgress* (1994). In those pages, hooks begins by discussing her feelings about and experiences of being a black woman moving from a schoolgirl "in the apartheid South" to a prominent black female in the Academy. She explains the significance of the work of the Brazilian thinker, Paulo Freire and the Vietnamese Buddhist monk, Thich Nhat Hanh, on her own developing thought. It was from Freire that she perceived the liberatory potentiality of education and developed her own "engaged pedagogy" emphasizing well-being. Using an engaged pedagogy, hooks challenges teachers and students alike to transgress the boundaries of conventional intellectual confinement and interact with each other honestly, respectfully, courageously, and creatively.

In Chapter 9, we discuss the continuities and discontinuities between these women's theories and identify emergent themes and common questions found in the book. We will discuss how the lived experience of each woman might have influenced her thought and how women's positions in society enable them to see other dimensions and aspects of societal issues and focus on features of a problem that had heretofore gone unrecognized as salient. Finally, we suggest what the field of philosophy of education in particular, and educational theory in general, has to gain from including these women, their theories, and their questions in its canon.

References

Martin, J. R. 1982. Excluding Women from the Educational Realm. *Harvard Educational Review* 52 (2): 133–48.

Rorty, R. 1984. The Historiography of Philosophy: Four Genres. *Philosophy in History*. Cambridge: University Press. 49–75.

Woolf, V. [1929] 1981. *A Room of One's Own.* Reprint, New York: Harcourt Brace & Company.

Chapter 2

CATHARINE MACAULAY

The Mere Production of Art

By Connie Titone

Introduction

> The very word respect brings Mrs. Macaulay to my remembrance. The woman of the greatest abilities, undoubtedly, that this country has ever produced. And yet this woman has been suffered to die without sufficient respect being paid to her memory. Posterity, however, will be more just; and remember that Catharine Macaulay was an example of the intellectual acquirements supposed to be incompatible with the weakness of her sex. In her style of writing, indeed, no sex appears, for it is like the sense it conveys, strong and clear. (Wollstonecraft 1792/1975, 200)

Catharine Sawbridge Macaulay,[1] who lived from 1731 to 1791, is best known as a political historian of seventeenth-century England, her homeland. Less known is her insightful and articulate work on the education of young people. This chapter presents Macaulay's theory of education as expressed in her noteworthy work, *Letters on Education*, printed originally in 1787 and in its revised form in 1790.

In *Letters on Education*, Macaulay articulated her philosophy of education, which integrated her metaphysical beliefs and her epistemological views with the pedagogy and practice they implied. Her ultimate hope from the educational process was to yield an educated person who had attained the character, morals, and knowledge that she valued for citizens and for individuals of both genders. She hypothesized "that the character of our species is formed from the influence of education" (Macaulay 1790, 84). She explicitly denied that differences in intellectual attainment and character were attributable to non-educational causes, such as God's partiality to certain parts of Creation, innate racial inferiority, or the geographic location of any group of people (Macaulay 1790, 257). Macaulay presented education as the remedy to the mistaken beliefs about limited capacities resulting from limited natures.

Catharine Macaulay expressed major revolutionary ideas in the field of the philosophy of education as it existed in an eighteenth-century England. She is one of a number of early women thinkers whose work is informed by centuries of philosophical thought—both in the topics she addressed and the previous works to which she referred. Like Plato and other philosophers who write about education, she considers questions about human nature, the human experience, what it means to know, and the role of education in the human process. Referring directly to Plato's plan of education, Macaulay argued in favor of her country's government becoming directly involved in the management of schools in order to develop with "children of the state" to "render them serviceable to its glory and prosperity" (Macaulay 1790, 15).

While the substance of Macaulay's work fits into the long tradition of philosophical inquiry, in many ways her work surpasses and refigures the tradition by taking a critical approach to its key concepts of human nature, virtue, and education. Citing Jean Jacques Rousseau's now classic work *Émile* (1762/1979), acknowledged as a major text in the development of modern education (Ulich 1982; Kaminsky 1993), Macaulay responded to educational questions raised in this work, but changed the focus of Rousseau's questions.[2]

Rousseau believed that male and female human beings possess two different human natures, each of which is predisposed to develop the specific characteristics needed to fulfill its socially defined, gender-specific role. The belief that these roles were defined by nature rather than by society was accepted by the general public in his time.[3] It justified the perpetuation of the masculine/feminine configuration as it then existed.

Macaulay's analysis reflected a deeper understanding of the complexity of those issues. In Part I of *Letters,* she made the following distinction and held to it throughout her work: human nature—the essential wholeness of the human being—is separate and distinct from the exhibited set of properties of boys and girls as observed in society. She recommended that the attitudes as well as the behavior of both boys and girls should change in order for each to enjoy a closer match between what was possible by nature and what was seen in conduct. She did not merely say that woman could be more like man if educated with him, but that both man and woman could be more fully human by striving to be more like her conception of the divine. Thus, part of Macaulay's accomplishment in *Letters on Education* was to bring to light how the differing conceptions and treatment of the sexes operated in her culture and how the prejudices against women and the limitations placed on them were maintained by social and educational arrangements. In this way, she went beyond changing the focus of Rousseau's questions, taking an interrogative stance toward the theory itself and problematizing it.

Macaulay did not accept the most historically fundamental philosophical dualism. This dualism predisposed socially constructed feminine qualities, such as tenderness, to a status inferior to that of masculine ones, such as rationality. Macaulay envisioned that the essential nature of the human being included the full expression both of what we commonly call "feminine" and "masculine" qualities. According to Macaulay, the discrete actions or attainments of both women and men reflected in large part their socialization. She argued that both men and women must change their concepts of themselves and of each other. They must become more open to their own possibilities, become fully educated and more fully human.

In her life and in her efforts to reconceptualize human nature, rationality, and the education of girls as well as boys, Macaulay played the role of pioneering feminist philosopher. Feminist philosophers today understand even more clearly the importance of attending to these fundamental concepts (Bryson 1992; Davis and Farge 1993; Gatens 1991; Harvey and Okruhlik 1992; Lowe and Hubbard 1983) because the "legacy of rationality has shaped and continues to influence conceptions of society, subjectivity, and knowledge" (Harvey and Okruhlik 1992, 1). Whereas the feminine had been defined to exclude full use of the rational powers, Macaulay insisted on girls' intellectual equality with boys and demanded that young girls receive an academically rigorous education to develop their innate capacities. One of her most powerful innovations, which I will discuss later in this chapter, came in defining "man" in relation to "woman" rather than following the long tradition of defining "woman" as a "male manqué."

Biographical Sketch

To understand how Catharine Macaulay did or did not fit into the social and political setting she inhabited has presented enormous challenges to scholars today. The most obvious obstacle is that no family papers, diaries, journals, or letters can be found. For specific, detailed information about Macaulay, I have had to depend on the scant references she made in her own writings and in what others have published about her, both during her lifetime and after. Writings by others offer contradictory assessments of her writings, her political activities, and her personal lifestyle. Unfortunately, we do not have access to her own voice as we would in her own private documents. We must depend instead on the images and analyses of observers and interpreters.

From Mary Hays, an eighteenth-century political and social philosopher and author of *Female Biography,* written in 1803, we learn that Macaulay was born in the English town of Kent, on March 23, 1731, the second daughter of Elizabeth Wanley and John Sawbridge. Macaulay's mother died in childbirth when Macaulay was two years old, and her father left the children in the care of a governess at the family estate, "Olintigh." The governess, "antiquated, well recommended, but ignorant . . . ill-qualified for the task she undertook" (Hays 1803, 288), provided Macaulay and her older sister with the education that was common for girls in the upper class (Reynolds 1920, 83). She taught them to read fairy tales, romances, and the Bible.

Catharine Macaulay

Apparently, Macaulay was not satisfied to let her education end with this instruction.[4] In the introduction to Volume I of her *History of England* (1763), written at the age of 32, Macaulay says this of her own education:

> From my early youth, I have read with delight those histories that exhibit liberty in its most exalted state, the annals of the Roman and Greek republics; studies like these excite the natural love of freedom which lies latent in the breast of every rational being. (quoted in Donnelly 1949, 177)

According to Hays, Macaulay was drawn to discussion of the laws and manners of the Greek and Roman republics and was inspired by their heroes (Hays 1803, 287). Identifying herself as a rational being who loved freedom, Macaulay thought it natural to delight in reading historical stories that inspired her own sense of independence. This self-awareness foreshadows her views presented in *Letters on Education,* in which she identifies personal characteristics such as reason, intellect, and tenderness as absolutely essential—though sometimes latent—to the nature of both girls and boys.

In 1949, Lucy Martin Donnelly, a professor of English at Bryn Mawr College, wrote an article called "The Celebrated Mrs. Macaulay." Speaking of Macaulay's education, she said, "her indulgent country squire of a father left the girl to educate herself" (Donnelly 1949, 177). Referring to Macaulay's relationship with her brother John, Donnelly wrote, "they read history side by side and talked together of liberty in the old library," and "she was probably the more intellectual of the two but lacked her brother's strong understanding, the sagacity which he learned from living in a man's world while she dwelt among books (Donnelly 1949, 178). It seems plausible, then, that Macaulay was aided in her education by her younger brother, John. He eventually became Lord Mayor of London and was afterwards a member of the British Parliament (Boos 1976, 50). His interests in politics obviously formed the focus of his own studies and quite possibly shaped his sister's as well. Their careers ran parallel in the London of the 1760s and 1770s, with the drastic differences that gender imposed.

Aside from these sketchy details, almost nothing is known of Macaulay's early upbringing or education. Because her lack of formal academic education coincides with the common practices for girls in England at the time (Reynolds 1920), it is safe to assume that Macaulay was largely self-motivated and self-taught.

In 1760, at the age of twenty-nine, Catharine married George Macaulay, a medical doctor fifteen years her senior. Although it is not known whether he psychologically and financially supported Macaulay's writing, it seems fair to assume that he did not hinder it, given that three years after the marriage the first volume of her *History of England* was published. This was a political history of seventeenth-century England, the first to be written by an English woman. This history was based on actual documents, handwritten manuscripts, as well as printed materials. A century later, W. E. H. Lecky, writing a history of the age in which Macaulay lived, described her as "the ablest writer of the new radical school" (Stenton 1957, 306).

Over a twenty-year period (1763–1783), Macaulay expanded her history to eight volumes, spanning 3,550 pages. Each volume was widely reviewed and enthusiastically received by many women and men in England, France, and the American colonies (Hill 1992, 39).[5] Horace Walpole, an eighteenth-century British writer and member of Parliament, articulates what he surely took to be a compliment when he said that "[Macaulay] exerted manly strength with the gravity of a philosopher" and that "she wrote the most sensible, unaffected, and best history of England that we have had yet" (*Dictionary of National Biography* 1908–1909, 408). In the American colonies, such leading thinkers as John Adams, Benjamin Franklin, Mercy Otis Warren, and George Washington read and esteemed it.

Letters on Education: Hortensia

> Every work published on education that affords one new idea which may be found useful in practice, is worthy the attention of the public. (Macaulay 1790, iii)

Macaulay's letters in *Letters on Education* are addressed to a woman by the name of Hortensia. Macaulay's biographers neither mention Hortensia nor speculate as to her identity. But after a few hundred pages of reading, and a growing recognition of Macaulay's careful scholarship and keen attachment to history's figures and stories, I became more interested in Hortensia. Several possibilities as to her identity exist.

One Hortensia lived in the last half of the first century B.C.E. She was the daughter of the Roman advocate and orator, Quintus Hortensius. She is remembered for her speech against the taxation without representation of 1,400 wealthy Roman women. Speaking before the triumvirate, for and on behalf of these women, Hortensia rebuked the rulers for taxing women to pay for a war that they had no part in initiating or conducting. The speech is said to have angered the triumvirs, but it also resulted in a reduction of the number of women liable to the tax. Finally, only 400 women were taxed, and a similar levy was imposed on wealthy Roman men (Appianus 1902, 32–34).

In keeping with Macaulay's deep interest in the history of Rome, it is plausible that she was familiar with and chose her correspondent intentionally. And if Macaulay was intentionally writing to the famous Roman Hortensia, she showed an insightful self-awareness of the historical importance of her own ideas, and perhaps aligned her hopes for change with those that Hortensia represented. In *Letters*, Macaulay presented her social analysis of the existing educational system: its false foundations and the resultant injustice of the differing educational outcomes based on gender and class.

In the introductory letter of this work, she first singled out the ruling men of her day. While speaking of her times as "enlightened days," and in keeping with Enlightenment ideals, she pressed for a critical examination of previously accepted doctrines in educating young people. Macaulay implored those in power to recognize the socially constructed basis of their beliefs regarding the different natures and capacities of boys and girls, and challenged them to apply their new-found understanding by radically changing their practices in educating young people. Since she believed that those who entered into an authentic teacher–student relationship had a unique opportunity to learn, she argued for open-mindedness and flexibility in teachers. But above all, she argued to convince the magistrates and legislators that the demonstration of humility was an essential first step in the character development of policymakers. She said:

> Oh magistrates! Oh legislators! admit of some variation in your views of interest; consider that in attempting to teach others, you may gain truths of the utmost importance yourselves. (Macaulay 1790, 13–14)

When addressing the parents among her readers, Macaulay also made strong recommendations for standardizing instruction and bringing boys and girls together to learn. She wrote:

> Confine not the education of your daughters to what is regarded as the ornamental parts of it, nor deny the graces to your sons. Suffer not prejudices to prevail on you to weaken Nature, in order to render her more beautiful; take measures for the virtue and the harmony of your family, by uniting their young minds early in the soft bonds of

friendship. Let your children be brought up together; let their sports and studies be the same; let them enjoy . . . all that freedom which innocence renders harmless . . . By the uninterrupted intercourse which you will thus establish, both sexes will find, that friendship may be enjoyed between them without passion. The wisdom of your daughters will preserve them from the bane of coquetry, and even at the age of desire, objects of temptation will lose somewhat of their stimuli, by losing their novelty. (Macaulay 1790, 50)

Macaulay cleverly included Hortensia as a silent student and confidante throughout the discussions she pursued. At times Macaulay seemed to use this conversational device to clarify her arguments, and in other instances to reinforce her ideas with the approval and sympathetic understanding of her "companion."

Overview of Macaulay's Thought

Macaulay was part of the radical political tradition that existed in eighteenth-century England, and she wrote about many of the issues faced by the state. Macaulay was a strong advocate for equality and freedom in the political arena, as demonstrated by her extensive writings on these topics and by her deep sympathy with the American colonists' cause. She became one of the early woman workers in a continuous tradition in British politics that reflected a broad disaffection with the monarchical and aristocratic nature of government. Her political vision extended the notions of equality and freedom to the nature and personal situations of women and men. While she implicated the existing social system and men's attitudes about women as two causes of the visible inequities between the sexes, she did not absolve any individual woman from her own complacent acceptance of the existing situation. She believed that there was only one human nature, though two certainly seemed to exist, and she understood the exceptional work and resistance required of each woman to achieve her innate potential—particularly in an environment that operated on false beliefs about that potential. The restricted lives that men and women lived and the partial natures that both expressed were, for Macaulay, a result of false education and social conventions. She gave her overall appraisal of girls' situation and education in *Letters*:

The situation of women, Hortensia, is precisely that which must necessarily tend to corrupt and debilitate both the powers of mind and body. From a false notion of beauty and delicacy, their system of nerves is depraved before they come out of their nursery; and this kind of depravity has more influence over the mind, and consequently over morals, than is commonly apprehended. (Macaulay 1790, 207)

In addition to her ambitious *History* and her *Letters on Education*, Catharine Macaulay responded to the works of past and contemporary philosophers, including

Thomas Hobbes and Edmund Burke, addressing social and political issues. In 1767, she wrote a response to one specific work of Hobbes on the topic of government and society, in which she questioned Hobbes' view of authoritarianism and the contracterian picture of the emergence of civil society. She subsequently supported the American colonists' cause during the American Revolutionary War period; after the war, she participated in extensive philosophical and political discussions about the newly forming republic with both English and American leaders. In 1784, she made a year-long trip to the United States, in part to prepare herself to write a history of the American Revolution (Hill 1992, 128). During that trip, she visited George and Martha Washington at their Mount Vernon home in Virginia. Following her ten-day stay, she corresponded with Mr. Washington specifically about the framing of the United States Constitution (Donnelly 1949, 174; Hill 1992, 226)[6]. In a June 1785 letter to Richard Henry Lee, an active member of the Continental Congress, George Washington said of Macaulay:

> I am obliged to you for introducing a Lady to me whose reputation among the literati is high, and whose principles are so justly admired by the friends of liberty and of mankind. (George Washington to Richard Henry Lee, June 28, 1785, in Fitzpatrick 1931–1944, 174)

In 1783, Macaulay wrote her *Treatise on the Immutability of Moral Truth*, in which she presented her metaphysical views. Some of the themes of this work were the nature of God, the correlation between God's nature and the nature of the human being, the origin of evil, and the debate concerning free will and moral necessity. She later revised the *Treatise*, which became the metaphysical groundwork for part of her last work, *Letters on Education* (1790).

In *Letters*, Macaulay proposed her coeducational system of educating youth and advocated for sexual egalitarianism. In *Letters*, she states:

> It is an absurd notion that the education of females should be of an opposite kind to males . . . [E]ducation should be the same for all rational beings. (Macaulay 1790, 205)

Her radical assertion denouncing what she called the absurd practice of educating females differently than males countered the ideas of two of her well-known contemporaries: Jean Jacques Rousseau (1712–1778) and the conservative English writer, Hester Chapone (1727–1801). Rousseau promoted the notion that girls' performance of their societal duties proved their restricted human natures (Rousseau 1762/1979). While Chapone intimated that women's restricted societal roles were not indicative of a restricted human nature, she nonetheless supported, and thus perpetuated, the training of young minds to accept the limited view of womanhood (Chapone 1773/1800). Macaulay's vision of human completeness necessarily exposed the limited and partial conception of humanity as defined by most of her contemporaries as false, unacceptable, and correctable. She asserted that "when the sexes have been taught wisdom by education, they will be glad to give up indirect influence for rational privilege" (Macaulay 1790, 215).

In *Letters on Education,* Macaulay naturally extended the concept of the requirement of equality to a specific treatment of the nature of women and of their educational rights. Her proposed coeducation, pedagogy, and curriculum all sprang from her beliefs about human nature and about the power of education to correct some of people's misconceived assumptions and practices.

It was not uncommon for women—even during the 1600s—to demand recognition of woman's capacity and her need to develop her intellect and her ability to reason,[7] but Macaulay also suggested a need for change in male education. This perspective was revolutionary at the time.

Macaulay's Views on Human Nature

In *Letters*, Macaulay argued that "the essential man"—both female and male—had been created in the image of one deity—not a male deity and a female deity. For Macaulay, this wholeness seemed to include the integration of those socially prescribed characteristics normally labeled "masculine" and "feminine." She used the terms "justice" and "equity" on the one hand and "benevolence," "sympathy," and "tenderness" on the other to describe two types of attributes of the one deity. She saw both types as elements of a perfect God and therefore as naturally occurring and equally valuable in human nature.

She identified the educational institution—rather than the family, legal system, or church—as the critical context for addressing and changing beliefs and behaviors. In fact, it was the formal educational process that she endowed with the power to "fashion" the human being. She argued that social man—male and female—

> is a mere artificial being, and when you have the power of molding
> him, it is your own fault if his fashion does not suit your purposes.
> (Macaulay 1790, 15)

Although she did not maintain that any traits belonged naturally to a specific gender, Macaulay acknowledged throughout her work that girls and boys were socialized by the world around them, by convention, by laws, and by their adult role models to see themselves as restricted in their ability to express all of their natural qualities. But Macaulay believed that "man"—both males and females—had the capacity, as well as the responsibility, to develop all of their natural qualities. In so doing, both males and females would successfully transcend the bonds of social customs and the prejudices of gender limitation. Macaulay further believed that it was only through education and individual effort that these universal capacities would be uncovered and cultivated. Conversely, the perpetuation of the existing educational system could also perpetuate the false limitations of manhood and womanhood.

Macaulay's argument separated the essential nature of the human being from the observable behavior of women and men. She did not exonerate women's "vices" or conduct; instead, she presented a well-reasoned defense of woman's completely sufficient nature qua human being. Just as she assigned responsibility to mankind for the creation of "social man," she also placed the responsibility for changed individual conduct with the women and men themselves:

> Though you have often heard me express myself with warmth in vindication of female nature, Hortensia, yet I never was an apologist for the conduct of women. (Macaulay 1790, 215)

While Macaulay provided a sharp social analysis and expressed compassionate understanding of woman's situation, she neither excused woman's conduct nor sacrificed her expectations of woman's potential.

Macaulay believed that girls and women of the laboring poor, as well as servants, possessed the same nature and capacity as any other rational being; however, her vision for education did not include the laboring poor or servants directly in its initial plan. She did expect, however, that they would receive educational benefits in time, as aristocratic girls became educated and created schools for them. She saw her proposed changes as a first step to universal education for all "classes of citizens." In the preface of *Letters,* she anticipated the charge of elitism and said this of her own ideas:

> Cavillers may raise objections to the author's rules of education on the following grounds—That the plan can alone be carried into general practice by the opulent; and that the needy, and those of moderate fortune, are by their circumstances precluded from attempting it. To these objections the answer is plain and fair. . . . That the education of the great, were it properly attended to, and pursued on the best rules, would be felt in the improved virtue of all subordinate classes of citizens—That there would be no end of framing rules of education for all the different ranks and situations of men. (Macaulay 1790, vi)

She acknowledged that the privileged would have first access to the education she proposed, but she did not expect that this new and true education would end with the people in the upper classes. She did not, however, address exactly how the laboring poor or servants would come to have access to the same education that she proposed. This stands today, as it was at her time, as a shortcoming of her work.

Macaulay's Views of the Educated Person

Catharine Macaulay's philosophy of education integrated her metaphysical and epistemological beliefs with the pedagogy and practice they implied. Her ultimate hope was to yield from the educational process an educated person—regardless of gender or class—who had attained the character, morals, and knowledge that she valued for citizens and moral individuals. She hypothesized "that the character of our species is formed from the influence of education" (Macaulay 1790, 84). She explicitly denied that differences in intellectual attainment and character were attributable to non-educational causes such as God's partiality to certain parts of Creation, innate racial inferiority, or the geographic location of any group of people (Macaulay 1790, 257). She envisioned

> a system of education, which aims at bringing the human mind to such heights of perfection as shall induce the practice of the best morals. (Macaulay 1790, 173)

Moral education was of critical significance in her educational system; she spoke extensively of educating the virtues in children.

Macaulay's vision advocated that both genders develop the complete human nature, integrating the commonly called "masculine" and "feminine" characteristics. She envisioned that the well-being of society would improve as a result of both men and women perceiving themselves and functioning as complete intellectual and emotional co-equals. She intimated that the naming of characteristics "masculine" or "feminine" was a matter of convention rather than necessity. And she stressed the importance of teaching boys what we usually label "girls' knowledge," such as tenderness and empathy, as well as teaching girls to exercise their powers of reason. She described the outcomes she expected of women and men educated by her method. Of woman, she says:

> I am sanguine enough to expect to turn out of my hands a careless, modest beauty, grave, manly, noble, full of strength and majesty; and carrying about her an aegis sufficiently powerful to defend her against the sharpest arrow that ever was shot from Cupid's bow. (Macaulay 1790, 204)

Macaulay's vision was of a "manly" woman, one who expressed qualities that society wrongly saw as fit only for men. Her woman foreshadows Charlotte Perkins Gilman's "manly" woman, who also possessed qualities generally associated with men.

Macaulay's vision for a "perfect man" was laid out with wit and creativity by turning the phrase of Alexander Pope. She says:

> When we compliment the appearance of a more than ordinary energy in the female mind, we call it masculine; and hence it is, that Pope has elegantly said a perfect woman's but a softer man. And if we take in the consideration that there can be but one rule of moral excellence for beings made of the same materials, organized after the same manner, and subjected to similar laws of Nature, we must either agree with Mr. Pope, or we must reverse the proposition, and say, that a perfect man is a woman formed after a coarser mold. (Macaulay 1790, 204)

She saw a "perfect man" as one who had successfully developed his innate capacity for "femaleness." Macaulay's innovation came in defining "man" in relation to "woman," rather than following the long tradition of defining "woman" as a "male manqué."

Addressing the "distortion" of gendered human nature that prevailed in her society, Macaulay offered a general indictment of people who allowed their prejudices to overrule their reason, focusing on the particular confusions and contradictions in Rousseau's view of gender differences. She set out the problem in this question: Why, despite maintaining that character is formed by experience, does the contradictory belief in innate characteristics of the female mind persist? Her analysis of this contradiction is explained thus:

> For though the doctrine of innate ideas, and innate affections, are in great measure exploded by the learned, yet few persons reason so clearly and so accurately on abstract subjects as, though a long chain of deductions, to bring forth a conclusion which in no respect militates with their premises. It is a long time before the crowd give up opinions they have been taught to look upon with respect; and I know many persons who will follow you willingly through the course of your argument, till they perceive it tends to overthrow of some fond prejudice. (Macaulay 1790, 203)

Macaulay's Views on Moral Education

In addition to discussing the practical and concrete aspects of educating youth, Macaulay's *Letters* addressed another important question: How can a person most effectively become virtuous? Macaulay stressed the importance of experience—and education—in developing virtuous character. She agreed with Locke's principle that all ideas are derived from sense impressions and argued that an understanding of virtue, as well as an environment that provides the kind of experience conducive to virtuous behavior, is essential. Therefore, she directed her analysis to the kind of experience and training of the human being from the cradle to adulthood that would provide such an environment.

In the nature–nurture debate, she considered nurture the predominant influence on intellectual and character development. She referred to the work of Lord Monboddo—an eighteenth-century pioneer anthropologist—agreeing with him that a human being is a social artifice. She said:

> The attention I have given to my own character . . . and to the means by which it has been formed, obliges me to subscribe to this opinion of the Scottish sage, viz. that a man in a state of society, is as artificial a being as his representation on the canvas of the painter. Nature indeed supplies the raw materials, and the capacity of the workman; but the effect is the mere production of art. No; there is no virtue or a vice that belongs to humanity, which we do not make ourselves. (Macaulay 1790, 10–11)

Macaulay also deemed physical nature as important as mental nurture. She said that "a conduct uniformly virtuous, must be the joint issue of a good head and a sound constitution" and praised the Spartans for endeavoring to improve the natural strength of their women, "instead of entailing the curse of feebleness on their women for the sake of augmenting their personal beauty" (Macaulay 1790, 24–25).

The Roles of Habit and Example in Moral Education

Let us now examine Macaulay's views on the role of habit and example in moral education. To begin with, she argued that the generally passive nature of sense perception effectively created habits of mind. She said:

> A common observer must be sufficiently acquainted with the human mind to know, that it is quite passive in receiving impressions through the organs of sense . . . they will necessarily be received by the mind, and laid up in the mental repository, where they will be ready to lead into the train of their associates; or when any corresponding impression is received by the mind; I can shut my eyes from seeing objects, but I cannot hinder the impressions which these objects, when they are seen make on my mind. Hence, we must be esteemed passive agents in the collection of by far the greater number of the ideas lodged in the storehouse of the brain; and the purity of the mind must chiefly depend on the discretion of those with whom we are entrusted in our youth. (Macaulay 1790, 163–64)

This being so, she advocated the encouragement of good habits by sensitively directed activities and by constant association with virtuous examples, including government, parents, and tutors. Of government she said:

> When the happiness of an individual is properly considered, his interest will be found so intimately connected with the interests of the society of which he is a member, that he cannot act in conformity to the one, without having a proper consideration of the other. (Macaulay 1790, 271–72).

She advised parents that

> the natural virtues and vices of parents commonly descend to the children. It ought therefore to be the task of every parent to examine carefully their own character, to find out its propensities, and to regulate the method of education in such a manner as shall guard particularly against the influence of those which they find censurable in themselves, unless experience should prove to them, that their children have a contrary tendency. (Macaulay 1790, 161)

Of the enduring relationship between parent and child and its educational value she said:

> Parents should not only lay aside the air of solemn dictator to their children, but when their reason begins to ripen and their affections to grow warm and vivid, they should enter into the familiarity of a companionable friendship . . . they will thus have opportunities to discover the true bent of their children's temper, inclinations and abilities; they will acquire their full confidence, and they will be able to introduce instructive observations in such a manner as is better adapted to steal on the mind and impress it with wisdom, than are the most laboured lectures of the schools. (Macaulay 1790, 154–55)

And of the tutor, she said:

> The tutor fit to raise mankind to that high degree of excellence of which his nature is capable, must himself partake of the excellence he bestows. (Macaulay 1790, 104)

Macaulay believed that habit was the basis from which understanding grew and strengthened, and she considered precept without example to be useless. True virtue, Macaulay argued, required a grasp of immutable principles, which, in turn, required the use of reason. She defined reason as being "always able to discern the moral difference of things, whenever they are fairly and plainly proposed" (Macaulay 1790, 193) and therefore, considered it essential in developing virtue. Macaulay thought that society needed truly virtuous people—whom she names philosophers—not merely to obey laws, but also to understand the principles underlying the laws and to be patriotic or religious on rational grounds. She argued:

> It is one thing . . . to educate a citizen, and another to educate a philosopher. The mere citizen will have learnt to obey the laws of his country, but he will never understand those principles on which they ought to be established; and without such an understanding, he can never be religious on rational principles, or truly moral; nor will he ever have any of that active wisdom which is necessary for co-operating in any reformation. (Macaulay 1790, 198)

Macaulay believed in the immutable principle of equity and expected philosopher–citizens to participate in reforming society. Another dimension of her well-educated person surfaces in this description of the philosopher.

Given the subjectivity of judgment, however, as seen, for example, in the many opposing views on the same object's beauty or goodness, she argued that habituation to right principles was required for securing right judgment. She described how the natural process of habituation occurred: "Children readily apply expressions of affection or aversion, or approbation or resentment," and "when these expressions are once connected by the same associations which connect words with their ideas," the sentiment follows the idea and hence attaches to whatever object the child has been "accustomed to apply the epithet." In this way, she said, moral sense is established—hence the crucial importance of developing habits of the appropriate associations (Macaulay 1790, 176–77). The philosophic tutor-teacher, Macaulay concluded, should therefore

> always annex the epithets of beautiful, charming, and lovely, to good actions; and of hideous, frightful, and deformed, to evil ones . . . Thus the maxim of the stoics, that the wise man alone is beautiful, will in some measure be felt in the child's sentiment. An association of ideas will prevail, which will serve to weaken the power of mere personal charms. (Macaulay 1790, 178)

In addition, Macaulay recognized the need to tailor the habituation process to the individuality and particularity of the child. Because the dispositions of children are so virtuous, she noted

> that mode of treatment which would rear some children up to honor and felicity, will be the ruin of others. (Macaulay 1790, 155)

Macaulay made no mention of the problematic concern that the teachers' views of "good" or "beautiful" might vary. In her mind, these concepts must have existed somewhat like Platonic forms, which were easily discernible to those with the proper preparation and thinking. In fact, she insisted, "There can be but one best" (Macaulay 1790, 462).

What Is the Aim of the Habituation Process? The Supreme Virtue of Benevolence

The aim of the habituation process, Macaulay stated, is to inculcate virtue. Though honesty and fortitude were emphasized, benevolence was considered the supreme virtue. Macaulay believed that discerning truth and falsehood required early training:

> As I have great opinion of the power of early impressions, I cannot agree with Rousseau in the notion, that it is right to keep children in ignorance on the subject of truth and falsehood. I should, on the contrary, be very particular in the explaining to them the nature of this moral difference. I should endeavor to make them feel forcibly, the obligation of observing the strict rules of veracity, by such reflections as were best adapted to convince them of the value of this virtue, and the degradation of character which must attend every departure from it. (Macaulay 1790, 85)

Of fortitude, she wrote:

> Encourage children to develop confidence and independence by
> avoiding either over-indulging in a child's every wish or terrorizing
> a child into obedience. (Macaulay 1790, 66–67)

She said this of benevolence, and explained why existing educational strategies did
not produce it:

> The reason then that education is found so deficient in producing
> benevolence is, that precept, without example, is of no use in the cul-
> tivation of this cardinal virtue. It is only example which can fire the
> mind to an emulation of disinterested actions, which can call its
> attention to distress without itself; and by a retrospect of its own
> capabilities of misery, can teach it with the clarity of thought to trans-
> port itself into the situation of the long suffering object. (Macaulay
> 1790, 115)

Her analysis of each virtue is Aristotelian in the sense that, for her, virtue is
a mean between excesses. Hence, to Macaulay, benevolence was neither avarice, a
reluctance to share what one has with others, nor prodigality, a reckless extravagance
(Macaulay 1790, 121), but rather the supreme virtue "of so comprehensive a nature,
that it contains the principle of every moral duty" (Macaulay 1790, 112). She argued:

> Certainly every tutor not drawn from the dregs of the people . . .
> would rescue a miserable insect or other animal from the tortures
> inflicted by a wanton fancy; but would he not suffer him to extend
> evil in other modes? . . . Would he shut out all habits of cruelty by
> keeping him from the chase and other sports of the field or from the
> hardened barbarity of putting worms on a hook as baits to catch fish?
> Would he set him the example both of a negative, and active good-
> ness in a total forbearance of every unnecessary injury and in seizing
> all opportunities to do acts of kindness to every feeling being?
> (Macaulay 1790, 121–22)

Macaulay found Rousseau's characterization of man's most important moral duty—
"that one should not do injury to any one" (quoted in Macaulay 1790, 113)—too
narrow. Agreeing that benevolence and doing injury were opposites that could never
exist simultaneously, she asserted that benevolence must be more than passively
refraining from doing harm, that it must also involve actually helping or protecting
from harm (Macaulay 1790, 113).[8] And this action was to extend beyond the human
realm to the treatment of animals.

Macaulay argued that the virtue of benevolence arose from the ability to sympathize with others in need, stating that

man has sympathy in his nature, and his knowledge of the relation of things causes him to put himself in the place of the sufferer, and thus to acquire ideas of equity and the utility of benevolence. (Macaulay 1790, 196–97)

Again, she asked why those educators did not focus on moral instruction:

Why does not education bend her whole care to produce a fruit thus advantageous to the possessor, and which when multiplied in private characters, would operate strongly in favor of public happiness? (Macaulay 1790, 114)

And she answered her own question:

The answer to the question is, that none can be acquainted with the happiness annexed to a truly benevolent mind, who is not in possession of it. We are all partially good, and some are more extensively so than others; but there are a few of the sons of men, who are benevolent. (Macaulay 1790, 114)

Implementation of the Vision

In *Letters*, Macaulay proposed an education that modeled in practice what it taught on several levels—from the coeducational system of instruction, to the type and content of the books used, and even to the tutor's method of disciplining and interacting with the students. Perhaps in response to Rousseau's work, she stated explicitly that her educational plan applied to women as well as men:

But I must tell you, Hortensia, lest you should mistake my plan, that though I have been obliged (in order to avoid confusion) to speak commonly in the masculine character, that the same rules of education in all aspects are to be observed to the female as well as to the male children. (Macaulay 1790, 142)

Macaulay believed that both girl and boy students educated by her system would be "life-long" learners who loved knowledge, had an insatiable appetite to learn, and would acquire "that active wisdom which is necessary for co-operating in any reformation" (Macaulay 1790, 198). She advocated using education as a means to reform society.

Curriculum

Macaulay recommended that formal instruction in reading and writing wait until the child was ten or twelve years old. Informal learning, however, was to begin at birth, and very young children were to be read to, talked with, and taught in a very careful manner. In her letter entitled "Literary Education of Young Persons," Macaulay quoted Rousseau as saying that "[t]he most critical interval of human life is that between the hour of birth and twelve years of age" (Macaulay 1790, 126). Macaulay had specific ideas about how those twelve years should be best spent educationally. And remember, while Rousseau's plan was intended only for the male child, Macaulay specifically broadened it to include the female learner as well. Assuming this, she agreed with Rousseau's notion that:

> We should not tamper with the mind till it has acquired all its faculties: for it is impossible it should perceive the light we hold out, while it is blind, or that it should pursue over an immense plain of ideas, that route which reason hath so slightly traced, as to be perceptible only to the sharpest sight. (quoted in Macaulay 1790, 126)

Of Rousseau's argument, she said:

> The arguments of the author are very ingenious; and I so far agree with him as to think, that till the mind has attained sufficient strength to co-operate with its instructor, in rejecting by the dictates judgment, improper associations of ideas, and in selecting such as are to be desired, it were better to leave it entirely to the simple impressions which it receives from example, and the experience of consequences. For opinions taken up on mere authority, must ever prevent original thinking, must stop the progress of improvement, and instead of producing rational agents, can only make man a mere ape of man. (Macaulay 1790, 127)

She explained the necessary consciousness of the teacher in recognizing his or her potential influence even in non-formal instruction:

> [T]o preserve as much as possible the independence of the mind, let us be very sparing of our precept to the credulous ears of infancy; and let us devote the first ten or twelve years of life to the strengthening of the corporal faculties, to the giving of useful habits, and to those attainments which can be acquired, without burdening the mind with ideas which it cannot well comprehend. (Macaulay 1790, 128)

In Macaulay's nursery and schoolroom, books were to be read to children, and the books were to be selected through a thorough process that considered the impressions and influence that the story and subject matter might have on the child. Neither mere entertainment nor satisfying the child's imagination was a valid standard for choosing the children's books.

Macaulay criticized much of the existing children's literature, arguing, for example, that fairy tales often frightened or deceived the youthful audience more than they inspired or instructed them. She also questioned the writers' ethics. She said:

> Tom Thumb, Jack Hickathrift, Jack the Giant Killer; and some few
> more histories of this kind, may be regarded as mere negatives as to
> their effects on the mind; but those tales which endeavor to recom-
> mend virtue, not from its intrinsic value; not from that tranquillity of
> soul which ever attends it; not from the mental enjoyment, which
> God has annexed to the practice and cultivation of the benign affec-
> tions; but from some carnal advantage with which its votaries are
> from every system of education. (Macaulay 1790, 53)

She claimed that many works implied that a person's motivation for being virtuous
was the material reward that he or she would receive as a result of his or her conduct.
She accused the writings and their authors of holding out an "imaginary bribe" that
could only misinform and possibly "corrupt the young mind" and "give it an erro-
neous idea of the ways of Providence" (Macaulay 1790, 53). She saw Jean de La
Fontaine's fables as

> so complicated and disproportionate to the capacities of children,
> that they might rather induce them to vice than virtue. The same may
> be said of Aesop's fables. (Macaulay 1790, 54)

It was Stephanie de Genlis' works of children's fiction that Macaulay specifically
recommended for young people's amusement and early learning. De Genlis was an
eighteenth-century French teacher and author of novels, plays, and works on education and politics. A teacher above all, it was her works on education that afforded her
the wide reputation she held during her own time (Chambaud 1901, 203–04).
Macaulay praised de Genlis' work, both for its ability to amuse and to teach. She
offered *L'Ami des Enfants* as exemplary:

> Madame Genlis . . . avoided the objections that lay against almost
> every previous work which has been published for the use of chil-
> dren. Her moral is pure and simple; her composition well adapted to
> the understanding of her readers; and though written in a stile [sic]
> and taste which might gratify a mature judgment, it is calculated to
> give pleasure and instruction to the most youthful mind. . . . I can
> venture to pronounce a decided judgment on the merits of a work
> entitled *L'Ami des Enfants*. Such indeed is the value of this publica-
> tion, that it must afford both pleasure and instruction to children
> from the period previous to their having acquired the art of reading,
> to the time when their taste and judgment are sufficiently matured to
> enter into a high line of literature. (Macaulay 1790, 55)

In addition to being read to during this zero to twelve year age span, Macaulay proposed that children study:

> The Latin grammar, geography taught in the easiest and pleasantest
> manner; such parts of physics as lie open to the attention of children;

writing, arithmetic, and the French language . . . are fully sufficient to
fill up the time of childhood; and to exercise its growing faculties
without the use of books, which I seldom introduce, but with the
view of amusement. (Macaulay 1790, 128)

If the child showed "any marks of a more than ordinary vigor of intellect," then at
age ten (but otherwise at age twelve) the students were to immediately begin reading
and writing using Plutarch's moral biographies as focus. Apparently, Macaulay
believed that the child who would have already enjoyed so much earlier work with
language would read easily and naturally.

In Letter XIV, "Literary Education of Young Persons," Macaulay began a detailed
description and discussion of the "mechanics" of her educational plan, which began
in the child's twelfth year and culminated when the student was approximately
twenty-one.

At age twelve, a very ambitious and rigorous formal education was to begin.
The students were to read and study selections of *Plutarch's Lives*, Addison's *Specta-
tors*, Guthrie's *Geographical Grammar*, and Mentelle's *Géographie Comparée* (in the
original French). At fourteen, students would begin to write themes in both Latin
and English on the topic of history. Rollin's *Ancient History* was to be read in French
and Livy's *History* in English. Roman history was also to be studied. At age fifteen,
students were to begin the study of Greek. At sixteen, a course in moral lectures
would be added, as would the study of Cicero, Plutarch, Epictetus, Seneca, and
Fénélon. Students would also study Shakespeare, Milton, Pope, Racine, Molière,
Voltaire, and others.

After this strenuous intellectual education was completed, students would learn
ancient geography and begin to study the globe, astronomy, philosophy, and natural
history. At eighteen, students would presumably have acquired a sufficient compe-
tence in Greek to read Plato's dialogues in the original. At nineteen, they would
study politics, including works by Harrington, Sydney, Locke, and Hobbes.

Macaulay suggested completely postponing reading the Bible until age twenty-
one. Anticipating much criticism for this part of her plan, she wrote:

And now, Hortensia, that I have concluded the mechanical part of
education, I have leisure to answer your objections, for I will not
compliment you so much, my friend, to suppose you have gotten
over every prejudice, which custom and general opinion impose on
the wisest of the human race. What! exclaim you, put off the perusal
of the sacred writings to so late a period of manhood as the age of one
and twenty, and run the risk of your pupil being snatched away from
the knowledge of Christianity by a premature death? (Macaulay
1790, 136)

She answered this challenge with the assertion that her design was meant to
make "true Christians" (Macaulay 1790, 137) of the students, waiting until they

have acquired the full vigor of their intellect, 'till they are capable of judging the subjects laid before them with precision, and 'till a full knowledge of the systems of religion which prevailed before Christianity, with the philosophical opinions of the ancients, enable them to discern plainly the advantages of those lights which have been gained by revelation.

In this state of unbiased mind, the evidence for and against Christianity will be examined with clearness; and the judgment which the mind forms on the question, will have a weight that no Sophistry can overthrow. (Macaulay 1790, 139)

Discipline

In Letter X, "Severity in the Education of Children, Improper-Indiscriminate Indulgence Censured," Macaulay called a teacher's use of corporal punishment the "ensign of pedagogue authority," and said that "in the last age," the "whole art of education was supposed to lie in whipping often and whipping with severity" (Macaulay 1790, 97). Though it had been the accepted manner of discipline, Macaulay was strongly opposed to "whipping" the child. She generally agreed with Locke, Rousseau, de Genlis, and other eminent writers of educational philosophy on this particular topic. She said:

> Mr. Locke has taken a great deal of pains to show the inefficacy, the ill tendency and the cruelty of the rigorous plan. Rousseau, Genlis, and all the later writers of eminence, who have treated on education; have either totally excluded the rod, or kept it for the punishment of hardened obstinacy and disobedience; and such has been the force of truth, supported by argument and eloquence, that severity is in general excluded from every mode of private education. (Macaulay 1790, 98–99)

When Macaulay discussed the treatment of the obstinate child, however, she said that corporal punishment might be necessary as a last resort, but added that

> this ought to be done with a delicacy, which should at once impress on the mind of the offender the advantage of character, and the friendly sentiments of the person by whom he is thus punished. (Macaulay 1790, 110)

Her major reason for objecting to the practice of whipping was that it showed a serious lack of "delicacy" or "tenderness" toward the child (Macaulay 1790, 97–99). She argued that withholding tenderness was more detrimental to a child's character formation than the whipping was in any obviously physical way (Macaulay 1790, 99).

So tenderness had somehow to be discerned in the tutor, even if whipping occurred. Her commitment to have the tutor express, and thus teach by modeling, the tender, softer, sympathetic aspects of human nature is, once again, articulated, this time in her methods of practice.

Macaulay believed that negative, long-term character traits in adults resulted from the improperly violent conduct toward children. Therefore, she argued that the interactions between teacher and student or parent and child were to be always respectful and affectionate. She explained her hypothesis:

> when the frame of mind is at an early period of life often disturbed and violently shaken by rigorous sensations, a perpetual irritation is produced, tranquillity gives place to restlessness, the temper becomes fretful and impatient, and the spirits are thrown into disorder by every thwarting incident which occurs.
> On the contrary, when during the state of infancy the mind is free from all painful commotion, it acquires a firmness and stability which is not easily shaken. Thus adults, who in their childhood have been tenderly and affectionately treated, commonly meet sorrow with constancy; but this is seldom, or perhaps never, the case with sensible minds who have experienced a contrary usage. (Macaulay 1790, 98)

She went on in the same letter to clarify that she was not recommending that the child should be spoiled or indulged or "doted upon" (Macaulay 1790, 102) in other inappropriate ways. She says that the

> most infallible way to make your child miserable, is to accustom him to obtain every thing that he desires; for those desires still encreasing [sic] from the facility of acquisition, your incapacity must sooner or later oblige you to the necessity of refusal; and that refusal, so new and uncommon, will give him more trouble than even the want of that which he desires. The sense of an imaginary injustice will sour his disposition. (Macaulay 1790, 101)

The Teacher

Who would be teaching in Macaulay's ideal school? The qualities and character of the teacher were clearly critical elements of instructional success. She said:

> When the task of education is given up by the parents and children are to be put into other hands, it is common in the choice of a tutor to look for no other qualities than those of learning and integrity. (Macaulay 1790, 104)

So, although Macaulay accepted that the tutor should possess the qualities of "learning and integrity," she thought that mere learning was insufficient unless united in the teacher with "judgment, penetration and sagacity" (Macaulay 1790, 104).

In Letter XI, "Necessary Qualities in a Tutor—Envy—Pride—Vanity—Punishment," Macaulay went on to say that the aforementioned "virtues of understanding" were not adequate unless accompanied by the "virtues of the heart." If all of these elements were not present in the mind and character of the teacher, then for Macaulay learning itself "becomes a dead letter, or a magazine of opinions," and she concluded that "the education of the pupil will be very incomplete" (Macaulay 1790, 104–05). She clearly tied the teacher's learning and character to the quality of the education that the student received.

Macaulay described the extraordinary balance of her ideal teacher's mind and heart:

> His learning must be accompanied with modesty, his wisdom with gaiety, his sagacity must have a keenness which can penetrate through the veil of prejudice, and attain to the high superiority of original thinking; and the virtues of the mind must be accompanied with that tenderness of feeling which produces the most valuable of all excellencies, an unconfined benevolence. (Macaulay 1790, 105)

Macaulay additionally recommended the manner in which the ideal teacher would go about teaching in order to diminish envy and competition among students:

> He will avoid the making of invidious comparisons and distinctions, or the bestowing of excessive praises on some particular person, in order to point him out to the pupil as an object of emulation, and consequently an object of envy. (Macaulay 1790, 105)

In addition to pointing out the negative effects of a teacher's exaggerated public praise of children, Macaulay commented on the negative effects of physical marking and labeling. Here she referred to the custom much used in schools for girls: "of putting various marks on little offenders, thus to point them out to their brethren and play fellows, as objects of contempt and ridicule" (Macaulay 1790, 109). Macaulay said that these methods served no positive purpose, and conversely only served to "blunt the feelings of shame . . . for when the mind has once lost its sensibility, there is no acting upon it with any success" (Macaulay 1790, 109–10).

If one equates learning and judgment with the "masculine" characteristics of the eighteenth century and "virtues of the heart" with the "feminine," then a picture of personal character integration in the teacher emerges in Macaulay's vision. According to Macaulay, this tutor, who had already accomplished the necessary character integration, would demonstrate and encourage by example the integration and development of those sometimes dormant qualities normally considered "masculine" and "feminine" in each student.

Assuming that the children were already socialized when they began to work with a tutor, and that they generally displayed only a part of their true nature, Macaulay's education was to work explicitly to rectify that situation. A girl was to be encouraged to cultivate not only her virtue and benevolence, but also her reason and intellect. Similarly, a boy was to be taught to nurture his capacity to be sympathetic and tender, as well as his leaning toward reason and justice. The tutor was presumably, regardless of gender, to demonstrate an integration of the aforementioned "reciprocally dependent" characteristics (Macaulay 1790, 216).

School Policy

In the second letter of Part I of *Letters*, called "The Question of Public and Private Education Considered," Macaulay argued in favor of the government becoming directly involved in the management of schools in order to create servants of and for the state. At the time she wrote this book, responsibility for educating children rested solely in the hands of individual parents. Again she refers to the work of the "ancients," thus reminding her reader that the notion that education was actually government's responsibility was not a new one. She said:

> The instruction of youth, Hortensia, was regarded by the ancients as an important part of the business of government, and many uniform plans of education have been given by Plato and other speculatifs, for the forming of the children of a state in such a manner as should best conduce to render them serviceable to its glory and prosperity. (Macaulay 1790, 15)

She did not specify exactly which social ills might be remedied by a public education or what "political advantages might accrue" to society as a result of it. She simply said:

> I will not expatiate here on all those various crimes which a public education, if well-planned, would prevent, nor on those enlargements of moral good, which it would effect. The subject is a fruitful one, and I could extend it to the size of a long letter, were I to explain to you the political advantages which might accrue from a wisely conceived, and a well administered plan of this kind, with the advancement which it must necessarily occasion in public and private happiness. (Macaulay 1790, 18)

Her proposal was motivated by her belief that the social being was formed out of his or her experiences and education. She argued, therefore, for a large-scale, systematic fashioning of educational experiences. For her, "social man" was both created by, and subsequently created, the social environment. Therefore, a young person's education could not be left to chance or to the differing levels of interest, capacity, or wisdom of individual parents. She inferred that the state must act as the "good parent" and do what was best by providing a thorough intellectual and moral education for all of its future citizens, wives, and mothers.

Macaulay understood the complexity of this issue and the implications of her proposal. A parent herself, she believed in the "unalienable right" a parent had to teach his or her own child as she chose. She said:

> [The parent] claims as his natural and unalienable right, the unmolested exercise of parental authority in the bringing up and tutoring of his offspring; and he says, he shall regard himself as materially injured in this right, if he does not use his pleasure in the making his child either a Turk, an Infidel, or a Christian; a rogue, or an honest man, as best suits his views and purposes. (Macaulay 1790, 18)

She conceded the parents' incomparable power, by virtue of the bond that naturally existed between them and their child, or the parents' interest in, and attention to, their child's development. However, she also understood that not all parents were inclined to take on the task of carefully overseeing the child's education, nor did some have the resources—material or otherwise—to hire tutors sufficiently capable, compassionate, patient, and virtuous to educate a child intellectually as well as morally. For her, natural rights did not take precedence over increasing the happiness of society. She wrote:

> It is true, Hortensia, that I have put the claim of my adversary in a very disadvantageous light; but though there is a great deal to be said on both sides of the question, I protest to you, that I never did hear any forcible argument urged against the expediency of vesting government with the charge of education; for it is absurd to oppose natural rights to any scheme of policy which would probably tend to encrease [sic] the happiness of society. (Macaulay 1790, 18–19)

This being the case, Macaulay suggested that a collective schooling system would require less money from each individual family and would ensure more uniform and equal opportunity for all children. She proposed a sliding scale of taxation to support the system, based on the individual's ability to pay. She said that

> numbers may be more easily provided for in the aggregate, than when they are separated into particulars; and therefore it would be lighter on the pockets of the people to pay a tax to government for the education of their offspring, than to take that charge on themselves, especially as such a tax might be regulated according to the rank, the fortune, and consequently the expectations of the citizens. (Macaulay 1790, 17–18)

Macaulay anticipated the controversial response to removing the right to educate one's child from the parents' strict domain. She entertained opposing arguments and offered her counterarguments to these positions. The first was the loss of freedom that parents would suffer in giving control of their child's education to the state. Her response chastised short-sighted, individualistic thinkers and focused the perspective from a personal to a societal one. She said:

> It is absurd to oppose natural rights to any scheme or policy which would probably tend to increase the happiness of society. (Macaulay 1790, 19)

The second argument against establishing public education was that the quality of a public education would necessarily be inferior to that of an individual education received in the home. Macaulay agreed that in many cases this was a valid argument, except for those parents she labeled as

> opulent idlers, who have neither the capacity nor the inclination to fulfill in their own persons, this most important of parental duties. (Macaulay 1790, 20)

Her goal was eventually to offer a uniformly excellent education to all children, and she hoped for an equally excellent educational outcome for all. She dreamed of a public system producing

> multitudes of finished citizens fitted for those various occupations which are necessary to support the glory and the prosperity of society. (Macaulay 1790, 17)

Conclusion

Philosophies of education come in three varieties. On one end of the spectrum are those works that remain theoretical and uselessly utopian. At the other end, one finds educational handbooks, "how to" manuals that may be practical but philosophically unreflective. Somewhere in the midst of this continuum are the most powerful educational philosophies, those that not only combine teaching and practice but also develop a theory, bearing in mind that practice must come from it. Catharine Macaulay's work approaches this ideal. She consistently modulated her proposed practices, bearing her theories in mind. Her *Letters* stands as a sound response to Rousseauian beliefs about human nature and the educational assumptions that emerge from those beliefs. We continue to correct many of the gender issues Macaulay noted, and in that sense alone, her work is relevant today.

Macaulay addressed issues of human nature and knowledge and their implications for education. Because of what we know about both her own personal experience and women's social and political situation of her time, *Letters On Education* speaks with passion and relevance. Her broad vision of humankind included a different model of masculinity as well as femininity. Her essentially holistic theory, which defined character elements as parts of one integrated human nature, anticipated the current discussion of these same lingering issues of gender differences, essential natures, and the synthesis of gender-constructed qualities within each individual. She proposed one single view of human nature, and in that sense we have not yet achieved her ideal.

Catharine Macaulay articulated and explained the source of her beliefs on human nature and knowledge, and, holding her beliefs as an immovable base, she proposed an educational practice that matched them. For example, she believed in justice and equity, which she said grew from her spiritual belief in a perfectly benevolent and just deity. In her *History of England*, she advocated a true democracy, denying the validity, the efficiency, and the fairness of a monarchical government. She applied this belief to other aspects of civil and social relations, such as gender differences.

Although Macaulay did not found a school, we can imagine how her ideas might look in practice through her detailed description of the curriculum, her method of disciplining students, and the characteristics of the tutor. *Letters* offers an estimable coherence among a philosophy of education with metaphysical foundations, a theory of education addressing epistemological questions, and specific practices of education—her pedagogy. The power of what underlay her practice was her belief in each child's unlimited potential. The recognizably unique component at each of these levels is the integration of so-called "masculine" and "feminine" characteristics, her rejection of what many people of her time accepted as truth.[9]

Today, it often seems that educational policies and the resultant practices are not based on beliefs—or if they are, the connection between beliefs and practices is not often carefully articulated. Too often, we discern in practice a belief in the child's incompleteness, especially when we design interventions to remedy their lack. Too often, we look at children and ask, "What do we need to give them, or do to them, in order to make them confident, literate, numerate, healthy, fully functioning socially or emotionally—WHOLE?" Macaulay first defined for us the nature of God, and from that starting point she outlined human nature and potential. Her description of "wholeness" in mankind was measured against the perfect and good deity. The "whole" we work to achieve is often defined by whatever potential we determine or whatever role we expect the child to occupy in society. If we were to begin instead with a belief in the child's completeness, soundness, and unconditional worth, reflective of the divine, and if we were committed to shaping our approach and our practices to coincide with those beliefs, as Macaulay suggested, how different might our schoolrooms and outcomes be?

Looking Forward

What do educators believe about the essence, the limitations, the potential of human nature? What informs those beliefs? Do we use them when we conceptualize school policies and practices? After confronting what we believe, we must ask ourselves some honest questions. Do we want to challenge ourselves and our beliefs about human nature, and rework them? If so, how will we construct our curriculum, our pedagogy, and our teacher education programs so that they match our beliefs in constructive ways?

Macaulay's method in *Letters on Education* of shaping her pedagogy and curriculum to match her explicitly stated beliefs is perhaps as valuable as her book's content. In her work, she studies her own beliefs and personal experiences, specifically regarding issues of human nature and knowledge. She then contemplates and makes explicit the rationale underlying her beliefs. Next, she proposes educational policies and practices that are based on, and that carefully honor, those beliefs. I believe that we could benefit from using the same process that she demonstrated.

Macaulay's philosophy of education, and her conceptualization of the role and character of the teacher, represent an intellectual act of liberation and reflect a deeply spiritual view of education. Her ideas show her dedication to conceptualize a structure in which every rational being is free to seek excellence and is taught to do so. If we enact her proposals, we might ready our students to seek excellence by first teaching them to question and reject the false notions of gender and racial limitation that some social norms accept as true. We might teach our pre-service teachers first to understand their own beliefs and, if necessary, to work intimately with them to eliminate all beliefs in gender and racial inequity and social restriction. Macaulay's philosopher teacher, in addition to teaching a rigorous academic curriculum, had the responsibility to develop attitudes, strengthen dispositions, and sharpen the insights of his or her students. Macaulay envisioned the act of education itself as the means to achieve full individual development and deep social change.

Notes

[1]In 1778, Macaulay married her second husband, William Graham. "Catharine Macaulay Graham" is the actual author of *Letters on Education;* however, because most scholars refer to her as "Catharine Macaulay," I use that name throughout this work.

[2]Other women living during Rousseau's approximate time period also disagreed with his ideas about women and wrote philosophical works countering both his premises and his conclusions about them. See, for example Chapone, 1773/1800; de Genlis, 1783/1804; Wollstonecraft, 1792/1975.

[3]The view that Macaulay rejected is today called the notion of sex complementarity. Mary Ellen Waithe, in her newest volume, *A History of Women Philosophers*, briefly describes this doctrine and its significance in Rousseau's work *Émile,* against which Macaulay argues in *Letters.*

This doctrine assumed that man and woman were biological and spiritual opposites, whose differences were totally innate and defined by essence, not by socialization. Furthermore, the doctrine categorized the unchangeable differences so that those "belonging" to woman were inferior in value to those "belonging" to man. Together, the distinct and different qualities composing each of their gender-based natures were thought to combine and complement each other to form one whole human being. As we have already seen, this view posed a serious problem for Macaulay, both in its metaphysical basis and in the educational and social outcomes it engendered.

[4]Mary Hays claims to have learned this information from Mrs. Arnold Leicester, a long-time friend of the Sawbridge family. Bridget Hill, Macaulay's recent biographer, says that the family papers were probably destroyed in the fire of the family home in Kent in the early part of this century.

[5]Bridget Hill (1992) lists the following positive reviewers of Macaulay's first volume of *History:* Thomas Hollis, Horace Walpole, William Pitt, Joseph Priestly, John Wilkes, Benjamin Franklin, Madame Roland, William Cowper, Elizabeth Carter, David Hume, Mary Wollstonecraft, George Washington, and Mercy Otis Warren.

[6]Macaulay was most concerned about the proposed organization of the U.S. two-body legislature. In a letter to Washington she asked, "May not your upper House in length of time acquire some distinction which may lay the grounds for political inequality among you?" (Sparks 1834–1837, 68)

[7]See for example, the works of Marie de Gournay (1622/1989), Margaret Cavendish (1622/1985), and Anna Maria van Schurman (1675).

[8]Macaulay was undoubtedly influenced by the Stoics in her views on moral duty in general and benevolence in particular. She referred specifically to Epictetus in the third section of *Letters on Education* and compared his views with those of "the Messiah." Though she did not endorse the Stoic's doctrines unreservedly, she argued in their favor regarding the manner of developing moral character. In speaking of the Stoics she said, "their principles of morality were more consonant to the purity of the Christian doctrine than that of any other of the philosophic sects, that they have been the only source from which both the ancient and modern moralists have drawn all their arguments for the intrinsic value and beauty of virtue" (Macaulay 1790, 448).

[9]The view that Macaulay rejected is today called the notion of sex complementarity. Mary Ellen Waithe, in her newest volume of *A History of Women Philosophers,* briefly describes this doctrine and its significance in Jean-Jacques Rousseau's work *Émile,* against which Macaulay argues in her *Letters.*

This doctrine assumed that men and women were biological and spiritual opposites, whose differences were totally innate and defined by essence, not by socialization. Furthermore, the doctrine categorized the unchangeable differences so that those "belonging" to woman were inferior in value to those "belonging" to men. Together, the distinct and different qualities composing each of their gender-based natures were thought to combine and complement each other to form one whole human being. As we have already seen, this view posed a serious problem for Macaulay, both in its metaphysical basis and in the educational and social outcomes it engendered.

Catharine Macaulay's Writings
Arranged in Chronological Order

History of England, from the Accession of James I to That of the Brunswick Line, 8 vols. (London, 1763-83): ii (1765), iii (1767), iv (1768), v (1771), vi (1781), viii (1783).

Loose Remarks on Certain Positions to Be Found in Mr. Hobbes' "Philosophical Rudiments of Government and Society." (London, 1767)

Observations on a Pamphlet "Thoughts on the Cause of the Present Discontents" [a review of *Thoughts on the Cause of the Present Discontents* by Edmund Burke] (London, 1770).

A Modest Plea for the Property of Copyright (Bath, 1774).

An Address to the People of England, Scotland, and Ireland on the Present Time, in a Series of Letters (Bath, 1775).

The History of England, from the Revolution to the Present Time, in a Series of Letters (Bath, 1778).

A Treatise on the Immutability of Moral Truth (London, 1783).

Observations on the Reflections of the Right Honorable Edmund Burke on the Revolution in France, in a Letter to the Earl of Stanhope (London, 1790).

Letters on Education, with Observations on Religious and Metaphysical Subjects (London, 1790).

References

Appianus, of Alexandria. 1902. *Civil Wars: Book I.* ed. J. Stracham-Davidson. Oxford: Clarendon Press.

Boos, F. S. 1976. *Catharine Macaulay's* Letters on Education *(1790): An Early Feminist Polemic.* University of Michigan Papers in Women's Studies, Ann Arbor: Women's Studies Program.

Bryson, V. 1992. *Feminist Political Theory.* New York: Paragon House.

Cavendish, M. [1662] 1985. Female orations. Reprint. In *Norton Anthology of Literature by Women,* ed. P. Gilbert and R. Gubar. New York: W. W. Norton.

Chambaud, L. 1901. *Mesdames de Maintenon, de Genlis, and Campan Leur Role dans l'Education Chretienne de la Femme.* Paris: Librairie Plon.

Chapone, H. [1773] 1800. *Letters on the Improvement of the Mind: Addressed to a Young Lady.* Reprint. Boston: William Green.

Davis, N. Z., and A. Farge, ed. 1993. *A History of Women: Renaissance and Enlightenment Paradoxes.* Cambridge: Harvard University Press.

de Genlis, S. F. C. [1783] 1804. *Adele et Theodore ou Lettres sur l'Education.* Reprint. Paris: Dufour.

de Gournay, M. [1622] 1989. The Equality of Men and Women and The Ladies Grievance, trans. Maja Bijvoet. In *Women Writers of the Seventeenth Century,* ed. G. Wilson and W. Warnke. Athens: Georgia University Press.

Dictionary of National Biography. Vol. 12. 1908–1909. ed. Sir L. Stephen and Sir S. Lee. New York: Macmillan.

Donnelly, L. M. 1949. The Celebrated Mrs. Macaulay. *William and Mary Quarterly* 6.

Ferguson, M. 1985. *First Feminists: British Women Writers 1578–1799.* Bloomington: Indiana University Press.

Fitzpatrick, J. C. 1931–1944. *Writings of Washington.* Vol. 28. Washington, DC: U.S. Government Printing Office.

Gatens, M. 1991. *Feminism and Philosophy: Perspectives on Difference and Equality.* Bloomington: Indiana University Press.

Gilman, C. P. [1915] 1979. *Herland.* Reprint. New York: Pantheon.

Graham, C. M. S. 1790. *Letters on Education, with Observations on Religious and Metaphysical Subjects.* London: Dilly.

Harvey, E. D., and K. Okruhlik, ed. 1992. *Women and Reason.* Ann Arbor: The University of Michigan Press.

Hays, M. 1803. *Female Biography.* Vol. 5. London: Phillips.

Hill, B. 1992. *The Republican Virago: The Life and Time of Catharine Macaulay, Historian.* Oxford, England: Clarendon Press.

Kaminsky, J. S. 1993. *A New History of Educational Philosophy.* Westport, CT: Greenwood Press.

Lerner, G. 1993. *The Creation of Feminist Consciousness: from the Middle Ages to 1870.* New York: Oxford University Press.

Locke, J. [1691] 1902. *Some Thoughts on Education.* Reprint. Cambridge: University Press.

Lowe, M., and R. Hubbard. 1983. *Woman's Nature: Rationalizations of Inequality.* New York: Pergamon Press.

Macaulay, C. 1763–1783. *History of England, from the Accession of James I to That of the Brunswick Line.* 8 Vols. London: Nourse.

_____ . 1783. *Treatise on the Immutability of Moral Truth.* London.

_____ . [1787] 1790. *Letters on Education.* London.

Plato. 1953. *The Republic.* London: Penguin.

Reynolds, M. 1920. *The Learned Lady in England, 1650–1760.* Boston: Houghton Mifflin.

Rousseau, J. J. [1762] 1979. *Émile.* Reprint. New York: Basic Books.

Sparks, J. 1834–1837. *The Writings of George Washington.* Vol. 4. Boston: Russell, Odiorne, Metcalf, and Hilliard Gray.

Stenton, D. M. 1957. *English Women in History.* London: Allen and Unwin.

Titone, C. 1992. Catharine Macaulay: Feminist Philosopher on Education. Unpublished qualifying paper. Harvard Graduate School of Education, Cambridge, MA.

Ulich, R. 1982. *Three Thousand Years of Educational Wisdom.* Cambridge, MA: Harvard University Press.

van Schurman, A. M. 1675. *The Learned Maid: A Logick Lesson.* London: John Redmayer.

Waithe, M. E. ed. 1991. *A History of Women Philosophers: 1600–1900.* New York: Kluwer.

Wollstonecraft, M. 1790. Letters on Education [a review of *Letters on Education* by Catharine Macaulay]. *The Analytical Review* 8: 244–47.

_____ . [1792] 1975. *A Vindication of the Rights of Woman*: 200. Harmondsworth: Penguin.

READING

Letter XXII
No Characteristic Difference in Sex

Catharine Macaulay

An excerpt from *Letters on Education*

The great difference that is observable in the characters of the sexes, Hortensia, as they display themselves in the scenes of social life, has given rise to much false speculation on the natural qualities of the female mind. —For though the doctrine of innate ideas, and innate affections, are in a great measure exploded by the learned, yet few persons reason so closely and so accurately on abstract subjects as, through a long chain of deductions, to bring forth a conclusion which in no respect militates with their premises.

It is a long time before the crowd give up opinions they have been taught to look upon with respect; and I know many persons who will follow you willingly through the course of your argument, till they perceive it tends to the overthrow of some fond prejudice; and then they will either sound a retreat, or begin a contest in which the contender for truth, though he cannot be overcome, is effectually silenced, from the mere weariness of answering positive assertions, reiterated without end. It is from such causes that the notion of a sexual difference in the human character has, with a very few exceptions, universally prevailed from the earliest times, and the pride of one sex, and the ignorance and vanity of the other, have helped to support an opinion which a close observation of Nature, and a more accurate way of reasoning, would disprove.

It must be confessed, that the virtues of the males among the human species, though mixed and blended with a variety of vices and errors, have displayed a bolder and a more consistent picture of excellence than female nature has hitherto done. It is on these reasons that, when we compliment the appearance of a more than ordinary energy in the female mind, we call it masculine; and hence it is, that Pope has elegantly said *a perfect woman's but a softer man*. And if we take in the consideration, that there can be but one rule of moral excellence for beings made of the same materials, organized after the same manner, and subjected to similar laws of Nature, we must either agree with Mr. Pope, or we must reverse the proposition, and say, that *a perfect man is a woman formed after a coarser mold*. The difference that actually does subsist between the sexes, is too flattering for men to be willingly imputed to accident; for what accident occasions, wisdom might correct; and it is better, says Pride, to give up the advantages we might derive from the perfection of our fellow associates, than to own that Nature has been just in the equal distribution of her favours. These are the sentiments of the men; but mark how readily they are yielded to by the women; not from humility I assure you, but merely to preserve with character those fond vanities on which they set their hearts. No; suffer them to idolize their persons, to throw away their life in the pursuit of trifles, and to indulge in the gratification of the meaner passions, and they will heartily join in the sentence of their degradation.

Among the most strenuous asserters of a sexual difference in character, Rousseau is the most conspicuous, both on account of that warmth of sentiment which distinguishes all his writings, and the eloquence of his compositions: but never did enthusiasm and the love of paradox, those enemies to philosophical disquisition, appear in more strong opposition to plain sense than in Rousseau's definition of this difference. He sets out with a supposition, that Nature intended the subjection of the one sex to the other; that consequently there must be an inferiority of intellect in the subjected party; but as man is a very imperfect being, and apt to play the capricious tyrant, Nature, to bring things nearer to an equality, bestowed on the woman such attractive graces, and such an insinuating address, as to turn the balance on the other scale. Thus Nature, in a giddy mood, recedes from her purposes, and subjects prerogative to an influence which must produce confusion and disorder in the system of human affairs. Rousseau saw this objection; and in order to obviate it, he has made up a moral person of the union of the two sexes, which, for contradiction and absurdity, outdoes every metaphysical riddle that was ever formed in the schools. In short, it is not reason, it is not wit; it is pride and sensuality that speak in Rousseau, and, in this instance, has lowered the man of genius to the licentious pedant.

But whatever might be the wise purpose intended by Providence in such a disposition of things; certain it is, that some degree of inferiority, in point of corporal strength, seems always to have existed between the two sexes; and this advantage, in the barbarous ages of mankind, was abused to such a degree, as to destroy all the natural rights of the female species, and reduce them to a state of abject slavery. What accidents have contributed in Europe to better their condition, would not be to my purpose to relate; for I do not intend to give you a history of women; I mean only to trace the sources of their peculiar foibles and vices; and these I firmly believe to originate in situation and education only: for so little did a wife and just Providence intend to make the condition of slavery an unalterable law of female nature, that in the same proportion as the male sex have consulted the interest of their own happiness, they have relaxed in their tyranny over women; and such is their use in the system of mundane creation, and such their natural influence over the male mind, that were these advantages properly exerted, they might carry every point of any importance to their honour and happiness. However, till that period arrives in which women will act wisely, we will amuse ourselves in talking of their follies.

The situation and education of women, Hortensia, is precisely that which must necessarily tend to corrupt and debilitate both the powers of mind and body. From a false notion of beauty and delicacy, their system of nerves is depraved before they come out of their nursery; and this kind of depravity has more influence over the mind, and consequently over morals, than is commonly apprehended. But it would be well if such causes only acted towards the debasement of the sex; their moral education is, if possible, more absurd than their physical. The principles and nature of virtue, which is never properly explained to boys, is kept quite a mystery to girls. They are told indeed, that they must abstain from those vices which are contrary to their personal happiness, or they will be regarded as criminals, both by God and man; but all the higher parts of rectitude, every thing that ennobles our being, and that renders us both innoxious and useful, is either not taught, or is taught in such a manner as to leave no proper impression on the mind. This is so obvious a truth, that the defects of female education have ever been a fruitful topic of declamation for the moralist; but not one of this class of writers have laid down any judicious rules for amendment. Whilst we still retain the absurd notion of a sexual excellence, it will militate against the perfecting a plan of education for either sex. The judicious Addison animadverts on the absurdity of bringing a young lady up with no higher idea of the end of education than to make her agreeable to a husband, and confining the necessary excellence for this happy acquisition to the mere graces of person.

Every parent and tutor may not express himself in the same manner as is marked out by Addison; yet certain it is, that the admiration of the other sex is held out to women as the highest honour they can attain; and whilst this is considered as their *summun bonum,* and the beauty of their persons the chief *desideratum* of men, Vanity, and its companion Envy, must taint, in their characters, every native and every acquired excellence. Nor can you, Hortensia, deny, that these qualities, when united to ignorance, are fully equal to the engendering and rivetting all those vices and foibles which are peculiar to the female sex; vices and foibles which have caused them to be considered, in ancient times, as beneath cultivation, and in modern days have subjected them to the censure and ridicule of writers of all descriptions, from the deep thinking philosopher to the man of ton and gallantry, who, by the bye, sometimes distinguishes himself by qualities which are not greatly superior to those he despises in women. Nor can I better illustrate the truth of this observation than by the following picture, to be found in the polite and gallant Chesterfield. "Women," says his Lordship, "are only children of a larger growth. They have an entertaining tattle, sometimes wit; but for solid reasoning, and good sense, I never in my life knew one that had it, or who acted or reasoned in consequence of it for four and twenty hours together. A man of sense only trifles with them, plays with them, humours and flatters them, as he does an engaging child; but he neither consults them, nor trusts them in serious matters."

Chapter 3

ANA ROQUÉ DE DUPREY

Let Us, Sisters, *Make* Another Life

By Maria del C. Garcia Padilla

Introduction

Ana Roqué de Duprey (1853–1933) was a Puerto Rican teacher, feminist, and social reformer. She was born in Aguadilla, a northwestern town on the Island. Daughter of a successful merchant, she received a privileged education and excelled as an educator, scientist, politician, journalist, and sociologist. She focused her work on finding solutions to the problems raised in a very particular Latin American context by educating Puerto Ricans (especially female teachers), calling Puerto Rican women to take a more active role in "making a homeland," and working in favor of women's right to vote. She hoped this project would extend to the rest of America and to the world.

Historical Background

For 500 years, Puerto Rico has been under colonial governments, first of Spain, and then of the United States. The Island became a Spanish colony in 1493. As with the rest of Latin American countries, our 400-year connection with Spain left us the Spanish language, Catholicism as the main religion, and a Hispanic cultural and political tradition. However, while during the nineteenth century all Spanish colonies in the New World became independent, in 1898 Puerto Rico became a territory of the United States. Roqué's long life spanned the last period of Spanish domination of the Island through the third decade of U.S. colonial rule. Thus, she lived through one of the most serious political transformations in our history.

Uncertainty about, and objections to, the way Spain conceived our relations were sources of constant debate on the Island since early in the colonial period. With the change of sovereignty, questions about what form the relationship with the United States would take echoed those of the Spanish period. The economic, political, and cultural implications of this connection as well as the role of the U.S. federal government in education and other areas of governance were all cause for serious concern.

Ana Roqué examined these issues from the perspective of a feminist educator. To an important extent, her work influenced political, sociological, and educational transformations on the Island. Her positions are illuminating in the context of Puerto Rico today, not only because of their logic, but also because they accentuate the historical roots of a debate that is still unresolved. In order to explain her answers to these problems of colonization, Roqué devised what I call her *project of civilization* for Puerto Rico. Before discussing Roqué's ideas and work, I will briefly discuss both colonization enterprises in our country that provide the context necessary to better understand the importance of her work.

Spanish and U.S. Rule in Puerto Rico

The Spanish crown imposed on Puerto Rico, and the rest of its colonies, a Catholic project of unification, centralization, and *civilization.* This project was nurtured by the notion that there are universal laws—originated by God—that govern the association of human beings and the constitution of their societies. Spain presented itself as the terrestrial empire representing those laws, in charge of civilizing its subordinated colonies.

As with the rest of Latin America, the Spanish colonization of Puerto Rico resulted in economic exploitation and arbitrary political rule. At the beginning of the nineteenth century, a general discontent with the Spanish monarchy, nurtured by republican ideas, gave rise to the first wars for independence and then to the first Latin American republics. By the end of the century, all the colonies had gained independence, except Puerto Rico and Cuba, where the same monarchic military authoritarianism remained in power (Scarano 1993, 516). During the last two decades of the century, an increasing number of Puerto Ricans and Cubans reinforced their demands for more autonomy. In 1898, fearing independence movements in its only two remaining colonies in the New World, Spain approved a series of reforms. The "Constitución Autonómica" granted both islands the right to have their own government. Spain, however, would remain sovereign with ample powers (Scarano 1993, 541).

That same year, in the midst of the Spanish-American War, the United States invaded Puerto Rico. A few months later, the Treaty of Paris was signed; through it Spain yielded to the United States its sovereignty over Puerto Rico.[1] There were many political, cultural, and economic reasons why the United States was interested in the islands of the Caribbean. The nation was in the midst of a rapid transition toward an advanced industrial capitalism, and new markets were needed. Cuba and Puerto Rico were valuable for military, agricultural, industrial, and business reasons. They constituted strategic points for the construction of military bases and of increased commerce.

Coexisting with its liberal and democratic tradition, the United States maintained widespread ideologies of cultural and racial superiority. The most important of them, the doctrine of Manifest Destiny, held that civilized peoples—Anglo-Saxons in particular—were called by God, nature, and history to rule over, guide, and educate the "barbarian," less-developed races. Nurtured by this view, the U.S. invasion of Puerto Rico became not only an economic and military enterprise, but also a *civilization* crusade, similar to the Spanish Catholic colonization project of the previous centuries. As historian Rosario Natal points out, William McKinley, who was president at the time, was impelled by a "patriotic and imperialistic euphoria" that was far more powerful than the protests of those North Americans who believed that a democratic republic had no moral right to own colonies (quoted in Scarano 1993, 252).

Interestingly, many Puerto Ricans on the Island—Ana Roqué among them—received U.S. troops with hope and cordiality. This was the case because, after centuries of arbitrary monarchic authority, there was a general feeling that Spain had betrayed and abandoned the Island and that the arrival of the United States would alleviate hunger, stimulate commerce, and bring prosperity, in addition to immediately installing its democratic governmental institutions.

General Nelson A. Miles, who was in charge of the invasion, nurtured this optimism in a famous proclamation that circulated around the Island:

> We have not come to make war upon the people of a country that for centuries has been oppressed, but, on the contrary, to bring you protection, not only to yourselves but to your property, to promote your prosperity, and to bestow upon you the immunities and blessings of the liberal institution of our Government. It is not our purpose to interfere with any existing law and customs that are wholesome and beneficial to your people as long as they conform to the rules of military administration of order and justice. This is not a war of devastation, but one to give to all within the control of its military and naval forces the advantages and blessings of enlightened civilization. (Negrón de Montilla 1970, 2)

In spite of people's initial optimism, hope began to vanish during the first months and years of U.S. rule on the Island. Immediately, a military government was organized. This first eighteen-month period was characterized by deep economic crisis, the establishment of measures promoting U.S. values and views of the world, and the elaboration of permanent colonial policies. In 1900, the consensus in Washington was that the capacity of Puerto Ricans for self-government was limited and that they should be submitted to a system of civil government controlled and supervised from Washington.

U.S. civil government in Puerto Rico was inaugurated with the Foraker Law in 1900. In its fundamental aspects, this law placed Puerto Rican affairs under the control of the United States and its representatives on the Island. With it, Puerto Rico became a nonincorporated territory of the United States, subordinated to it in every order, as it had been to Spain before. Among other things, the Foraker Law established that people born on the Island were "citizens of Puerto Rico" and that as such they had the right to be protected by the United States. This law was partly inspired by an idea of mentorship, whereby power would be concentrated in the hands of North American individuals who, like "good mentors," would "teach" Puerto Ricans to fulfill the demands and duties of democracy.[2] In 1917, in the particular context of the First World War, the Jones Act was approved, introducing changes within the new colonial regime, and implanting U.S. citizenship in Puerto Rico.

From its very beginning there were those who foresaw that the results of the U.S. invasion would be a new colonial domination. But the great majority of the Island's leading and middle classes had the hope that the United States would treat Puerto Rico with dignity, and either contribute to its independence or allow it to enter the Union, first as a territory and later as a state. The United States, however, established a colonial system that was essentially very similar to the Spanish regime.

Education under U.S. Colonization

In 1898, when the Spanish domination of the Island ended, there were relatively few Puerto Ricans who had acquired formal instruction. There was an enormous shortage of teachers and of schools; the government spent very little money on public instruction; there were very few educational opportunities beyond those found in the larger towns; and girls' access to education was much more limited than boys', especially if they were born to rural workers.[3] In 1898, between 80 to 85 percent of the Island's inhabitants were illiterate (Scarano 1993, 490).

Under U.S. rule, the educational system began to expand. More public schools were built and the number of teachers and students increased. One of the reasons for this change was an interest among many Puerto Ricans to learn and adopt the educational approaches and methods utilized in the United States. Here again, their idealization, not only of what was going on in the United States, but also of what that country would be willing to grant and stimulate on the Island, led them to hope that the American educational system would contribute to the development of a more autonomous Puerto Rico.

The U.S. government welcomed this interest. It saw instruction as an essential tool to transmit U.S. values, language, and views of the world, as a road to *Americanize* [4] Puerto Ricans. Education was conceived by many as the essential vehicle through which Puerto Ricans would be converted into "good Americans." Victor S. Clark, author of many of the educational reforms implemented during U.S. military rule, wrote a statement that for many years provided the content and main objective of educational policies on the Island:

> If the schools are made American and the teachers and pupils are
> inspired with the American spirit . . . the island will become in its
> sympathies, views and attitude toward life and toward government
> essentially American. The great mass of Puerto Ricans are as yet pas-
> sive and plastic. . . . Their ideals are in our hands to create and mold.
> (quoted in Negrón de Montilla 1970, 13)

Since the 1900s education in Puerto Rico was centrally administered by Commissioners of Education, who were appointed by the President of the United States.
These commissioners, most of whom shared the view that the "native" culture was
inferior to theirs, had very extended powers and were in charge of most decisions
regarding appointments, curricula, and educational programs of all sorts (Negrón de
Montilla 1970).

Ana Roqué's political, sociological, and educational work sought to respond to a
number of problems within the circumstances just described. She searched for
solutions to the difficulties affecting the Island through three closely intertwined
endeavors: an effort to educate Puerto Ricans, especially female teachers; a call to
women to fulfill their *duties;* and a struggle in favor of women's vote. Her work in
these three endeavors constitutes, in my view, her *project of civilization* for Puerto Rico.
After independence from Spain, Latin American intellectuals and politicians were
profoundly discontent with the results of Spanish colonization in America. A series of
debates emerged dealing with the question of the relationship between cultural and
political emancipation from Spain and with the problems of defining the roads to be
taken for the development of the new nations. A number of *projects of civilization,* defined
and interpreted in different ways by many thinkers, resulted from this nineteenth-
century effort to develop a new human being and a new society in Latin America. My
view is that Ana Roqué de Duprey takes a place within this debate proposing, through
her political and educational work, her own *project of civilization* for Puerto Rico.

Biographical Sketch

As Ana Roqué herself tells us in an autobiographical article, since she was very
young she felt a passion for learning and for sharing her knowledge with others.
During the first seven years of her life, her grandmother, who had been a teacher for
thirty years and who was "one of the most illustrious women of her times . . . [who]
knew three languages, including Italian . . . [and for whom] reading was the center of
her life," was in charge of her instruction. Roqué tells us:

> I entered school . . . when I was seven years old and had learned
> already from my grandmother almost the entire elementary school
> program. It was a private school, every girl paid $2 a month. The first
> month my father sent $10 to the teachers telling them: "My daughter
> has a passion for books and for studying; I can only pay this amount
> for two years, and in that time I want her to learn everything the

Ana Roqué de Duprey

teacher can teach her." The teacher had been a student of an illustrious French man and had knowledge superior to her time. I left that
school when I was nine years old, knowing Spanish with perfect
spelling; 8 Maps from the Atlas because there [were] no Geography
[texts] at the time; quite broad [knowledge of] History, elementary
Arithmetic and sewing . . . Religion and Education. I had already
taken [introductory] notions of piano with another professor . . . I
spent two years at home learning Arithmetic with my father and
learning piano . . . I reentered school at eleven as a teacher aide and to
learn French . . . But I would teach advanced Arithmetic to my
teacher while girls wrote . . . When I was thirteen this teacher closed
her school and I established my own school at home with all her
pupils. . . . (Roqué 1932/1941, 7)[5]

Three years later, at the age of sixteen, she married a young trade clerk who had
recently finished his studies in Spain. Her husband's father was the owner of several
coffee and sugar cane farms, one of which became her home. She left her teaching
and her hometown and spent the next fifteen years of her life raising her children,[6]
working at home and spending as much time as she could reading and studying
botanics, geography, philosophy, and, most of all, astronomy (Meléndez 1941, 11).
Later, in 1879, she moved with her family to San Juan, where she continued her studies and participated actively in the intellectual and cultural life of the city. By 1880, at

the age of thirty, she had become one of the few women publishing in Puerto Rican journals and newspapers. She wrote short stories and articles about modern philosophy of education, botanics, astronomy, and other issues.

Roqué taught during most of her life. After her first experience teaching at home, she abandoned formal instruction until 1884 when, after completing the equivalent of her high school diploma, she reentered the teaching career. Later on, she obtained her teaching license. By 1887, and for reasons that are not altogether clear, she was separated from her husband and was in charge of her four children. One of her daughters says:

> All her children received from her elementary and high school instruction, we had no other teacher . . . At home, talks about studying to attain the highest levels of education were constant, inspiring us to try and conquer . . . She directed us in our chores . . . persuading us to exercise our duty to help and giving us a little money weekly to stimulate us . . . She was the teacher . . . [H]er critique was severe because she always demanded from each of us the most and the best: this was her pedagogy. . . .
>
> She believed that both men and women should work with their hands as they prepared for higher studies. She herself provided an example of this. I remember her ironing our clothes. . . . The book from which she was studying for an exam was on the iron board, this was almost always at night. . . .
>
> She did not want to see us inactive during the day . . . [and she] chose the books we should read . . . in our free time. She was restless . . . during the day she taught at school and during the evenings she gave classes to prospective teachers. . . .
>
> She was never weak with us, in spite of her immense love which she always expressed because she was very affectionate; but she demanded strict fulfillment of the house rules. . . .
>
> Only her grandchildren made of her a tender and consenting grandmother . . . [But], she also was their teacher. (Duprey de López 1941, 13)

Overview of Roqué's Thought

Positivism: an Intellectual Influence

The second half of the nineteenth century was a period of great cultural plenitude for intellectual minorities in Puerto Rico and the rest of Latin America. A spirit of social reform, an interest in the advancements of science, and a faith in progress were nurturing intellectual and political life. In her effort to find solutions to the Island's problems, and in her search for sound theories of social structure and organization,

Ana Roqué, as many intellectuals of her time, took up European philosophical, political, and educational thought and reinterpreted it to accommodate the particular needs of her country. In particular, Roqué adopted aspects of Liberalism and French Positivism and integrated them with her Catholic and Hispanic tradition.

Positivism, a school of thought founded by French philosopher August Comte (1798–1857), spread throughout Latin American countries during the nineteenth century.[7] Roqué found in Positivism a philosophy whose main goal was the complete reorganization of humanity. She shared with it the view that human beings and their societies are governed by natural laws and immutable scientific principles, as well as its conception of evolution as a progressive, inevitable, and irreversible force. Defining civilization as "a country's moral, material and intellectual stage of culture," Roqué posited with Comte that societies are classified as savage, barbarian, or civilized according to the level of progress they have reached (Roqué 1888, 53). She says, "With the passing of time, the hearts and minds of men and their ways of thinking evolve towards perfection" (Roqué 1917a/1941, 19).

> [Civilized are those] . . . who make progress in science, the arts, and
> all the fields of human knowledge; civilized peoples respect women,
> the law, and religion, rewarding talent, effort, service, and merit.
> (Roqué 1888, 54)

About those individuals and societies who try to "extinguish the meridional light of modern advancements," she adds:

> But in their foolish attempt to hold at bay both the overwhelming tide
> of what must be and shall be—for it is the sign of the time—and the
> unavoidable fulfillment of Fate, they will only call upon themselves
> the ridicule of History and the contempt of their contemporaries with
> any gray matter. (Roqué 1917a/1941, 19)

In this perspective, Puerto Rico, subject as it was to these invariable laws of successive and perfecting stages, was still in an early stage of its development. The Positivist notion that "developed" rational minds could accelerate the evolution process and make it more effective, and that the level of development of the social order depends to a great extent on the level reached by the human mind, gave Roqué an explanation for the unacceptable situation on the Island and a focus for her educational efforts. In a country where political subjection, economic crisis, and almost universal illiteracy had obstructed any attempt to bring forward order and progress, the Positivist idea that human beings are made for action and that through observation and reason they are capable of understanding the laws governing individual and social progress had to be strongly appealing to Roqué. The notion that the intellectual and active faculties of Puerto Ricans could contribute to the reorganization of their society permeated her political and educational endeavors.

Roqué's Educational Philosophy and Practice

Roqué believed that schools, and education in general, were main auxiliaries of the civilization process because they disseminate knowledge, cultivate reason, and initiate children from all social classes into what they need to know in life (Roqué 1888, 54). She shared with Positivism the view that the systematic study of the natural sciences provides an objective approach to the order of the world and contributes to the adequate development of human rational capacities. She coincided in this respect with English Positivist philosopher Herbert Spencer, who thought that education should prepare for life and scientific knowledge—which, according to this philosophy, had made progress possible—should become a primary part of the curriculum. Reacting against a tradition that had halted the fruitful development of the Island, Roqué emphasized with Spencer and Puerto Rican Eugenio María de Hostos[8] the position that saw science as the only possible educator of the rational faculties, and thus as an essential motor for social progression. Roqué says:

> I would like my people to love Natural Sciences because therein lies the future. Young nations think with their hearts; older nations are dedicated to science. We, unfortunately, belong to the former group; we still think like poets. (quoted in Chardón 1941, 9)[9]

Music and art, according to Roqué, humanize individuals and draw them away from their savage period. But while music and art *inspire* creation, science leads to *enact*. It is to science, this "magician of the centuries," that we owe "towns . . . cities . . . cultivated fields . . . monuments and civilization" (Roqué 1918b, 3).

However, Roqué argued, as important as the natural sciences are, if schools were to contribute in a significant way to the progress of society, they also had to teach morality. Here Roqué, a devoted Catholic, moves away from Positivism. This school of thought was based on a conception of the world and society that viewed the natural law of science—not of God—as the epistemological and sociological tool to establish order and further progress. For Roqué, however, scientific principles and laws are created by God and contain in them a moral order to which all human beings are subordinate. In this perspective, human conscience, as human reason, is subject to development. This conviction led her to ask, "What is the point of making progress in Science and the Humanities if none is achieved in Ethics and Culture?" (Roqué 1918c, 12).

Her whole conception of morality was based on the idea that the absolute laws governing nature have an ethical finality and necessarily lead to the good. Although recognizing that what she, like Hostos, called "the sciences of morality" had not been adequately studied, she underscored the importance of moral education to direct human natural forces and to reform human conduct. "We firmly believe that the soul, the spirit, that intelligent cause inside us all is so powerful when duly educated, and has such an excellent effect on our being, that it is capable of overcoming all our vices, whichever they may be, with strong determination and a well guided education" (Roqué 1904, 103–4).

Through her articles and speeches, Roqué exhorted Puerto Rican society to unite in demanding from Commissioners of Education the implementation of moral education in every school, so that each could become a "hallowed seat of virtue and knowledge where children may seek learning and walk the path of honor and duty paying homage to their country, which provides them with instruction and guidance" (Roqué 1918c, 13).

Roqué believed, thus, that education was indispensable for the progressive development of individuals and their societies. Moreover, in a country where, for centuries, the majority of women had had no access to instruction, she states:

> If culture is what sets one country apart from another, then educate women and you shall have a school in every home, for it is she who shapes the family and stamps upon society the seal of her culture. (Roqué 1899, 5)

However, she underscored that Puerto Rico could not develop without the *unified* efforts of both women and men (quoted in Andreu 1941, 29). She favored the same instruction for boys and girls except for "slight differences regarding particular jobs" (Andreu 1941, 29)[10] and believed that for both, intellectual work should be accompanied by manual work. Although Roqué did not question girls' need to learn house chores such as cooking, doing the laundry, and sewing, in a world where women were considered weak and fragile and where their capacity to think was seriously contested, she maintained that the education of boys and girls should stimulate *both* to use their reason, to work hard—the best they could—and to fulfill their duties at home, at school, and in the rest of society (Duprey de López 1941, 13).

Roqué's grandmother had taught her to read when she was three years old. An avid learner since then, reading and relentless study had been for her sources of self-development and freedom. As one of her students and biographers says, Roqué's own experiences led her to believe that, through education, individuals learn to be free. Through education, human beings learn to struggle for their happiness, to choose "the most transparent, beautiful and dignified" road in life, and to help other human beings choose that road (Negrón Muñoz 1941, 16). This sense that education liberates is, as her own students attest, what she sought to transmit to her pupils (Cadilla 1941, 25; Andreu 1941, 29).

She taught children and adults both in primary schools and at home in several towns of the Island. But her main passion was teacher education. She prepared many teachers during the last years of Spanish rule, and subsequently founded several Normal Schools throughout the Island. In 1899, a year after the U.S. invasion, she was appointed director of one of the first Normal Schools under the new system. And in 1903, she established a private Normal School, el Liceo Ponceño, which she directed for several years. At a time when the teaching profession had opened up as a professional opportunity for women, Roqué chose as one of her main missions in life to contribute to their professional development.

The passionate testimonies of her female students[11] (many of them prospective teachers at the Liceo Ponceño) reveal aspects of her educational philosophy and practice. In her teaching, Roqué wanted to stimulate their reason and intelligence, their will to act in accordance with their consciences, and their sense of duty. She tried to transmit to them an enthusiasm for learning and discovery and encouraged them to pose questions. She struggled to make them realize the importance of teaching and of infusing children and youth with a love for life and the vigor and energy to live it and with a feeling of patriotism. She treated them with respect, courtesy, and sincerity; she taught her classes with a "magnetic enthusiasm," awakening students' interest and conveying a great deal of knowledge in a simple but profound ways. She wanted women to confront successfully the responsibilities of modern life while realizing their right to learn, to be free, and to participate actively in the construction of a free society (Betances de Córdoba 1941, 23; Andreu 1941, 29–30; Duprey de López 1941, 13–14; Negrón Muñoz 1941, 15–17).

One of her students remembers her expressing her passion for teacher education and its importance in a society aiming to govern itself:

> Were it within my power to create a teacher, I would make teachers out of every Puerto Rican. My concern is not only that they may desire to acquire a degree, but that they may also practice the sacred mission of teaching. That would be my greatest joy, for thus the nation that governs us would find in us an educated people, able to assume responsibilities, and prepared for self-government. (Betances de Córdoba 1941, 24)

Within the framework of these perspectives about reason, science, development, progress, education, women, freedom, self-government, and of her own practice as teacher and teacher educator, Roqué, as most Puerto Ricans at the time, had a mixed reaction toward the educational policies of both colonial governments on the Island. On the one hand, she kept the illusion that both Spain and the United States would fulfill what she saw as their duty to treat Puerto Ricans with dignity and to grant to the Island the same rights their citizens were enjoying. She embraced the causes of the liberal sectors of both countries, thinking that those who favored democracy, progress, and freedom for themselves would assist the Island in the carrying forward of those same ideals. In spite of dictatorial rules and economic profiting, and aware of the inconsistencies of both governments, Roqué utilized tools such as letters, petitions, articles, and speeches, to demand justice from Spain and the United States and to further the ideals that in her view would lead Puerto Rico to democracy and freedom.

Recognizing, as both Spain and the United States had recognized, the political implications of education, she held to her practice as a teacher and encouraged women to join this profession and to contribute, through it, to the reconstruction of Puerto Rico. During the Spanish regime, she used—and encouraged other teachers to use—instructional materials more adequate to Puerto Rican realities than those approved by Spain. In 1889 she wrote a book, *Explicaciones de Gramática Castellana,* to be used in elementary schools. This book intended to provide a simpler and more complete Spanish grammar explanation than the one offered by the official text of the Real Academia Española. Because she feared its not being approved by the Spanish government, and given the urgency of a better text, she published it in fragments in a teachers' journal so that all would have access to it (Roqué 1890). In 1888, she published a geography text, *Elementos de Geografía Universal*, that she had written when she was thirteen and had used at her own school. Many years later, the book was approved by the Spanish government and was used in schools until the arrival of the United States.

Roqué also encouraged teachers to write petitions to the Spanish queen demanding justice at work. In an article in which she argues in favor of equal salaries for male and female teachers, both of which earned less than male teachers in Spain, she says:

> The law is the law, and as such, it should protect us all equally. Justice is what we should demand, not just through our members of Parliament, but in a proffer before our Queen by all the female teachers in Puerto Rico . . . This is what we must require of our government day after day; no more graces—the time has come for justice to be done on our behalf. (Roqué 1889, 4–5)

The issue of *Americanization* and the imposition of the English language in schools aroused protests from many quarters: from those like Roqué, who sought to affirm a sense of patriotism and a Puerto Rican nationality; from teachers; and from high school and college students. They argued that teaching in English created confusion and obstructed learning, in part because of the students' resistance to it. Furthermore, they challenged the imposition of North American values, which simultaneously disregarded those of Puerto Rico (Scarano 1993, 608–09). Roqué, who had been teaching and preparing teachers around the Island since she was thirteen years old, was convinced of the need—and inevitability—of teaching in Spanish (Chardón 1941, 46).

Thus, in the case of the United States, a nation that took pride in its liberal and democratic institutions, Roqué's reaction, as that of many Puerto Ricans, went from initial hope to gradual disillusionment. She ended up assuming that although the U.S. government in Puerto Rico had been dominated by the "will to exploit" the "commercial part" of that nation, most of its people were "humane and just" (Roqué 1931/1941, 22). She believed that people such as Commissioner of Education Clark, with their insulting educational policies, had obstructed the "relative Americanization" process that could take place on the Island. She recognized that with the government's effort to *Americanize* through means like the Foraker Law[12] and the imposition of English in schools, Puerto Ricans, who were proud of themselves as a people and of their Hispanic heritage, had been profoundly offended and had resisted and resented that imposition (Roqué 1918a, 3).

Nevertheless, Roqué kept hope until the end of her life that with Democrats in power in the United States (with Roosevelt in particular), that the Nation, which in her view represented "Humanism, Generosity, Freedom and Democracy" (Roqué 1918a, 3–4) would finally contribute to the development, democratization, and freedom of the Island. One of Roqué's students reminds us once again of the ideals nurturing this hope and guiding her lifelong educational philosophy and practice:

> It was from her lips that I first heard these causes . . . democracy, justice for the people, defense of children, equal rights for both men and

women, fostering the mind equally for all, be they rich or poor, black or white. Freedom for all the peoples of the world. (Negrón Muñoz 1941, 16)

A Call to Women

Until the 1930s, open and legal participation of Puerto Rican women in public decisions was prohibited. Female subordination was taken as a given among most men and women. During the nineteenth century ideas opposing patriarchy and denouncing the moral, material, and social effects of female subordination began to spread among learned women. However, it was not until the beginning of the twentieth century, with the changing position of women in the work force, that the first feminist movements were organized in Puerto Rico.

During the second half of the nineteenth century and until the 1920s, most women workers were employed in the tobacco industry. Between 1900 and 1930, employment opportunities there, as well as in the needlework industry, brought about an increase in the number of women workers. The difficult conditions under which these women worked awoke in them an awareness of the need to organize in order to fight for common causes. Anarchist, Sindicalist, and Marxist doctrines, as well as French Revolution influences, nurtured the thought of these working-class women, who founded the Liga Feminista Democrática. They defended a new order based on economic and political justice for all and proposed a plan to attain social and juridical equality for women.[13]

During the first decades of the 1900s, the service sector expanded and opened up professions such as nursing and teaching for women. In order to work in these sectors, women needed higher education. At first, these positions were occupied mainly by women whose families could provide such an education in recently created institutions and universities.[14] These women, most of them from the upper classes, formed professional and civic organizations that became centers for discussing and disseminating reformist ideas of all kinds.

Thus, less radical ideas than the ones supported by working-class women began to gain support in the most privileged sectors of society. In 1893, Roqué, who had been interested in women's issues for years, founded a journal called *La Mujer*, written, printed, administered, and distributed by women. Its objective was to improve teacher preparation and to defend and create awareness of women's rights. In 1902, in collaboration with other women, she founded, directed, and administered another publication, *La Evolución*, in which women wrote articles about social problems, literature, and pedagogy. In 1917, Roqué[15] founded the Liga Femínea, an organization aimed at creating awareness of women's issues and exhorting women to become active participants in the struggle for their rights. The Liga Femínea published journals such as *La Mujer del Siglo XX* and *Nosotras*.[16] It also called for massive rallies, wrote to politicians, and sent petitions regarding women's suffrage to the legislature and to the Congress of the United States.

In a 1917 address to women, Roqué stated:

Committed since childhood to constant study and used to sleeping only four or five hours a day and working the rest, I have much reflected upon the tough problems of human knowledge and the condition of women's lives on this earth. My most firm convictions have led me to conclude that the civil status of women in society is an injustice of our times, a contradiction of what we call civilization, and a misinterpretation of what we define as human rights. . . . Thus, after well-pondered reflection I remain the most ardent feminist, the firmest defender of the rights of women, eroded by laws and societies created by men that have fallen prey to inhuman selfishness, perhaps through habit; not ill nature, but basing their exclusive advantage on sheer force as when Barbarians ruled. (Roqué 1917a/1941, 19)

Concerned with women's lack of economic independence as well as with the unfairness of a social order that did not allow for the development of what she conceived as their natural human powers, Roqué took up the mission of "awakening up women for the future" and helping them "raise their spirit and nurture their intelligence" (Roqué 1917a/1941, 20). She wanted to stimulate women to search for progress and to realize that, using their innate faculties, they could accomplish their aspirations. This objective was served in her classrooms, in her articles, and in her political rallies and speeches. In one of the latter she stated:

Bearing in mind that God provided you with a brain to reflect and a will to follow the dictates of a righteous conscience; you should resolve to lead a useful life, a life of awareness as befits a rational being that seeks light through her efforts, her actions, by work and by the resolute and fair use of the will. (Roqué 1917a/1941, 19–20)

And, reminding women of the importance of working toward their moral well-being, she stated:

Let us be clear and persistent . . . Let us banish from our hearts forever the selfishness that blinds our consciousness, the envy that would shatter our soul, the unbounded ambition that would cause unfairness and the frivolousness that would make us naught. (Roqué 1929/1941, 21)

Through her speeches addressed to women, through her teaching, and through her own personal example, she struggled to convey the message that human beings have a duty to fulfill. She believed that both men and women have the duty to work "first for humanity and then for their homeland; first for their homeland and then for their family; first for their families and then for themselves" (Roqué 1917a/1941, 19–20). Although conceiving the whole world as a homeland and all human beings as siblings, she believed that the immediate and particular duty of Puerto Rican women was to work for that which surrounded them, for that upon which the future of their sons and daughters depended. God, in her view, had commended Puerto Rican women with the mission of regenerating their people through education and through the enhancement of civic virtues (Roqué 1917a/1941, 19–20). Puerto Rican women had the duty to form a "dignified and noble homeland . . . big for its deeds . . . [n]otable for its civic virtues . . . [c]ivilized and rich for the conduct, honesty and laboriousness of its sons and daughters" (Roqué 1929/1941, 20)[17]

From Roqué's perspective, one of the forces that impels human beings to fulfill their duty is "the saint love" that God has placed in every human heart for his or her homeland (Roqué 1929/1941, 20). "[T]hat intimate love . . . ", she believed, "is born spontaneously in our being by a natural law that no human convenience can suffocate nor invalidate" (Roqué 1918a, 4). Appealing to this feeling of patriotism in women, she exhorted them to contemplate their "unfortunate" and "unhappy" land, to work relentlessly toward its development, and to awaken in men their love for their country:

> Our foremost duty is to instill in the hearts of our children, our husbands, our brothers and fathers, the sacred love of country that will stir their hearts. Let patriotism be their lofty guide until our land is saved. (Roqué 1931/1941, 22)

One of the duties of Puerto Rican women was to recognize that Puerto Rico had a large population which could actively contribute to the construction of a better country. Puerto Rican men, she thought, were "intelligent, enthusiastic, virile, and patriotic." Recognizing their human attributes and strengths, Puerto Rican women should awaken them to Christian virtues and engage their hearts and their consciences so that they would contribute to the progress and development of the Island (Roqué 1929/1941, 20).

At a time when the majority of Puerto Ricans thought that women had neither the capacity nor the interest to intervene in political matters, and that contact with those issues would deprive them of their *feminine qualities*, Roqué posited not only that women had this capacity but also that they had the *duty* to participate in politics. In her own words:

> Is it a woman's duty to become involved in her country's politics? Yes. Without a doubt her goal should be to unite our wills, to draw us closer in the ideal pursuit of progress, honesty, and dedication, that all citizens born under the same sun may claim their well-being. (quoted in Cadilla 1941, 26–27).

The idea of unifying wills to regenerate the Island was shared by many Puerto Ricans at the beginning of this century. The view was that Puerto Ricans should unite as a people to counterbalance the effects of U.S. political, economic, and educational policies on the Island.[18] In 1904, a group of individuals founded the

Union Association, which later became the Union Party, the dominant political institution in the country at the time. Joining the Party's call for unity among Puerto Ricans, Roqué tells women:

> Our essential duty is to unite the wills of Puerto Rican men and women. While our country remains destitute, while each Puerto Rican, seeking his or her own benefit, think alone, we will achieve nothing, we are and we will be nothing. (Roqué 1931/1941, 22)

In addition to struggling for the unity of the people, Roqué argued that women's political activity should include letters and petitions to the government voicing their views and demanding justice for the Island. In 1931, during her last public address to Puerto Rican women, Roqué reminded them of the current political situation: Puerto Rico was still a colony, surrounded by twenty-one Latin republics. She reminded women about the "exploitation," "lack of freedom," "suffering," and "unhappiness" on the Island under the government of "the biggest nation in the world." Here, as in previous instances, she exhorted women to write letters and petitions to "noble" North Americans, "who may not be aware of our misfortunes," asking for their support in demanding from the United States government the resolution of the status of the Island. She advised Puerto Rican women to tell the Congress of the United States:

> Heed the voices of the women of this land that you have saddened by letting others exploit what little we have. American Congress: we do not want to be a colony! . . . We want a status that will make us owners of our land; we want sovereignty to freely determine our acts; and, with all our strength and by our own decisions, we want to work to industrialize our island until it is safely ours; a better place in which to live. (Roqué 1931/1941, 22)

In spite of her indignation with the United States government, she encouraged women not to lose hope and to endorse a petition to the Congress of the United States, stating their aspirations:

> They truly listen to women there, trust the nation that calls itself the land of the free, where women are listened to, where each can pursue his or her own happiness. Doubt not that they will heed the women of this ailing Puerto Rico. (Roqué 1931/1941, 22)

Women's Vote

The issue of women's vote was a very important element in the development of a feminist movement in Puerto Rico. Although in the United States, women's right to vote was recognized by constitutional amendment in 1920, many legislators in Puerto Rico were fiercely opposed to it. They argued that women themselves did not want to vote and that if they entered the "dirty" world of politics, they would lose their feminine qualities. This reaction prevailed throughout most of the 1920s.

During the 1920s, and inspired by suffrage struggles in other countries, Puerto Rican women began to organize themselves to demand equal political rights. Roqué, who became the leader of the suffragist movement, thought that this was, for several reasons, the right moment to begin this kind of struggle on the Island: the international situation during the First World War had demanded women's cooperation; the Jones Act, granting more rights to Puerto Rican people,[19] had been recently approved by the United States; women were beginning to participate in industry and commerce and their numbers were increasing at the universities (Andreu, 1941, 28). In 1917, Roqué wrote:

> I see among all women a contained aspiration, suffrage; but they are shy, none of them daring yet to start confronting opposition. That is the mission that I must fulfill before dying. (quoted in Andreu 1941, 28)

Organized around entities such as Roqué's Liga Femínea, the suffragist movement was actively supported by thousands of women. While working-class organizations such as the Liga Feminista Democrática were demanding universal female suffrage, the first program of the Liga Femínea admitted the possibility of excluding illiterate women from voting.

In the first 1917 issue of her feminist revue *La Mujer del Siglo XX*, Roqué wondered if Puerto Rico would be the first Latin American country to grant women the right to vote. She wondered whether Puerto Ricans "who love progress and justice so much" would show the "highest levels of culture" by "granting the right to vote to all 21 year old women who [knew] how to read and write in Spanish or English" (quoted in Andreu 1941, 29–30). Her view was that the prospect of enjoying the rights of all citizens would stimulate illiterate women to educate themselves. However, in 1921, the Liga Femínea, under the name of Liga Social Sufragista (and at that point, the most important feminist organization in the country), amended its program to favor universal female suffrage.

With the increase of female participation in the work force, suffragists were able to present to the legislature of Puerto Rico projects of law for female suffrage annually from 1919 to 1927 with no results. In 1929, their project of law was presented for the fifth time and approved, allowing only literate females the right to vote. These women voted for the first time in 1932, a year before Roqué's death. Her feminist friend, Isabel Andreu, tells us a bittersweet story:

> When the Governor of Puerto Rico signed the project of law granting Puerto Rican women the right to vote . . . Doña Ana received as a present the pen with which the project was signed. Finally our illustrious leader had succeeded in her last struggle for the women of her land. She did not want to die without exercising [her] right to

> vote . . . [T]he day of the elections she was ready early on . . . My husband, Angela Negrón and myself went with her . . . and how deeply surprised we were when we were told that Ana Roqué de Duprey was not on the lists of that electoral school. From that school we were sent to another and then to another, until it was so late that all electoral schools were closed . . . without the vote of the first leader of women's suffrage. In order to prevent her from receiving what would probably had been the biggest disappointment in her life, we made her sign an affidavit making her believe she was voting. She never knew. . . . (Andreu 1941, 30).

In 1935, two years after Roqué's death, a law was approved that extended the right to vote to all women.

Although Roqué believed the act of voting should be voluntary, there were several reasons why female suffrage was particularly significant in her view. In 1929, after the right to vote had been granted to literate Puerto Rican women, she addressed them in these terms: "Fellow women: we are voting women; we are people" (Roqué 1929/1941, 20). And later on, in 1931, she affirmed:

> Puerto Rican women are beginning to take up their difficult, new mission. And the world does not fully realize what women's suffrage really means. We were almost pariahs, meaningless beings in the civic life. Today we are women, with reason and with a conscience. Women with the right to vote, and thus free to work for the future and happiness of our children and the homeland where they will live.
>
> Doesn't your heart overflow with gladness? Isn't your spirit totally overjoyed? (Roqué 1931/1941, 21)

To Roqué, women's exercise of the right to vote was a concrete manifestation of their capacity to think, to follow the principles their consciences dictated, and to put these principles into practice. The action of voting was by its very nature rational and ethical, the utmost political manifestation of their civic powers.

Roqué's position was that the action of voting *gives* life to women in the sense that it opens up for them a social space in which to express their personhood, their rational and social nature, their natural tendency to develop and to act toward that development. Voting is in this sense a source of life and of profound happiness for women. But voting also *makes* life, it *constructs* homeland. It is conscious and informed political action through which women fulfill what in Roqué's view is their mission of contributing to the betterment of the world (Roqué 1929/1941, 20). In this way, with each vote, every woman moves from the private to the public, from being a mother in the private to being a mother in the public, from being responsible for her home to being responsible for her homeland. Voting, for Roqué, constitutes a road toward emancipation and civilization while being its most basic and necessary manifestation.

According to her, female suffrage would bring to the people of Puerto Rico the "advancements of the times." Some women and men could fear or oppose progress, but trying to stop it would be gullibly denying what for her was the inevitable development of the Island toward more advanced levels of civilization:

> Women who wish it and desire it, will march in the vanguard of the times; and those who love to be stationary can remain counting their beads, in the enervating hammock, living without conscience in a faded past: it is their choice. (Roqué 1917b, 7)

Conclusion: Roqué's *Project of Civilization*

I have tried to show that Ana Roqué's political and educational work sought to provide solutions to the problems raised in a very particular Latin American context. While at the end of the nineteenth century all Spanish colonies in the New World had become independent and were involved in the reconstruction of their recently constituted nations, Puerto Rico had become the site of still another *colonization crusade*. In the context of a country that had been colonized for centuries, Roqué embarked on her own *civilization project*, one that, unlike those undertaken by Spain and the United States, would pursue in actuality the ideals both nations had hindered.

In response to the problems and needs of the Island, and nurtured by Liberal and Positivist thought, Roqué's *civilization project* took up a threefold form: educating children and preparing teachers; persuading and mobilizing women to fulfill their individual and social *duties;* and striving for their right to vote.

As in the work of many other Latin Americans of the time, Roqué's project centered on education. If Puerto Ricans were to consciously contribute to the progressive development of the Island, their mental faculties had to be strengthened, a love for science had to be developed, and a sense of freedom, duty, patriotism, and morality had to be cultivated. Schools were, in this perspective, essential loci for civilization, and their teachers were primary civilizing agents. As we have seen, teacher preparation was for her one leading area of effort and concern.

Interestingly, unlike other nineteenth century endeavors, Roqué's project placed in the hands of *educated* women the responsibility for the development of the country. Although she did not question the common assumption that women are naturally inclined toward motherhood, child-rearing, and family life, she redefined and broadened that role. In her view, within the domestic sphere, women are in charge of the well-being of their children and their families. Whether they are formally educated or not, they are all teachers who deeply influence the intellectual and moral development of their children. This is, in her view, one of the reasons why all women should receive formal education.

But in the public sphere, women, Roqué thought, are also mothers. Conceiving the universe as a homeland and a homeland as a home, she equated women's role in society to that in the domestic sphere. In this perspective, Puerto Rican women are not only mothers—and teachers—of their children, but also mothers—and teachers—of every Puerto Rican child; they are not only responsible for their own family, but also for the whole Puerto Rican family. Their "motherly" responsibilities in this "extended home" are fulfilled through active participation in social and political issues and through inspiration of the civic virtues and duties in every member of the "extended family." Puerto Rican women in this project are committed, not only to self-development, but also to the progressive evolution of men, children, and the whole society.

Although Roqué based her work on Positivist notions of progress, reason, and science that are questionable; although she did not focus, as feminist women workers did, on an effort to attain radical economic transformations for the Island; and although her feminism is in many respects conservative, her work was, in my view, particularly significant. Her *project of civilization* was a project for action and a project of conviction. It consisted of Roqué's actions themselves: her teaching and her child-rearing; her writings; her founding of feminist organizations and journals; her speeches, political petitions, gatherings, and rallies; and her call to women and her appeal to men. It consisted of the actual teaching of her student-teachers and of those who became teacher educators, as well as of the actions of women who, joining Roqué's struggles, became agents of social transformation.

But this enterprise was also a project of conviction. It was nurtured by a profound belief in democracy and freedom and in the power of reason, science, and education. It was strengthened by a confidence in the possibility of inspiring and engaging men and in the political potential of a unified people. The project was also sustained by the conviction that reasonable and persistent arguments could persuade governments to transform their policies in the Island, and that petitions, letters, and articles were all effective vehicles for social and political change. Naive as these convictions might have seemed, they reinforced Roqué's and others' efforts to transform the life of Puerto Rican women and men.

Ana Roqué believed that through this civilization project of action and conviction, Puerto Rico would become a civilizing homeland responsible for its own development. Thinking of the universe as a home and all human beings as siblings, she hoped that Puerto Rican women would set an example of culture, practical wisdom, and civilization for the rest of the world to follow. Proposing the universal maxim: "Liberty, Sincerity and Patriotism," she exhorts women to join her once again:

> Let us all work for the well-being, morality and progress of all . . . Let us . . . fulfill our duties with our land. . . Let us, sisters, make another life. Let us make a homeland. (Roqué 1931/1941, 21)

Notes

[1]Cuba became independent of Spain that same year while the Philippines, another Spanish colony, fell under United States domination.

[2]Interestingly, the "Carta Autonómica" granted by Spain a few months before the invasion had given Puerto Ricans broader rights and powers than those provided by the United States with the Foraker Law. See Scarano 1993, 574.

[3]Most of the schools were urban and those in the country were mainly for males. The first rural school for girls was inaugurated in 1880. Peasant girls had very little opportunity for instruction. See Scarano 1993, 493.

[4]"The process by which people of alien culture acquire American ways, standards of living, and national allegiance; or the assimilation of American culture by people of foreign birth of heritage." Fairchild, *Dictionary of Sociology* (New York: Philosophical Library, 1944) 10. Quoted in Negrón de Montilla 1970, ix.

[5]Translations from Roqué's Spanish texts into English are by Guiomar Emedán.

[6]She had seven children, of which only four reached adulthood. See Duprey de López 1941, 13.

[7]Richard Morse says that Positivism in nineteenth century Latin America "appeared to offer a unitary, constructive, systematic, scientific approach to the problems of stratified societies, stagnant economies, and archaic school systems" (Morse 1964, 167).

[8]Eugenio María de Hostas (1839-1903) was a Puerto Rican philosopher, educator, and politician.

[9]Interestingly, Roqué's ongoing study and promotion of disciplines such as astronomy, cosmography, and botany places her in a position within an educational debate that had been taking place for years in Latin America, between those who believed in the more classical curriculum that had prevailed since the sixteenth century, and those who favored a more "scientific" approach to educational matters.

[10]In addition to common subjects, girls had to learn domestic work such as cooking and sewing, while boys learned carpentry and the like.

[11]In 1941, the Revue of the Association of Women Graduated from the University of Puerto Rico dedicated an issue to the memory of Ana Roqué, and several of her students wrote articles in her honor.

[12]The Foraker Law was generally seen as one of the most "anti American things . . . done here" (quoted from the Journal *La Correspondencia* in Scarano 1993, 577).

[13]Luisa Capetillo and Juana Colón became national figures who disseminated a feminist and at the same time Sindicalist message.

[14]The University of Puerto Rico was founded in 1903.

[15]She worked in collaboration with Isabel Andreu and Mercedes Solá, among others.

[16]In addition to her educational work, Roqué wrote innumerable articles and several didactic stories and novels. She founded five journals: *La Mujer* (1893), *La Evolución* (1902), *La Mujer del Siglo XX* (1917), *Album Puertorriqueño* (1918), and *Heraldo de la Mujer* (1920).

[17]Although Roqué uses the form "hijos" here, we must assume she meant it in its neutral sense of "hijos" and "hijas." (It has been the norm in Spanish to use the masculine on a generic form referring to both.)

[18]Rosendo Matienzo Cintrón was the main exponent of this position.

[19]Among them, U.S. citizenship. See the Jones Act on page 46.

References

Andreu, I. 1941. Defensora del sufragio femenino. *Revista de Mujeres Graduadas* IV(I): 28–30.
Betances de Córdoba, C. 1941. Ana Roqué de Duprey, forjadora de maestras. *Revista de Mujeres Graduadas* IV(I): 24.

Cadilla, M. 1941. Doña Ana Roqué como feminista. *Revista de Mujeres Graduadas* IV(I): 25–27.

Chardón, C. 1941. *Biografía En Cuatro Tiempos.* San Juan: Asociacíon de Mujeres Graduadas: 8–9, 46.

Duprey de López, A. 1941. Ana Roqué de Duprey en el Hogar. *Revista de Mujeres Graduadas* IV(I): 13–14.

Meléndez, C. 1941. *Biographía En Cuatro Tiempos.* San Juan: Asociacíon de Mujeres Graduados 10–12.

Morse, R. 1964. The Heritage of Latin America. In *The Founding of New Societies,* ed. L. Hartz. New York: Harcourt, Brace and World.

Negrón de Montilla, A. 1970. *Americanization in Puerto Rico and the Public School System, 1900–1930.* Río Piedras: Editorial Edil.

Negrón Muñoz, A. 1941. Mis primeras impresiones de la maestra de toda mi vida. *Revista de Mujeres Graduadas* IV(I): 15–17.

Roqué, A. 1888. *Elementos de Geografía Universal.* Humacao: Imprenta de Otero.

_____ . 1889. *El Magisterio de Puerto Rico* 1(7): 4–5.

_____ . 1889. Explicaciones de Gramática Castellana. *El Magisterio de Puerto Rico* II(24): 3.

_____ . 1899. *El Magisterio de Puerto Rico* 1(7): 5.

_____ . 1904. *Luz y sombra.* Río Piedras: Editorial de la Universidad de Puerto Rico.

_____ . [1917a] 1941. A mis compatriotas. Reprint. *Revista de la Asociación de Mujeres Graduadas* IV(I): 19–20.

_____ . 1917b. *Album Puertorriqueño* I(2): 7.

_____ . 1918a. Algo de política. *Album Puertorriqueño* I(5): 3–4.

_____ . 1918b. Ciencias y artes. *Album Puertorriqueño* I(2): 3–4.

_____ . 1918c. La asignatura de moral en nuestras escuelas. *Album Puertorriqueño* I(2): 12–13.

_____ . [1929] 1941. A la mujer puertorriqueña. Reprint *Revista de la Asociación de Mujeres Graduadas* IV(I): 20–21.

_____ . [1931] 1941. A la mujer puertorriqueña. Reprint *Revista de la Asociación de Mujeres Graduadas* IV(I): 21–22.

_____ . [1932] 1941. Autobiografía de Ana Roqué de Duprey. Reprint *Revista de la Asociación de Mujeres Graduadas* IV(I): 7.

Scarano, F. 1993. *Puerto Rico. Cinco siglos de historia.* México: McGraw Hill.

READING

Mensaje al aprobarse la ley concedieno el Sufragio Femenino, 1929

De Doña Ana Roqué de Duprey

A la Mujer Puertorriqueña

"Compatriotas nuestras, somos mujeres votantes; somos personas.

"Compatriotas nuestras, ha llegado la hora en el Reloj de los Tiempos, en que el Destino por orden de Dios, llama a la Mujer Puertorriqueña a cumplir con el deber que tiene todo nacido de contribuir con su voluntad, con su inteligencia, con su esfuerzo y con el santo amor que Dios puso en el corazón de cada ser por la patria en que vió la luz.

"Bien considerado nuestra patria es el mundo, y todos los humanos, nuestros hermanos son; pero nuestros deber ineludible es trabajar por lo que nos rodea, por todo lo que ataña al porvenir y felicidad de nuestros hijos.

"Somos Madres, serán madres las jóvenes algún día, y nuestro deber es formar un patria grande, digna y noble para los seres que nos debarán la vida.

"Hacer de nuestra islita, este búcaro de flores que Dios nos regaló, una tierra de Amor y Bendición. Grande por sus hechos. Notable por sus virtudes ciudadanas. Civilizada y rica por la conducta, honradez y laboriosidad de sus hijos.

"Nosotras, la primera gran Antilla donde se ha reconocido el veto para la mujer, nosotras, las puertorriqueñas, tenemos que dar un ejemplo al mundo y a la América de cordura y de civismo.

"Para hacer de esta tierra un paraíso, tenemos la materia prima que es el exceso de población; y luego, nuestros puertorriqueños son inteligentísimos entusiastas, viriles y patriotas. Llamemos a su corazón, interesando su conciencia, despertándola para todas las virtudes cristianas.

"Y ese puertorriqueño digno y noble, cooperará con nosotras en el engrandecimiento patrio.

"A los analfabetos debemos decir que todas las mujeres de Puerto Rico, nos interesaremos, como es nuestro deber, en la campaña del A. B. C., para hacer de nuestros paisanos, hombres y mujeres conscientes, para que participen en la gloria y el honor que vamos a conquistar por nuestro patriótico esfuerzo.

"Es grande, es inmensa la Misión que Dios ha puesto en manos de la mujer puertorriqueña.

"Poco podrá ayudaros vuestra Presidenta honorario, hijas mías de la Asociación Insular de Mujeres Votantes, pues su vida toca a su fin. Pero es nuestro deber, y lo cumple vuestra Presidenta Honoraria, de llamaros al cumplimiento de vuestros deberes.

"Ahora que tenemos el voto, poderosa palanca que todo lo remueve, ahora, creemos que la mejor forma de ayudar al país, será formar ese gran núcleo de que ya me habéis hablado hace tiempo, núcleo patriota, noble y digno de la mujer puertorriqueña, sin distinciones de clases ni credos, sin estridencias, sin partidarismo ni sectarismo, con un sólo objetivo: El Bien de la Patria que ha de ser el hogar de nuestros hijos. Tratemos de unir en esa bendita aspiración a todos los puertorriqueños.

"Trabajemos por el bienestar, moralidad y progreso de todos, altos y bajos.

"Levantemos con amor y fe nuestra alma al Todopoderoso y El nos ayudará a cumplir nuestros deberes con la patria, el bendecido hogar de los seres que más amamos.

"Hagamos, hermanas nuestras, otra vida.

"Hagamos patria.

"No trabajemos jamás por prebendas utilitarias. Nada de rencores, ni de auras tontas, que ningún valor tienen en la vida, ni ante las personas sensatas.

"Seamos sencillas y perseverantes, unidas fraternalmente para el bien.

"Desterremos para siempre de nuestro corazón el egoísmo que ciega la conciencia; la envidia que despedaza el alma; la ambición desmedida que nos haría injustas, y la frivolidad que nos anula.

"Que sea la Cordura, la Reflexión y el Patriotismo Y EL SANTO AMOR A NUESTROS HIJOS los que guien nuestros pasos.

"Trabajemos por el bien de todos sin interés de lucro alguno, como nos enseñó Jesús, y cumplamos a conciencia nuestros deberes en la vida, para que Dios nos ayude, y la Divina Providencia nos sonría y aliente, desde el templo de su Excelsitud.

"Procuremos que nuestra bella isla dé la nota más alto de su cultura y civilización.

"Vengan a nosotras todas las madres; todas las mujeres puertorriqueñas de alma levantada y noble.

"LEMA: Libertad, Sinceridad, Patriotismo."

En ocasión de la Asamblea Anual de la Asociación de Mujeres Votantes, celebrada en Mayagüez en 1931

Mujeres puertorriqueñas, hermanas mías muy queridas de mi corazón.

Desde mi habitación de enferma dirijo un cariñoso saludo a esa Asamblea feminista, para decirles que al ver la actitud y el entusiasmo de la mujer puertorriqueña en esa ocasión, estoy orgullosa de mis paisanos.

Qué tesoro de patriotismo y amor a esta tierra querida que nos vió nacer existe en vuestros corazones!

No me engañé en 1917 al llamaros a la lucha reivindicadora de nuestros derechos.

Contemplad, hermanas días, nuestra amada tierra. Siempre irredenta, siempre desgraciada y siempre dulce y bella entre sus palmas y sus flores!

Unámonos todas en apretado haz para trabajar por la felicidad de esta tierra infeliz.

La mujer puertorriqueña está empezando a hacerse cargo de su nueya, difícil misión. Y el mundo no se da cuenta exacta de lo que significa la franquicia del voto para la mujer.

Nosotras éramos casi parias. Seres casi insignificantes en la vida cívica.

Hoy somos mujeres: personalidades con razón y conciencia. Mujeres con voto, y por tanto con libertad para trabajar por el porvenir y felicidad de nuestros hijos, y por la patria donde ellos han de vivir.

¿No se ensancha vuestro corazón? ¿No se expande vuestro espíritu con la plenitud de vida que embarga vuestro ser?

Y lo más grande, en que quizás pocas personas hayan pensado: Nosotras estamos rodeadas de veintiuna repúblicas latinas, y aún somos colonia: una colonia que sufre, pobre e infeliz, bajo la bandera estrellada de la nación más grande de la tierra que permite nuestra explotación y no nos da libertad bastante ni nos deja casi desarrollar nuestras iniciativas para buscar nuestra felicidad.

Y esta colonia, girón de tierra americana desprendida de los Andes, es la primera tierra americana que proclama la reinvindicación de la mujer de este continente.

Nuestra islita amada, brillante de vívidos cambiantes, engarzado en flores y rodeado de las espumosas ondas del Caribe, ha sido la tierra elegida por Dios para marchar a la cabeza de la reivindicación de la mujer latino americana.

Y nosotros tenemos que hacernos dignas de ese gran honor a ningún otro comparable, cumpliendo con entereza y sensatez la gran misión que Dios nos ha confiado.

Nuestro esencial deber es unir voluntades. Mientras nuestro pueblo esté desunido, mientras cada puertorriqueño, attendiendo a su propia conveniencia, piense a su manera, nada conseguiremos, nada somos y nada seremos.

Nuestro primer deber es infiltrar en el corazón de nuestros hijos, esposos, hermanos y padres, ese patriotismo santo y sagrado que vibre en sus corazones. Que sea el amor patrio el sentimiento más grande que nos aliente, mientras no veamos reivindicada a nuestra patria.

Ante el cual todo interés personal toda aspiración, ambición, todo egoísmo vano debe ceder.

Nuestro pueblo puertorriqueño, nuestra isla idolatrada está al borde del abismo...

¡Y la vamos a dejar morir!

Esta tierra llena de fertilidad y belleza, donde agoniza el nativo falto de justicia y piedad, la vamos a dejar convertirse en una colonia extranjera victima de la explotación y mala fé de la parte del pueblo comerciante de Norte América que sólo atiende a su provecho?

Pero pensad, queridas compatriotas, que la mayor parte del pueblo de nuestra metrópoli, es humano y justo. Pidamos las mujeres, de esta tierra infeliz, TODAS A UNA, a la parte noble de ese pueblo, que quizás ignora nuestras desgracias, que se una a nosotras para demandar a la nación, el status no resuelto desde que tomó la responsabilidad de nuestro porvenir.

Y digámosle al Congreso americano: Oye la voz de las mujeres de esta tierra que habéis contribuído a hacerla infeliz permitiendo que exploten lo poco que tenemos.

Congreso americano: ¡no queremos ser colonia! Cuando nos arrebatásteis del poder de España, no éramos colonia: el serlo nos avergüenza.

Queremos un status que nos haga dueños de nuestra tierra; queremos la soberanía para determinar libremente nuestros actos y trabajar por industrializar nuestro isla según nuestras fuerzas y nuestro criterio propio, hasta reivindicarla y hacerla apta para vivir feliz en ella, un pueblo que tiene cuatrocientos años de civilización.

Un status digno de nuestra cultura y nuestro derecho; donde vivíamos modestamente sin ser humillados y explotados.

Y que por vuestra conveniencia estáis obligados a darnos protección en un caso de emergencia, desde que nos arrebatásteis a nuestra nación descubridora, que jamás nos hubiera abandonado.

Mujeres puertorriqueñas, endosemos un escrito con nuestras aspiraciones al Congreso, si lo creéis pertinente. Allí se atiende mucho a la mujer, y confiad en la nación que se dice Patria de los Libres, donde cada uno puede buscar su felicidad.

Ella atenderá a las mujeres de la infeliz Puerto Rico. No lo dudéis.

¡Vivan nuestras mujeres valientes y decididas!

¡Trabajemos con fé por nuestra isla idolatrada!

READING

Address on the Occasion of the Passage of the Women's Suffrage Act of 1929

Doña Ana Roqué de Duprey

Translated by Guiomar Emedán

An excerpt from *To Puerto Rican Women* (1929)

Fellow citizens: we are voting women; we are people.

Fellow citizens: the clock of time has struck the hour when Destiny, through the will of God, calls upon Puerto Rican women to fulfill what is their birthright and to make their contribution of virtue of their good will, their intellect, their dedication, and God's Divine love instilled in the hearts of all human beings for the country of their birth.

Rightfully, our country is the world and all human beings our brothers, but inevitably we are bound to labor for those near us, for all that which affects the future and happiness of our children.

We are mothers, as our young daughters tomorrow will be, and it is our duty to create a great, proud, and honorable country for those who one day will owe their lives to us.

To make our dear Island, that garden of flowers, that gift from above, into a land of love and blessings, great for its deeds and renown for its civil virtues, civilized and nurtured by the conduct, honesty and industry of its children.

This being the first of the great Antilles where women's suffrage has been recognized, we, Puerto Rican women, have to set an example of reason and civic duty for America and the world.

To create this Paradise, we have the raw materials—our abundant population; Puerto Rican men are enthusiastic, virile and patriotic. Let us call upon their hearts, appealing to their consciences, that they may be awakened to all the Christian virtues.

And those Puerto Rican, noble and proud, will come to our aid as we strive to build a greater homeland.

To the illiterate we must say that all the women of Puerto Rico will be interested in the literacy campaign as is our duty, that we may turn our countrymen into men and women able to partake of the honor and glory resulting from our patriotic endeavors.

For great, indeed immense, is the responsibility that God has placed in the hands of Puerto Rican women.

Your honary president, my dear voters of the Insular Association of Women Voters, can hardly be of help at this time when her own life nears the end. But we remain duty-bound by her example to call upon you to honor your duties.

Now that we have the vote, that powerful lever that changes all things, now we are convinced that the best way to help the country lies in creating that great circuit mentioned so long ago. That patriotic, proud and noble group of Puerto Rican women without concern for differences of class or creed, without shrill partisanship or sectarianism, with only one objective: the well-being of this country, the future home of our children! May we strive to bring all Puerto Ricans together in the pursuit of this blessed goal.

Let us work for the well-being, morality and progress of all, tall and short. Let us fulfill our duty with our land, the sacred home of our beloved.

Let us, sisters, make another life.

Let us make a homeland.

May we never be tempted by convenient rewards nor bear resentment or put on foolish airs; all of no value to sensible persons in this life.

Let us be clear and persistent. Let us banish from our hearts forever the selfishness that would blind our consciousness, the envy that would shatter our soul, the unbounded ambition that would cause our unfairness and the frivolousness that would make us naught.

May patriotism, common sense, reflection and the blessed love of our children be our sole guide.

Let us work for the common good without concern for personal gain, as Jesus taught. Let us fulfill our duties in life to the best of our abilities that God may help us and Divine Providence smile upon our fate and bring us courage from His exalted throne.

May we endeavor that our beautiful Island will ring the highest note its culture and civilization can produce.

Join us, all mothers, all Puerto Rican women of noble heart and superior spirit.

Motto: Liberty, Sincerity, Patriotism.

Address on the Occasion of the Annual Assembly Meeting of the Association of Women Voters Held in Mayaguez in 1931

Puerto Rican women, my very dear sisters, from my ailing room I bring you my warmest greetings expressing great pride in your demeanor and enthusiasm on this occasion.

What treasures of love and patriotism for this beloved land of ours lay cradled in your hearts!

How right was I in 1917 when calling upon you to join the struggle to restore our rights!

Behold, dear sisters, our adored land, forever unredeemed; unfortunate yet beautiful amidst its splendor of flowers and palm trees!

Let us be joined in a united front endeavoring to bring joy to this unhappy land.

Puerto Rican women are beginning to take up their difficult, new mission. And the world does not fully realize what women's suffrage really means. We were almost pariah, meaningless beings in the civic life. Today we are women with reason and with a conscience. Women with vote, and thus free to work for the future and happiness of our children and the homeland where they will live. Doesn't your heart overflow with gladness? Isn't your spirit totally overjoyed?

And what's more, what few may call to mind, we are surrounded by twenty-one Latin American Republics while being a colony still; a suffering, poor, unhappy colony under the starry flag of the biggest nation on this earth which permits our exploitation and allows us little freedom for the development of our initiatives or the pursuit of our happiness.

This colony, a shred of land stripped from the Andes, is the first on American soil to proclaim women's rights on the continent.

Our beloved Island, bright in its vivid and ever-changing hues, crowned in flowering glory and bordered by the foamy waves of the Caribbean, has been chosen by God to lead in the struggle to uphold women's rights in Latin America.

We thus have to rise to the height of that unprecedented honor by wisely fulfilling this God-given mission to the end.

Our essential duty is to unite our wills. While our country remains destitute, while each Puerto Rican, seeking his or her own benefit, thinks alone, we will achieve nothing, we are and will be nothing.

Our foremost duty is to instill in the hearts of our children, our husbands, our brothers and fathers, the sacred love of country that will fill their hearts. Let patriotism be their lofty guide until our land is saved.

Second to any personal concern or aspirations, ambition or vain selfishness, we hold this our first duty.

Puerto Rican people, our beloved Island is at the brink of disaster . . . Will we let it die?

This land, as fertile as it is beautiful, whose native children suffer for lack of justice and compassion—will we let it become a foreign colony, the victim of exploitation and the ill designs of that part of North America to be found in its self-seeking peddlers?

My fellow citizens, most of the people in the nation that governs us are humane and just. Let us, the women of this unhappy land, cry out single-voiced to the noblest part of that country, which perhaps knows not our misfortune. May they unite in requiring of their nation the status that remains unresolved for us ever since their country took charge of our destiny.

And let us say to the American Congress: Heed the voices of the women of this land that you have saddened by letting others exploit what little we have.

American Congress: we do not want to be a colony! When you seized us from Spain we were not a colony: we are ashamed by this status.

We want a status that will make us owners of the land, sovereignty to freely determine our acts, that we may fight with all our strength and by our own decisions to industrialize our island until it is safely ours; a better place in which to live, a land of 400 years of civilization.

We want a status deserving of our culture and our rights that we may enjoy humbly without fear of humiliation or exploitation.

For the sake of your own convenience you are now obliged to protect us in an emergency since you seized us from the nation of our discoverers which would have never abandoned us.

Puerto Rican women, let us sign a declaration of our aspirations to the Congress, if you deem fit. There they truly listen to women. Trust the nation that calls itself the land of the free, where women are listened to, where each can pursue his or her own happiness.

Doubt not that they will heed the women of this ailing Puerto Rico.

Long live our women, courageous and steadfast.

May we all work in faith for our beloved Island!

Chapter 4

ANNA
JULIA COOPER

Not the Boys Less, but the Girls More

By Nicole Pitts

Introduction

Anna Julia Cooper (1858–1964), who lived to the age of one hundred and six, faced many challenges and triumphs throughout her long life. From her birth in 1858 as a slave on a North Carolina plantation, she went on to earn both a bachelor's and master's degree from Oberlin College in Ohio. In 1892, at the age of thirty-four, she published *A Voice from the South: By a Black Woman of the South*, a collection of her writings and speeches about the regeneration of the Black race and the role of Black women in that effort. Later, she was one of the founding members of the Black Woman's Club Movement, the only Black female member elected to the American Negro Academy out of 40 prominent male "scholars, poets, clergymen, journalists, academicians and bibliophiles" (Hutchinson 1981, 110), the second Black female principal of the Washington Colored High School, and the fourth Black woman in America to obtain her Ph.D., defending her dissertation in French at the Sorbonne in Paris at the age of sixty-seven. Cooper believed that she could achieve the goals she set out to accomplish in spite of her sex, her race, and her slave beginnings. The fact that she succeeded in her personal endeavors proved to her that others could also. It is no surprise, then, that Cooper dedicated her life to teaching and inspiring children and adults to work toward their highest potential.

Anna Julia Cooper

From the age of ten until her retirement at age eighty-two, Anna Julia Cooper was an educator of school-age children, college students, and working adults. This career allowed her to do more than merely educate; being a teacher positioned her as a role model to the thousands of individuals she touched in the community and in the classroom. From her personal writings we know that some of her students went on to attend colleges such as Harvard, Yale, and Dartmouth on scholarships that she personally sought out; countless others became productive members of the community, well-rounded citizens, and thinkers. Cooper inspired and uplifted people of all ages and various backgrounds as she, herself, climbed the ladder of success and accomplishment. Her life of teaching, inspiring others, and enhancing herself is reflected in the motto of the Black Woman's Club Movement, "Lifting as we climb."

Biographical Sketch

Only recently has there been agreement on when Cooper was born. Louise Daniel Hutchinson, the most thorough biographer of Cooper's life and contributions, has established her date of birth as August 10, 1858 (Hine et al. 1993, 276). Her mother, Hannah Stanley Haywood, was a domestic slave of Dr. Fabius J. Haywood of Raleigh, North Carolina. Fabius Haywood is also thought to have been Cooper's father; however, even Cooper herself was not certain of her parentage. In one of her autobiographical writings she says, "Presumably my father was [my mother's] master, if so I owe him not a sou & [my mother] was always too modest and shame-faced ever to mention him" (Hutchinson 1981, 4). This aspect of Cooper's life—miscegenation—was common in the South during slavery.[1] The plantation on which Cooper lived was, however, uncommon.

The Haywood plantation was one of the sizable plantations of the South and was kept up by 271 domestic and field slaves (Hutchinson 1981, 9). Modern readers often envision the pre-Civil War South as having abundant plantations and massive colonial homes with hundreds of servants and slaves. Actually, this was the exception rather than the rule. "The extremely wealthy families who owned more than a hundred slaves numbered less than three thousand, a tiny fraction of the southern population" (Stampp 1956, 30–31). An account of the Haywood residence reveals the fabulous wealth and prosperity of this plantation. It boasted

> stables, barns, a carriage house, and the slave quarters. A flower garden, vegetable gardens, and fruit trees were planted for household and family use. Beyond the flower garden there was a family cemetery . . . The scene of social and political gatherings, the slaves were kept busy caring for the house and its master and mistress, grooming the horses, keeping the carriage in good repair, milking the cow, tending the gardens, and preparing the "sumptuous breakfasts." (Hutchinson 1981, 9)

Although the Haywood plantation sounds idyllic, for the enslaved—both the domestic and field slaves—it was a life of forced labor and hardship.

According to Cooper's later writings, Hannah Haywood worked hard after Emancipation in 1865 to give young Anna the "advantages [her mother] had never enjoyed" as a slave. Anna's biographer, Louise Hutchinson, surmises that Hannah Haywood probably sent her child to the Episcopal Church's parochial school, which may have, in turn, allowed Cooper to pass the examination required to enter St. Augustine's Normal School and Collegiate Institute (Hutchinson 1981, 22–23). It is here that Cooper's lifelong teaching career began.

In 1868, at the young age of ten, Cooper took her first step toward teaching by becoming a tutor at St. Augustine's Normal School and Collegiate Institute,[2] receiving $100 a year—this privilege was granted to only two other fellow pupils (Chitty 1983, 154). Although Cooper was not yet a "teacher," she served as a "coach" to her schoolmates, instructing students who were oftentimes older than she how to read (Hutchinson 1981, 19–23).

Cooper's early schooling and teaching career were a sign of the times. She was one of many exceptional examples of ex-slaves, mostly young girls, who ventured early into the world of academia though the normal school. Often, this route was chosen to escape the threat of White male promiscuity that was continually met in domestic service (Davis 1983, 90). At that time, teaching in schools for Black children and domestic service were the only two vocations Black women were allowed to pursue (Giddings 1984, 101).[3]

The normal school was the equivalent of elementary and secondary school, and Cooper attended and taught at St. Augustine's from 1868 to 1881, a total of thirteen years. These years channeled her energy for learning and contagious enthusiasm into her preparation for becoming a teacher. Yet, her great desire to learn was a mixed blessing. While attending St. Augustine's, Cooper often found herself "with a good deal of time on [her] hands," according to *A Voice from the South* (Cooper 1892/1988, 76). She goes on to say, "I had devoured what was put before me, and, like Oliver Twist, was looking around to ask for more. I constantly felt (as I suppose many an ambitious girl has felt) a thumping from within unanswered by any beckoning from without" (Cooper 1892/1988, 76). Here is Cooper's description of her studies at St. Augustine's:

> Besides the English branches and Latin: Caesar, seven books; Virgil's Anead, six books; Sallust's Cataline and Jugurtha; and a few orations of Cicero; [and in] Greek, White's first lessons; Goodwin's Greek Reader, containing selections from Xenophon, Plato, Herodotus, and Thucydides; and five or six books of the Iliad . . . [In] mathematics: Algebra and Geometry entire . . . I have filled the post of both matron and teacher. (Chitty 1983, 55)

The study of ancient languages and math would eventually become Cooper's areas of expertise in the classroom as an accomplished student and teacher.

Anna Cooper had high standards for herself and those responsible for her education. Her dissatisfaction with St. Augustine's curriculum and the amount of work she was given had a lot to do with the low priority given to Black women's education at that time. At St. Augustine's and elsewhere, the Black male students who were being prepared for the ministry were strongly encouraged, while the female students received little or no encouragement (Cooper 1892/1988, 77).

In 1871, at the age of thirteen, Cooper graduated from St. Augustine's. She then stayed on as a teacher, one of three alumni teachers. In 1877 Cooper married George A. C. Cooper, a teacher at St. Augustine's. Within two years, her husband died. It is interesting to note that, had George Cooper lived, Anna J. Cooper would not have been able to pursue her teaching career; a law barring married women from the classroom was not abolished until 1923 (Hutchinson 1981, 49).

After Cooper graduated from St. Augustine's, her desire for higher education continued. One college existed in the late 1800s for the education of Black women—Spelman College in Atlanta, Georgia. Yet, Cooper was focused on attending a northern college rather than a southern school.[4] She chose Ohio's Oberlin College. In a letter dated July 27, 1881, asking Oberlin's President Fairchild for financial assistance in exchange for teaching services, Cooper's enthusiasm and drive to get more from her education is apparent:

> I have, for a long time, earnestly desired to take an advanced course
> in some superior Northern college, but could not see my way to it for

lack of means. However, I am now resolved to await no longer, if there is any possibility of my accomplishing my purpose . . . I expect to have money enough to keep me one or two years at your College, provided I can secure a favor mentioned by Mrs. Clarke, of free tuition and incidentals . . . Please let me know if you think it likely that I can get any way of keeping myself after I come, by teaching, or something similar, during vacation. I desire to remain to be able to complete the course, if possible. (Hutchinson 1981, 34)

Cooper's life in Ohio proved itself quite different in many ways from the one she had in North Carolina. Although she paid for her studies, room, and board at Oberlin by teaching, as she had while at St. Augustine's, the similarities ended there. Oberlin was one of the nation's finest and most revolutionary colleges for men and women *and* Black and White students.[5] Unlike St. Augustine's, which underestimated the ability of its female students, Oberlin set a new standard for women's education. In 1833 Oberlin became the only college in America to allow women to take classes and receive degrees, though they could only take prescribed classes toward a degree. This curriculum was appropriately called the "Ladies' Course." The male students took what was then called the "Gentlemen's Course."

In a move that was to become trend-setting, Oberlin later allowed its women students to take the "Gentlemen's Course," a choice Cooper readily made. In her essay, "The Higher Education of Woman," Cooper tells of how women came to be admitted to Oberlin and then to the "Gentlemen's Course":

[The admission of women to Oberlin College] was felt to be an experiment—a rather dangerous experiment—and was adopted with fear and trembling by the good fathers. . . .

But the girls came, and there was no upheaval. They performed their tasks modestly and intelligently. Once in a while one or two were found choosing the gentlemen's course. Still no collapse; and the dear, careful, scrupulous, frightened old professors were just getting their hearts out of their throats and preparing to draw one good free breath, when they found they would have to change the names of [the "Gentlemen's Course" and "Ladies' Course"]; for there were as many ladies in the gentlemen's course as in the ladies', and a distinctively Ladies' Course, inferior in scope and aim to the regular classical course, did not and could not exist. (Cooper 1892/1988, 49–50)

Cooper graduated from Oberlin College with her B.A. in Mathematics in 1884.

Declining an offer from St. Augustine's to return as "teacher in charge of girls," Cooper went instead to Wilberforce University in Greene County, Ohio[6] as Professor of Modern Language and Literature (Chitty 1983, 156). Wilberforce was touted by one alumnus as "a community with an atmosphere of culture and refinement hardly equaled elsewhere among Negroes of the United States" (Gatewood 1990, 266).[7]

After teaching at Wilberforce University for the 1884–85 academic year, Cooper returned to St. Augustine's and plunged into a "full schedule of classroom teaching" (Chitty 1983, 156). It is uncertain why she spent such a short time at Wilberforce only to return to St. Augustine's. However, we do know that her time and energy at St. Augstine's were used both inside and outside the classroom.

Cooper's many efforts outside of the classroom arose from the less-than-ideal circumstances that surrounded Black education in the South. Due to the lack of funds for teachers' salaries throughout the Southern states, Cooper was inspired to become "active in the North Carolina Teachers Association which sought unsuccessfully to secure equal treatment and salaries" (Chitty 1983, 156). Besides designing "outreach programs in the black community of Raleigh," Cooper also spoke against "the failure of lawmakers to appropriate 'reasonable and just provisions for the training of colored youth'" through the North Carolina Teacher's Association (Chitty 1983, 156; Hine et al. 1993, 277). These types of activities were built into the profession of teaching in the South:

> The dominant social vision among African Americans in the period before World War II projected expectations and responsibilities for the race's teachers that extended far beyond the classroom setting. Over and over during this half-century writers reiterated the concept of the activist African American teacher. Examples abound, all highlighting this central theme: "the genuine teacher knows that his duty is not bounded by the four walls of the classroom. He is dealing with boys and girls to be sure, but he is dealing with something more— with social conditions . . . the school is held responsible for the mental, moral, religious, and physical status of the people immediately touching it." (Fultz 1995, 406)

All her life Cooper worked tirelessly to foster changes in education, the condition of her pupils, and the members of her race.

In 1887, after having received her M.A. in Mathematics from Oberlin *in absentia*, Cooper was recruited by the superintendent for Colored Schools to teach Latin at M Street Colored High School (first known as Washington Colored High School, then as M Street Colored High School, and later as Dunbar High School) in Washington, D.C. The highly regarded "M Street High School enjoyed a national reputation among professionals who knew it as having an academically oriented curriculum and teaching staff" (Morgan 1995, 134).

The four decades following Anna Julia Cooper's move to Washington, D.C. are the years in which she is most vigorously intellectual, social, and political. During these years, Cooper came into contact with one of the most influential figures of her adult life, Dr. Alexander Crummell. A member of one of the most prominent religious, academic, and politically active Black families in Washington, Crummell was pastor and founder of St. Luke's Episcopal Church (Brotz 1992, 171). Through her association and residence with Dr. Crummell, Cooper came to know and study his sermon, "The Black Woman of the South: Her Neglects and Her Needs," in which he advocates uplifting Black women through spiritual, domestic, and social education. This sermon was the namesake of Cooper's book, *A Voice from the South*,[8] the only collection of her writings.

Cooper's life in the 1880s and 1890s was intensely productive. She contributed editorial material to *Southland*, based in Raleigh, North Carolina, which Cooper later called "the first Negro Magazine in the U.S.A" (Cooper, Negro College Graduates, 1938a, Question 55). In 1890 she was the sole writer and editor of *Southland's* Woman's Department, and in 1891 she became co-editor of the magazine with S. G. Atkins. She was also the summer editor of *Southern Workman* from 1893 to 1896 (Cooper, 1921).[9] Both of these publications represented the social, intellectual, and political voice of the Black community, and by writing for them Cooper helped put into print the Black, female point of view, which had not been allowed such a forum. Also in the 1890s, continuing to affect change for Black women, Cooper became an important part of the Black Women's Club Movement, helping to organize the Colored Woman's League of Washington, D.C., in June 1892.

During this period, Cooper also spoke before a wide variety of audiences across the United States on the subject of African American uplift. In 1886 she gave the talk "Womanhood: A Vital Element in the Regeneration and Progress of a Race" to a group of African American Episcopal clergymen at their Fourth Annual Convocation. In 1890 she spoke on "The Higher Education of Woman" to the National Conference of Educators, a group of (mostly male) African American educators. In 1892 she delivered the address "The Status of Woman in America" before the Lady Board of Managers at the building dedication ceremony of the Columbian Exposition. Also in 1892, Cooper spoke to the Bethel Literary and Historical Association of Washington, D.C., on the portrayal of the African American in contemporary literature. In 1893, Cooper gave a talk on "The Needs and the Status of Black Women" (this speech was taken from her essay "Woman versus the Indian"), again to the Lady Board of Managers, as well as the Congress of Representative Women, at the Columbian Exposition.

All of these speeches appear in modified form in her one published book, *A Voice from the South*, which she privately published in 1892. The book consists of eight essays that serve as testament to Cooper's vast store of knowledge on many fronts, as she takes on the specific issues of race, gender, and class in a progressive way. Because of her triple identity as former slave, female, and Black in turn-of-the-century America, Cooper's voice is both powerful and constrained in her public speaking, in *A Voice*, and in other articles and essays. Cooper is forced at almost every turn first to demonstrate her intelligence as an African American and a woman, and then her earnestness, before she can begin to make her plea for the Black men and women of the South, whom she described as suffering in silence and ignorance. Whether she was speaking to African American men, European American women, African American male religious leaders, or African American intellectuals, Cooper had to mediate her voice because these audiences could not immediately and totally sympathize with her gender, race, and class. Fortunately, Cooper's step-by-step style of presentation allowed her voice to emerge from the pages of *A Voice* with rhetorical strength.

Although her resonance was not always as strong as a modern reader might wish, given her racial, gender-based, and social limitations, Cooper was remarkably vocal.

In examining *A Voice* in this way, the contemporary reader can begin to appreciate the forces against which Cooper, as a highly-educated Black woman and former slave, had to contend. White people's prejudices against Black people in general, the prejudice of Black men against Black women, the prejudices of wealthy, upper-class Blacks against lower-class Blacks, White women's organizations against Black ones, and the educated against the uneducated are all forces confronting Cooper in *A Voice*.

After publication of *A Voice*, Anna Julia Cooper continued to speak widely on issues relating to the African American community. In the summer of 1900, she went abroad to the Pan-African Conference held in London, England, to voice her views on "The Negro Problem in America," an issue she felt compelled to bring to the world. Cooper was one of only two female presenters at this conference.[10] Their being invited to speak at such a groundbreaking, international event was unusual in that women, either "black or white, were not invited to play dominant roles along with men" (Hutchinson 1981, 111). This first international event at which Cooper spoke was organized by "Du Bois and a group of his intellectual followers" to write a "formal protest against Western imperialism and the colonization of African nations. Their mission was to promote self-government for all nations" (Morgan 1995, 103). *The Times* (London) reported on the groundbreaking Pan-African Conference, stating "for the first time in the history of world black men [and women] had gathered together from all parts of the globe with the object of discussing and improving the condition of the black race" ("Pan-African Conference" 1900, 7). This event marked the first of Cooper's many travels abroad.

In 1902, Cooper made the transition from teacher to administrator, becoming principal of M Street School (Chitty 1983, 152). She was the second woman to hold this position and was largely responsible for M Street's superior status. According to Gatewood (1990, 249), "Aristocrats of color in Washington had few qualms about sending their children to the racially segregated M Street High School, which was probably superior to white high schools in the city."

Cooper's contribution to M Street High School during her tenure as principal is summarized best in her own words. In a survey question—What suggestions have you "made to your superiors as to improvement in [the] organization of school or department?"—which she answered in her later years, Cooper hand wrote the following answer:

> Standardization of curriculum in the "M Street" High School so that the opportunity for the same or equivalent work be afforded the colored children of Washington as might be found if they were white. Result: M Street High School admitted to list of accredited High Schools for the first time in 1902 and pupils from that school training direct for Harvard, Yale, Brown and Oberlin without intervening year in a northern academy. (Cooper 1921, Question 2c2)

There is no evidence to establish whether Cooper "suggested" these changes, as the above question is worded; she simply did it.

What followed these radical changes in curriculum was dubbed "The M Street Controversy," which lasted from 1902 to 1906. This philosophical conflict had two distinct sides. The existing curriculum at M Street was one that Cooper believed would put the Black "pupils [at M Street High School] on a lower footing in scholarship than white schools of similar grade" ("Support Mrs. Cooper," 1905). To the contrary, Percy M. Hughes, the White director of Washington High Schools, believed that the curriculum was fine because, in his words, "the students [at M Street] are incapable of taking the same studies in the same time as the other schools of like grade in the city" ("Support Mrs. Cooper," 1905). After four years, in 1906, the Board of Education sided with Hughes and dismissed Cooper from her principalship amidst a flurry of newspaper articles, gossip, and administrative hearings. Cooper promptly left Washington, D.C., to teach and serve as Chair of Classical and Romance Languages at Lincoln Institute in Jefferson City, Missouri, from 1906 to 1910.

In 1910, Cooper again found herself teaching Latin at M Street High School. However, while teaching, she was laying the foundation for obtaining her Ph.D. from the Sorbonne in Paris. During the summer and other school vacations, Cooper made trips back and forth to France from 1911 to 1917, taking classes in French literature, phonetics, philology, and preparing "a college edition of 'Pelerinage de Charlemagne' an epic of the XIth Century" at La Guilde International in Paris (Cooper n.d., 3–4). During these years, Cooper fought a serious bout of influenza and physical exhaustion resulting from the new responsibilities of raising five orphaned grand-nieces and nephews, ranging in age from six months to twelve years old (Cooper n.d., 4–5).

At age sixty-seven, on March 3, 1925, Anna Julia Cooper received her Ph.D. from the Sorbonne, the fourth African American woman to do so. Acquiring the necessary leave time from M Street High School on top of family responsibilities made getting her Ph.D. intensely difficult. At one point, toward the end of this ordeal, Cooper was given notice that she would be fired if she did not return to M Street from Paris in sixty days (Cooper n.d., 6). Cooper did finish her dissertation and her defense. In her dissertation, as she tried to do in much of her writing, "she meant to reflect a woman's interpretation of events and a woman's perception of historical meaning about the confrontation over slavery between France and her colony" (Keller 1975, 168).

In 1930 Cooper took on the position of President of the struggling Frelinghuysen University in Washington, D.C. The institution's mission meshed with Cooper's interest in adult education for working men and women, for most of its students were poor and Black (Chitty 1983, 158). However, because of competition from Howard University and an inability to acquire accreditation, Frelinghuysen was forced to close its doors in the 1940s, and Cooper entered retirement.

Cooper continued to be as active as she could in her eighties, writing articles and compiling her memoirs. In anticipation of her death, Cooper wrote a poem called "No Flowers Please," stating she wanted to be remembered as "Somebody's old Teacher on Vacation now! Resting a while, getting ready for the next opening of a Higher School" (Hutchinson 1981, 173). Cooper's strong desire to be remembered in life and in death as a teacher above all else exemplifies her belief in the essential and far-reaching nature of education.

Overview of Cooper's Thought

Cooper's Contributions to Black Education in the South

Although Anna Julia Cooper was a writer, public speaker, intellectual, feminist, and political activist, of all these, the role of teacher allowed her to fight for what she believed was "the inherent right of every soul to its own highest development" (Cooper 1892/1988, 108). At the turn of the century, when Cooper was teaching Black high school students, there were several ideas of how best to educate Black people in the South. One of these, voiced by Booker T. Washington,[11] was an "industrial education." The other, whose primary advocate was W. E. B. Du Bois,[12] was an "academic" or "classical" education. The clashing of these vastly different philosophies was dubbed the "Washington–Du Bois Controversy." Cooper, unlike many of her contemporaries, believed in and contributed time and energy to both philosophies.

Academic and industrial education are two particular paths of learning that Cooper validated in her writings because they allow for individuals to attain and use their talents and capabilities to their highest potential. Just as Cooper's own life exemplified, she believed that the role of education in society is to make productive use of individual talents, capabilities, and desires for knowledge. Unlike many of her contemporaries, especially Du Bois and Washington, Cooper was able to see the value of *both* an academic and an industrial education for Black people. She did not see these two types of education in opposition precisely because her philosophy of education starts with the individual and moves out. First, find out what the individual is interested in and capable of, then fashion the education accordingly. In this way each individual's education will be appropriate, and it can also enable each person to contribute his or her best to the uplift of the race. As Cooper explains in the essay "What Are We Worth?", an academic education is not for everyone; an industrial education involving the learning of trades is also a viable alternative. Cooper states:

> I believe in allowing every longing of the human soul to attain its utmost reach and grasp. But the effort must be a fizzle which seeks to hammer souls into preconstructed molds and grooves which they have never longed for and cannot be made to take comfort in. The power of appreciation is the measure of an individual's aptitudes; and if a boy hates Greek and Latin and spends all his time whittling out steamboats, it is rather foolish to try to force him into the classics . . . It is a waste of forces to strain his incompetence, and smother his proficiencies. If his hand is far more cunning and clever than his brain, see what he can best do, and give him a chance according to his fitness; try him at a trade. (Cooper 1892/1988, 259)

Cooper's approach to the Washington–Du Bois Controversy was to recognize the worth of both types of education, as they were appropriate to the individual. Many believe that curriculum development for Black youth has been unquestionably tied to Black America's experience of slavery and oppression in the United States. Contrasting viewpoints have reflected socio-political perspectives that existed during Cooper's time (and continue to exist today) (Watkins 1993). For her own education and teaching career, Cooper purposely sought out schools with academic-centered curricula—St. Augustine's, Oberlin, Wilberforce, M Street Colored High School, and the Sorbonne in Paris. However, Cooper is also known to have said, "I believe in industrial education with all my heart . . . We can't all be professional people. We must have a backbone to the race" (Giddings 1984, 103). To illustrate her belief that both industrial and academic types of education are valuable, Cooper convincingly argues that complex trades such as farming need to be taught and will benefit the young learners, their families and neighbors, and, in turn, the entire community:

> The youth must be taught to use his trigonometry in surveying his own and his neighbor's farm; to employ his geology and chemistry in finding out the nature of the soil . . . to apply his mechanics and physics to the construction and handling of machinery—to the intelligent management of iron works and water works and steam works and electric works. (Cooper 1892/1988, 262)

At this time in Black education, words like Cooper's were unusual. The debate among philosophies of education specifically for Black people was so intense, in part, because education was seen as the best way to overcome the ravages of slavery.

Human Nature, Social Equality, and "Like Seeks Like"

Cooper saw all races and classes as having the same nature. During newspaper interviews conducted by White reporters, Cooper admits she was often asked to give some "points" about *"your people"* (Cooper 1892/1988, 111). Her response explains her views on human nature in great detail:

> My "people" are just like other people—indeed, too like for their own good. They hate, they love, they attract and repel, they climb or they grovel, struggle or drift, aspire or despair, endure in hope or curse in vexation, exactly like all the rest of unregenerate humanity. Their likes and dislikes are as strong; their antipathies—and prejudices too I fear, are as pronounced as you will find anywhere; and the entrance to the inner sanctuary of their homes and hearts is as jealously guarded against profane intrusion. (Cooper 1892/1988, 112)

Cooper goes a long way in "humanizing" Black people at a time when Blacks were thought to be incapable of complex thought, less than human, and sometimes lower than animals. She goes on to show that Black people do not relish race separation but do relish having the choice to enjoy the company of those with similar needs, desires, talents, and aspirations. She states:

> What the dark man wants then is merely to live his own life, in his own world, with his own chosen companions, in whatever of comfort, luxury, or emoluments his talent or his money can in an impartial market secure. Has he wealth, he does not want to be forced into inconvenient or unsanitary sections of cities to buy a home and rear his family. Has he art, he does not want to be cabined and cribbed into emulation with the few who merely happen to have his complexion. His talent aspires to study without proscription the masters of all ages and to rub against the broadest and fullest movements of his own day. (Cooper 1892/1988, 112)

Finally, Cooper asserts the Black communities' desire for "oneness" with God, "raceless" male and female ideals, and "classless" personal and intellectual attainment. She says:

> Has he religion, he does not want to be made to feel that there is a white Christ and a black Christ, a white Heaven and a black Heaven, a white Gospel and a black Gospel—but the one ideal of perfect manhood and womanhood, the one universal longing for development and growth, the one desire for being, and being better, the one great yearning, aspiring, outreaching, in all the heart-throbs of humanity in whatever race or clime. (Cooper 1892/1988, 112–13)

Overall, Cooper believes that Blacks, like Whites, seek out people, philosophies, and environments that meet their needs and desires, and that the individual longing for development is a part of universal human nature.

Cooper's perception of basic human nature, I believe, gives her a blueprint of the highest potential that Black women and men can aspire to. Because she sees Blacks and Whites as having the same nature—not to be confused with their needs, desires, and social circumstances—they also have the same growth potential. Unfortunately, what prevents society as a whole, but Blacks especially, from realizing that potential is another aspect of human nature that Cooper names: "Like seeks like" (Cooper 1892/1988, 110). "Like seeks like" is what causes a lack of social equality[13] among classes, races, and genders. However, this has nothing to do with their essential human nature. Because people are often different when it comes to the categories of class and race (and, in some cases, gender), people will seek out, associate with, and behave civilly toward those who are like them, discriminating against others who are not like them.

Cooper gives a scenario in her essay "Woman versus the Indian" that explains why the phenomenon of "like seeks like" prevents—and at the same time forces the issue of—social equality. When upper-class Blacks such as Cooper find themselves desiring "first class accommodations on a railway train" but cannot secure a seat in first class, this is a result of *different* races (even though they are of the *same* social class) seeking similar treatment (Cooper 1892/1988, 111). Using herself as an example, she explains her motivation for seeking similar treatment:

> I do so because my physical necessities are identical with those of other human beings of like constitution and temperament, and crave satisfaction. I go because I want food, or I want comfort—not because I want association with those who frequent these places; and I can see no more "social equality" in buying lunch at the same restaurant, or riding in a common car, than there is in paying for dry goods at the same counter or walking on the same street. (Cooper 1892/1988, 111)

However, because of socially constructed racial difference (in spite of class similarity), social equality is not possible.

Black Women's Education

Women's versus men's education functions in much the same way—the potential is the same for both genders, but one group is discouraged from meeting its potential while the other is encouraged. In Cooper's opinion, the problem is as follows: Although human nature is universal, social inequality prevents people who are alike in their needs from having those needs met. The impossibility of like meeting like prevents all groups from meeting their highest potential, which requires social equality.

From her vantage point as a Southern, educated Black woman, Cooper experienced the hardships of getting an education. She recounted the lack of encouragement she received at St. Augustine's with passion and humor:

> A boy, however meager his equipment and shallow his pretensions, had only to declare a floating intention to study theology and he could get all the support, encouragement and stimulus he needed. . . . While a self-supporting girl had to struggle on by teaching in the summer and working after school hours to keep up with her board bills, and actually to fight her way against positive discouragements to the higher education . . . And when at last that same girl announced her desire and intention to go to college it was received with about the same incredulity and dismay as if a brass button on one of those candidate's coats had propounded a new method for squaring the circle or trisecting the arc. (Cooper 1892/1988, 77–78)

Cooper gave her opinions on the lack of support among African American males for female higher education: "It seems hardly a gracious thing to say, but it strikes me as true, that while our men seem thoroughly abreast of the times on almost every other subject, when they strike the woman question they drop back into sixteenth century logic" (Cooper 1892/1988, 75).

It wasn't only Black men that the Black woman of the South had to contend with. White women also had difficulty seeing the necessity for Black women's uplift. Knowing that White women couldn't fully appreciate how their cause and the Black woman's causes were linked, while at the Congress of Representative Women in 1893, part of Chicago's Columbian Exposition, Cooper explains that her goal of uplifting Black women of the South is part of a universal cause that all women share:

> The colored woman feels that woman's cause is one and universal; and that not till the image of God, whether in parian or ebony, is sacred and inviolable: not till race, color, sex and condition are seen as the accident and not the substance of life; not till the universal title of humanity to life, liberty, and the pursuit of happiness is conceded to be inalienable to all; not till then is woman's lesson taught and woman's cause won—not the white woman's, or the black woman's, nor the red woman's, but the cause of every man and of every woman who has withered silently under a mighty wrong. Woman's wrongs are thus indissolubly linked with all undefended woe, and the acquirement of her "rights" will mean the final triumph of all right over might, the supremacy of the moral forces of reason, and justice, and love in the government of the nations of earth. (Lowenberg and Bogin 1976, 330–31)

Cooper chose to emphasize education as women's means of advancement. She and her many contemporaries—including Crummell, Washington, and Du Bois—agreed that social equality would be a natural result of an education. Cooper expressed this belief in her eloquent speeches and articles directed to philanthropists, women's groups, religious groups, and the Black intellectual community. She writes, "every attempt to elevate the Negro, whether undertaken by himself of through the philanthropy of others, cannot but prove abortive unless so directed as to utilize the indispensable agency of an elevated and trained womanhood" (Cooper 1892/1988, 28–29). Echoing Crummell, Cooper characterizes society as totally reliant on women (both Black and White) and the purity of the home in which they reign. She claims that:

> The atmosphere of homes is no rarer and purer and sweeter than are the mothers in those homes. A race is but a total of families. The nation is the aggregate of its homes. As the whole is sum of all its parts, so the character of the parts will determine the characteristics of the whole. (Cooper 1892/1988, 29)

With this assertion, all people—males and females of all heritages—are dependent on the quality of the (child-bearing) women in their society.

Cooper asserts that by educating women, the feminine influence of women will augment the overwhelming masculine influence "which has dominated . . . for fourteen centuries" (Cooper 1892/1988, 5). She concludes that the woman's educated voice and unique influence is necessary to give "symmetry" to a presently unbalanced society. This assertion forms the basis for the gendered aspect of her philosophy of education. For all races, not just the African American race, both genders must be educated for equality to shine on all facets of civilization.

However, Cooper narrowly escapes being entangled in an ideological straitjacket in her attempt to define the essential natures of men and women. She comes alarmingly close to asserting that the fundamental virtue of men is reasoning while women's is "sympathy." As in another essay in *A Voice*, "The Status of Woman in America," Cooper here betrays her adherence to Victorian notions of womanhood. To say that men are the original and exclusive possessors of higher thought would demolish her entire argument, her entire crusade for women's education. Cooper makes an astonishing, although not complete, recovery. She reclaims woman's power of reason by saying that men and women possess varying degrees of both intellectual and emotional qualities, each obtained from the corresponding male or female parent (with this latter statement she falls back into the trap). In the case of men, she cautiously writes that a man's sympathetic inclination is the result of his mother's influence on him:

> Now please understand me. I do not ask you to admit that these benefactions and virtues [of sympathy and caring] are the exclusive possession of women, or even that women are their chief and only advocates. It may be a man who formulates and makes them vocal. It may be, and often is, a man who weeps over the wrongs and struggles for the amelioration: but that man has imbibed those impulses from a mother rather than from a father and is simply materializing and giving back to the world in tangible form the ideal love and tenderness, devotion and care that have cherished and nourished the helpless period of his own existence. (Cooper 1892/1988, 59–60)

From this standpoint, Cooper shows the necessity of having both genders equally educated so that their respective "natures—related not as inferior and superior, but as complements"—can assert their full impact on America and work to create a virtuous national conscience, viable institutions, and a society based on fairness and equality (Cooper 1892/1988, 60).

Cooper's final words on the subject are to privilege the value of women teachers, homemakers, wives, mothers, and even the Republican but "silent influences" from women to their husbands over that of the theologian:

> The earnest well trained Christian young woman, as a teacher, as a home-maker, as wife, mother, or silent influence even, is as potent a missionary agency among our people as is the theologian; and I claim that at the present stage of our development in the South she is even more important and necessary. (Cooper 1892/1988, 79)

In these offices of teacher, homemaker, and wife, Cooper seems to imply that the educated Black women of the South need to fill the even more important, powerful, and necessary position in society as teachers of womanly values and that these standards are more "important and necessary" than religious teachings. This is a very high claim for the voice of Black womanhood. But then, "The Higher Education of Woman" is Cooper's empowering claim for womanhood as an institution in and of itself. Yet womanhood is an institution that must still realize its full development and potential. Cooper fittingly closes this essay (the second essay of *A Voice*) with what she sees as the first step in the progression toward the evolution of the female force through higher education: "Let us then, here and now, recognize this [female] force and resolve to make the most of it—not the boys less, but the girls more" (Cooper 1892/1988, 79).

It is Cooper's belief that she can be an essential part of the important work of Du Bois, Washington, and others by focusing on Black women's uplift which will, in turn, uplift the entire race. She goes on to say:

> A race cannot be purified from without. Preachers and teachers are helps, and stimulants and conditions as necessary as the gracious rain and sunshine are to plant growth. But what are rain and dew and sunshine and cloud if there be no life in the plant germ? We must go to the root and see that it is sound and healthy and vigorous; and not deceive ourselves with waxen flowers and painted leaves of mock chlorophyll. (Cooper 1892/1988, 29)

The Black woman of the South is the "root" of the race, the most critical aspect of the race's ability to grow. For this essential group of women, Cooper advocates industrial and domestic training schools and explains the need to tap into the potential of the Black woman:

> Now I would ask in all earnestness, does not this force potential deserve by education and stimulus to be made dynamic? Is it not a solemn duty incumbent on all colored churchmen to make it so? Will not the aid of the Church be given to prepare our girls in head, heart, and hand for the duties and responsibilities that await the intelligent wife, the Christian mother, the earnest, virtuous, helpful woman, at once both the lever and the fulcrum for uplifting the race. (Cooper 1892/1988, 45)

Another of Cooper's beliefs about women's higher education is that if women are educated, their generosity and open-mindedness will ensure that they do not become discontented mothers and wives (which was the prevailing thought on women's education) but rather better, happier mothers with more tidy homes:

> [Educated women] deny that their education in any way unfits them for the duty of wifehood and maternity or primarily renders these

conditions any less attractive to them than to the domestic type of woman. On the contrary, they hold that their knowledge of physiology makes them better mothers and housekeepers; their knowledge of chemistry makes them better cooks; while from their training in other natural sciences and in mathematics, they obtain an accuracy and fair-mindedness which is of great value to them in dealing with their children or employees. (Cooper 1892/1988, 71–72)

This type of argument, while extinguishing the threat of female superiority to men by way of education, is rooted in "the cult of true womanhood." As Harriet Beecher Stowe did in *Uncle Tom's Cabin,* Cooper is drawing a parallel between the orderliness of a home and the morality and tranquillity of the nation (Tate 1992, 23). But Cooper's ultimate vision for educated women is for them to contribute their intellect to society rather than their domestic talents to the nation's households:

Now I claim that it is the prevalence of the Higher Education among women, the making it a common everyday affair for women to reason and think and express their thought . . . that has given symmetry and completeness to the world's agencies. . . . Religion, science, art, economics, have all needed the feminine flavor; and literature, the expression of what is permanent and best in all of these, may be gauged [*sic*] at any time to measure the strength of the feminine ingredient. You will not find theology consigning infants to lakes of unquenchable fire long after women have had a chance to grasp, master, and wield its dogmas. (Cooper 1892/1988, 57–58)

The reality of the late nineteenth century causes Cooper's dream of women participating in religion, science, art, and economics to be deferred. However, Cooper's higher vision for women's achievement and influence is inspiring even today.

Qualities That Should Be Emphasized— Religion, Morals, Manners, and Perseverance

A thirty-six-year-old Cooper stood before a group of Hampton teachers and students, asking the question: "Can we succeed under our special disadvantages[?]" Her answer to that question of Black success shows the importance of doubled effort and perseverance:

We can [succeed], provided we work just twice as hard. We are at the beginning of the race, to do the unheard of thing; to extemporize a perfect civilization in thirty years time to compete with a civilization centuries old. Once the Anglo Saxons stood where we stand, at the beginning of the race. Julius Caesar thought they would never amount to anything—that they were not fit even for slaves. But they went to work and made themselves what they now are. We now have our record to make. We ought not to be discouraged because we are a later race. To have a later start is no disgrace. We do not despise a child because he is not a man. ("Our Most" 1894, 54–55)

Throughout her writings, Cooper also emphasizes the importance of cultivating religion, morals, and manners as sources for racial uplift. When Cooper speaks of "religion," she is very specific. Religion is not dogmatic or formulaic. She writes, "Religion must be *life made true;* and life is action, growth, development—begun now and ending never. And a life made true cannot confine itself—it must reach out and twine around every pulsing interest within reach of its uplifting tendrils" (Cooper 1892/1988, 299). In other words, what one believes should be made an integral part of one's life and all of the actions that he or she executes in life. Cooper gives a philanthropic example:

> Do you *believe* that the God of history often chooses the weak things of earth to confound the mighty, and that the Negro race in America has a veritable destiny in His eternal purposes—then don't spend you time discussing the "Negro Problem" amid the clouds of your fine havanna, ensconced in your friend's well-cushioned arm-chair and with your patent leather boot-tips elevated to the opposite mantel. Do those poor "cowards in the South" need a leader—then get up and lead them! Let go your purse-strings and begin to *live* your creed. (Cooper 1892/1988, 299–300)

As for manners, Cooper quotes Lord [*sic*] Bryce, who asserts that manners affect the execution of laws and social interaction directly:

> As regards social relations, law can do but little save in the way of expressing the view the state takes of how its members should behave to one another. Good feeling and good manners cannot be imposed by statute. When the educated sections of the dominant race [Whites] realize how essential it is to the future of their country that the backward [lower classes of Blacks and Whites] be helped forward and rendered friendly, their influence will by degrees filter down through the masses and efface the scorn they feel for the weaker.
>
> A philosopher may say "let who will make the laws if I make the manners; for where manners are wholesome the laws will be just and justly administered. Manners depend on sentiment and sentiment changes slowly. Still it changes." (Cooper 1938b, 148)

With manners there is civility, which, as Cooper has written, implies social equality (Cooper 1892/1988, 109). And social equality, as discussed previously, is the bridge that society must cross in order for all groups to reach their true, highest potential.

Conclusion

On her one-hundredth birthday, during an interview by a *Washington Post* reporter, Cooper stated: "It isn't what we say about ourselves, it's what our life stands for" (quoted in Hutchinson 1981, 175). Anna Julia Cooper's life spanned the first hundred years of freedom for African Americans in this country. Her unwavering commitment throughout her long life was to the progress of the Black race through education. Mary Helen Washington describes Cooper's contribution to the tradition of women's thought and work:

> Cooper wrote in a college questionnaire in 1932 that her chief cultural interest was "the education of the underprivileged," and indeed the fullest expression of her feminism and her intellectual life is to be found in her work as an educator. Still, I do not want to minimize the accomplishment of *A Voice From the South*. It is the most precise, forceful, well-argued statement of black feminist thought to come out of the nineteenth century. (Washington 1988, li)

Notes

[1]According to Kenneth Stampp (1956), "To measure the extent of miscegenation [during slavery] with precision is impossible, because statistical indexes are crude and public and private records fragmentary. But the evidence nevertheless suggests that human behavior in the Old South was very human indeed, that sexual contacts between the races were not the rare aberrations of a small group of depraved whites but a frequent occurrence of all social and cultural levels" (350–51).

[2]St. Augustine's first school session began in May 1868. Cooper later described St. Augustine's educational mission "to prepare teachers for colored youth, furnish candidates for the ministry, and offer collegiate training for those who should be ready for it" (quoted in Hutchinson 1981, 22). One writer describes the curriculum in the following way: "the boys cultivated 45-acre farm of corn and oats. The following subjects were taught: reading, writing, arithmetic, spelling, defining, geography, grammar, algebra, geometry, composition and Latin" (Bennet 1974, 416).

[3]Cooper was privileged to have been born in North Carolina, because this state encouraged young women to pursue teaching as a profession. The state school superintendent made it a point to form schools such as St. Augustine's to educate Southern teachers for Black children so that they would not be reliant upon an unpredictable pool of Northern teachers. His opinion was correct; a decade after the Civil War, "only a few" Northern teachers remained in the South (Huntzinger, 8).

[4]Du Bois, one of Cooper's noteworthy contemporaries, explained the difference between Northern and Southern schools in a speech he gave to Northern philanthropists:

> [T]he great mistake which some of you and many others make, when they talk and think about the South, is to assume that there are in the South the same

facilities for the transmission of culture from class to class and man to man as exist in the North . . . [R]acial separation in the South means voluntary and persistent isolation of those who most need to learn by race contact . . . In the North, of course, in the last twenty-five years, the development has been exactly in the opposite way: it has been toward greater and more frequent and broader contact of the more favored classes of society with the less favored . . . There is in the South a social separation between workman and employer, the ignorant and the learned, society and its servants, the high and low, white and black, whch goes to an extent and reaches a degree quite unrealized by those who have not studied the situation. (Du Bois 1973, 35–36)

[5]"From its establishment in 1833 until the Civil War, blacks constituted about four or five percent of the student body [at Oberlin]. . . . Despite the college's celebrated role in the Abolition movement, black students at Oberlin 'were never treated the same as whites.' Nevertheless, the atmosphere was probably freer of prejudice than at virtually any other predominantly white institution in the country" (Gatewood 1990, 251).

[6]A racially segregrated school, Wilberforce University was named after "Britian's premier abolitionist, Bishop William Wilberforce" (Lewis 1993, 151). "The village of Wilberforce was about twenty miles southeast of Dayton and three dusty miles of buggy tracks from Xenia, the nearest incorporated town" (Lewis 1993, 151).

[7]It is important to note that schools such as Spelman College, Clark College, Atlanta Baptist (Morehouse), Atlanta University, Fisk University, and Howard University could boast the same high standards (Gatewood 1990, 266).

[8]The following quote from Crummell's sermon, "The Black Woman of the South: Her Neglects and Her Needs," vividly explains the status of Black women in the South and what he sees as their needs:

The eighteen years of freedom have not obliterated all slavery's deadly marks from either the souls or bodies of the black woman . . . [The Black woman of the South] has rarely been taught to sew, and the field labor of slavery times has kept her ignorant of the habitudes of neatness, and the requirements of order. Indeed, coarse food, coarse clothes, coarse living, coarse manners, coarse companions, coarse surroundings, coarse neighbors, both black and white, yea, everything coarse, down to the coarse ignorant, senseless religion, which excites her sensibilities and starts her passions, go to make up the life of the masses of black women in the hamlets and villages of the rural South. (Crummell 1978, 58)

[9]Both of these publications were venues for earlier versions of the essays that appear in *A Voice from the South.*

[10]Anna H. Jones of Missouri, "a long-time friend" of Cooper's, was the other presenter; the title of her paper was "The Preservation of Race Individuality" (Hutchinson 1981, 110–11).

[11]The year 1890 marked the rise of Booker T. Washington and his philosophy of education, one that advocated industrial and mechanical training for Blacks to prepare them to function practically in the real world of work (labor) rather than that of academia. In his own words, in the historic "Atlanta Compromise" speech at the Cotton States International Exposition on September 18, 1895, he expressed his vision for the Southern Black:

Our greatest danger is, that in the great leap from slavery to freedom we may overlook the fact that the masses of us are to live by the productions of our hands, and fail to keep in mind that we shall prosper in proportion as we learn to dignify and glorify common labor, and put brains and skill into the common occupations of life; shall prosper in proportion as we learn to draw the line between the superficial and the substantial, the ornamental gewgaws of life and the useful. No race can prosper till it learns that there is as much dignity in tilling a field as in writing a poem. It is at the bottom of life we must begin, and not at the top. Nor should we permit our grievances to overshadow our opportunities. (quoted in Ploski and Kaiser 1971, 134)

[12]William Edward Burghard Du Bois had a drastically different idea of what African Americans' academic attainments should encompass. As a Boston-born Black man and the first African American to earn a Harvard doctorate, W. E. B. Du Bois saw the goal of African American education as that of "developing 'a class of thoroughly educated men according to modern standards . . . [the] standards of white colleges'" (quoted in Lewis 1993, 549).

[13]Cooper takes great pains in this essay to explain that social equality does not mean forced association but "civility," which she sees as two very different ideas (Cooper 1892/1988, 109–11).

References

Bennet, R. A. 1974. Black Episcopalians: A History from the Colonial Period to the Present. *Historical Magazine of the Protestant Episcopal Church* 43: 231–45.

Brotz, H., ed. 1992. *African-American Social and Political Thought, 1850–1920.* New Brunswick: Transaction Publishers.

Chitty, A. B. 1983. Women and Black Education: Three Profiles. *Historical Magazine of the Protestant Episcopal Church* 52: 153–65.

Cooper, A. J. [1892] 1988. *A Voice from the South: By a Black Woman of the South.* Reprint. New York: Oxford University Press.

———. 1921. Data Desired Relative to Group B Examination, December 17, 1921. Howard University, Moorland-Spingarn Research Center. Anna Julia Cooper Papers, Box 1.

———. 1938a. Negro College Graduates: Individual Occupational History. Howard University, Moorland-Spingarn Research Center. Anna Julia Cooper Papers, Box 1.

———. 1938b. Angry Saxons and Negro Education. *The Crisis* (May): 148.

———. n.d. *The Third Step (Autobiographical).* Booklet. Privately printed.

Crummell, A. 1978. The Black Woman of the South: Her Neglects and Her Needs. In *An Introduction to Black Literature in America from 1746 to the Present,* ed. L. Patterson. Cornwells Heights, PA: Publishers Agency.

Davis, A. 1983. *Women, Race, and Class.* New York: Vintage.

Du Bois, W. E. B. 1973. *The Education of Black People: Ten Critiques, 1906–1960,* ed. H. Aptheker. New York: Monthly Review Press.

Fultz, M. 1995. African American Teachers in the South, 1890–1940: Powerlessness and the Ironies of Expectations and Protest. *History of Education Quarterly* (Winter): 401–22.

Gatewood, W. B. 1990. *Aristocrats of Color: Black Elite, 1820–1920.* Bloomington: Indiana University Press.

Giddings, P. 1984. *When and Where I Enter: The Impact of Black Women on Race and Sex in America.* New York: Morrow.

Hine, D. C., et al., ed. *Black Women in America: An Historical Encyclopedia.* 2 Vols. Bloomington: Indiana University Press.

Huntzinger, V. M. Portraits in Black and White: A Micro and Macro View of Southern Teachers Before and After the Civil War. Pre-Conference Draft. *ERIC* Document Reproduction Service, ED 390 856: 1–29.

Hutchinson, L. D. 1981. *Anna J. Cooper: A Voice from the South.* Washington, DC: Smithsonian Institution Press.

Keller, F. R. 1975. The Perspective of a Black American on Slavery and the French Revolution: Anna Julia Cooper. *Proceedings of the Annual Meeting of the Western Society for French History* 3: 165–76.

Lowenberg, B., and R. Bogin, ed. *Black Women in Nineteenth-Century Life: Their Thoughts, Their Words, Their Feelings.* University Park: Pennsylvania State University Press.

Lewis, D. L. 1993. *W. E. B. Du Bois: Biography of a Race 1868–1919.* New York: Holt.

Morgan, H. 1995. *Historical Perspectives on the Education of Black Children.* Westport, CT: Praeger.

"Our Most . . ." 1894. Editorial. *Southland* (June) 54–55.

"Pan-African Conference." 1890. *Times* (London) (July 24): 7.

Ploski, H. A., and E. Kaiser, ed. 1971. *The Negro Almanac.* 2nd ed. New York: Bellwether.

Stampp, K. M. 1956. *The Peculiar Institution: Slavery in the Ante-Bellum South.* New York: Vintage.

"Support Mrs. Cooper: Colored People Aroused over High School Inquiry." 1905. *Washington Post* (September 29): n. p.

Tate, C. 1992. *Domestic Allegories of Political Desire: The Black Heroine's Text at the Turn of the Century.* New York: Oxford University Press.

Washington, M. H. 1988. Introduction to *A Voice from the South,* by A. J. Cooper. New York: Oxford University Press.

Watkins, W. H. 1993. Black Curriculum Orientations: A Preliminary Inquiry. *Harvard Educational Review* 63(3): 321–38.

READING

Our Raison d'être

Anna Julia Cooper

An excerpt from *A Voice from the South*

In the clash and clatter of our American Conflict, it has been said that the South remains Silent. Like the Sphinx she inspires vociferous disputation, but herself takes little part in the noisy controversy. One muffled strain in the Silent South, a jarring chord and a vague and uncomprehended cadenza has been and still is the Negro. And of that muffled chord, the one mute and voiceless note has been the sadly expectant Black Woman,

> An infant crying in the night,
> An infant crying for the light;
> And with *no language—but a cry.*

The colored man's inheritance and apportionment is still the sombre crux, the perplexing *cul de sac* of the nation,—the dumb skeleton in the closet provoking ceaseless harangues, indeed, but little understood and seldom consulted. Attorneys for the plaintiff and attorneys for the defendant, with bungling *gaucherie* have analyzed and dissected, theorized and synthesized with sublime ignorance or pathetic misapprehension of counsel from the black client. One important witness has not yet been heard from. The summing up of the evidence deposed, and the charge to the jury have been made—but no word from the Black Woman.

It is because I believe the American people to be conscientiously committed to a fair trial and ungarbled evidence, and because I feel it essential to a perfect understanding and an equitable verdict that truth from *each* standpoint be presented at the bar,—that this little Voice has been added to the already full chorus. The "other side" has not been represented by one who "lives there." And not many can more sensibly realize and more accurately tell the weight and the fret of the "long dull pain" than the open-eyed but hitherto voiceless Black Woman of America.

The feverish agitation, the perfervid energy, the busy objectivity of the more turbulent life of our men serves, it may be, at once to cloud or color their vision somewhat, and as well to relieve the smart and deaden the pain for them. Their voice is in consequence not always temperate and calm, and at the same time radically corrective and sanatory. At any rate, as our Caucasian barristers are not to blame if they cannot *quite* put themselves in the dark man's place, neither should the dark man be wholly expected fully and adequately to reproduce the exact Voice of the Black Woman.

Delicately sensitive at every pore to social atmospheric conditions, her calorimeter may well be studied in the interest of accuracy and fairness in diagnosing what is often conceded to be a "puzzling" case. If these broken utterances can in any way help to a clearer vision and a truer pulse-beat in studying our Nation's Problem, this Voice by a Black Woman of the South will not have raised in vain.

Tawawa Chimney Corner, Sept. 17, 1892

Chapter 5

CHARLOTTE PERKINS GILMAN

The Origin of Education is Maternal

By Karen E. Maloney

Introduction

Charlotte Perkins Gilman (1860–1935) was well known as a feminist and social reformer from the 1880s through the early 1900s.[1] During her many tours on the lecture circuit, thousands of people came to hear her speak on such topics as "The New Motherhood," "Heroes We Need Now," "How to Get Good and Stay So," and "Woman Suffrage and Man's Sufferings." Dozens of her poems and short stories appeared in the popular journals and magazines of her day, and hundreds of her articles were published in such periodicals as *Woman's Journal*, *Century Magazine*, and *American Journal of Sociology.* She also published her own journal, the *Forerunner,* from 1909 to 1916, writing all thirty-two pages of each monthly issue. Thousands also bought her many books, the most successful of which was her first, *Women and Economics*, which went through three printings in two years and was translated into Danish, Italian, Dutch, German, and Russian within five years of its publication in 1898 (Gilman 1898/1966). More than a dozen books followed, but none achieved the attention and acclaim of this first. Gilman continued writing and speaking up until her death in 1935, but she never again reached the height of attention that she enjoyed from 1898 to 1910.

Gilman was a bold and original thinker, the power of whose ideas, as biographer Ann Lane explains, "comes from their stark originality and jolting freshness"

Charlotte Perkins Gilman
_____

(Lane 1991, 232). In her day she was described as possessing the "most original and challenging mind which the movement produced" by suffragist organizer Carrie Chapman Catt (Hill 1980, 4). Noted writer, editor, and critic William Dean Howells was particularly impressed with Gilman, writing to Gilman that her first book of poems, *In This Our World,* contained "the wittiest and wisest things that have been written this many a long day and year . . . you speak with a tongue like a two-edged sword" (quoted in Lane 1991, 145). H. G. Wells, Jane Addams, Edward A. Ross, and Theodore Dreiser also praised her thought and work (Lane 1991, 6–7).

Biographical Sketch

Gilman was born in 1860 into the famous New England Beecher family that shaped nineteenth-century culture through the writings and oratory of ministers Lyman Beecher and his son Henry Ward Beecher, and his daughters Harriet Beecher Stowe, author of *Uncle Tom's Cabin;* educator and author Catharine Beecher; and suffragist Isabella Beecher Hooker. Gilman's father, Frederic Beecher Perkins, was the grandson of Lyman Beecher. Gilman's father left the family soon after she was born, and her life was shaped by financial instability and frequent moves from the home of one relative to another. Gilman was involved in the family's precarious finances from a young age, teaching young children, painting greeting cards for sale, and giving art lessons as means of helping the family financially. At the age of twenty-two, Gilman met Walter Stetson, a painter. They were married two years later in 1884. Their child,

Katharine Beecher Stetson, was born a year later. However, Gilman was terribly unhappy and depressed in the marriage, and in 1887 she and Walter agreed to separate. Several years later they legally divorced. Walter remarried, and Gilman sent Katharine, then nine years old, to live with Walter and his wife in 1894. Gilman was viciously attacked as an "unnatural mother" because of this act, for by this time she had become a public figure. Her first poem was published in the suffragist publication the *Woman's Journal* in 1882. In 1886 she attended her first suffrage convention and began contributing articles for the *Woman's Journal*. In 1890 her first theoretical poem, "Similar Cases," was published in the *Nationalist*, and she joined the Nationalist lecture circuit in California, where she was living. In 1892 Gilman published *The Yellow Wallpaper*, a gripping account of a young mother's struggle with insanity while enduring the popular "rest cure" of the day. Gilman is most often known in connection with this work, which is commonly assigned reading in women's studies and literature classes. Her reputation grew from this point on, with the publication of a book of poetry, countless articles and columns in newspapers, and hundreds of lectures and addresses, including an invited address at the Twenty-Eighth Annual Woman's Suffrage Convention in 1896 and attendance at the International Socialist and Labor Congress of 1896 in London. In 1898 Gilman published her first and most important theoretical work, *Women and Economics*, in which she analyzes the limited roles and functions of women and how these hinder social progress. The book, reprinted seven times in seven years and translated into seven languages, received effusive praise from women reformers, suffragists, and social reformers in the United States and Europe. From 1898 on, Gilman traveled across the United States on the paid lecture circuit, a grueling but financially rewarding occupation. She continued her heavy writing schedule, publishing in the *Saturday Evening Post* and *Cosmopolitan* and publishing her second book of poetry, her book on educating children, her book on the home, and her book on human work between 1898 and 1905.

In 1900 she married Houghton Gilman, and they remained happily married until his death in 1934. In 1909 she began publishing her own journal, the *Forerunner*, writing all the copy for each monthly issue for the next six years. Gilman's last theoretical work, on religion, was published in 1923. Her autobiography was published in 1935, soon after her death. Gilman took her own life in 1935 after living with incurable breast cancer for more than three years. She was determined not to suffer needlessly once the pain made any work and contribution to society impossible.

Gilman's prominence diminished after the First World War, and after her death she faded into oblivion, with all her books out of print, until historian Carl Degler reintroduced Gilman to the world in 1956 with his article "Charlotte Perkins Gilman and the Theory and Practice of Feminism" (Degler 1956). Degler played a central role in the resurgence of interest in Gilman's work through this article and through the publication of his 1966 reprint edition of *Women and Economics* (Gilman 1898/1966). Since that time, numerous articles have been written on Gilman. In the 1960s scholars focused on her feminist thought, its place in the feminist thinking of her time, and its contribution to feminist studies today. In the 1970s and 1980s, as Gilman and her writings became more widely known and available, scholars began to focus on specific disciplinary topics within Gilman's overall thought, analyzing such topics as her social evolutionary theory, her social ethics, her domestic science, her social science, and her understanding of the role of science in society.[2] Gilman's educational philosophy has received attention as well. Philosopher Jane Roland Martin has analyzed what Gilman contributes to a theory of the ideal of the educated woman. Martin devotes a chapter to Gilman's theory of education as presented in her utopian novel *Herland,* in her book *Reclaiming a Conversation: The Ideal of the Educated Woman* (Martin 1985).

   In this chapter I will present, analyze, and evaluate Gilman's philosophy of education and discuss what it has to offer us today. In order to fully understand her educational theories, it is necessary to be acquainted with her social reform theories in general, so I will begin with a brief overview of her general thought. In elucidating Gilman's educational theory, I will focus on the basic questions of educational philosophy: the purpose of life, the role of the individual in society, the role of education in society, beliefs about human nature and knowledge, and her pedagogical theory. Within this larger discussion I will also present Gilman's central and powerful insights about women and the place of women in society. I will then evaluate her educational theory and discuss what it has to offer us today. Through this discussion I hope to provide those familiar with Gilman's feminist theories with a deeper understanding of the role of education in her thought, and to introduce those familiar with educational theory to the contributions that this nineteenth-century feminist's insights can make to our understanding of the critical issues facing educators today.

Overview of Gilman's Thought

The most fundamental description of Gilman is that she was a nineteenth-century social reformer. All her efforts during her career as an author and lecturer were based on her belief in the possibility of individual and social progress. Since she believed that society could direct its progress through the application of reason to social problems, her goal was to understand society and its workings so that she could improve it. In the course of her life's work, Gilman analyzed numerous social institutions, customs, and beliefs. Her educational theory is embedded in her overall theory of the meaning of being human and the nature of society because this was the mental arena in which she worked.

   Gilman held many of the same beliefs and prejudices as other nineteenth-century reformers. She steadfastly believed in the tenets of social evolutionary theories as articulated by sociologist Lester Frank Ward, with whom she had a relationship of mutual respect. Social evolutionists believed that they could take the principles of evolution from the biological world and apply them to the social world. This type of thinking dominated social reformist thinking from the 1860s, when the evolutionary theories of Charles Darwin gained widespread notice, until the turn of the century. Social evolutionists viewed society as a complex social organism that functioned in the same way that biological organisms functioned, and so was subject to the same rules and principles.

Many social evolutionists of this period also believed that evolution and its laws were not random, but were purposive or telic—that is, occurring toward some end or purpose. In the case of social evolution, they believed that the end was a better society. Liberal-minded social evolutionists such as Gilman further believed that if they could identify the scientific laws of evolution that applied on the social level and convince individuals and society to follow these laws, great and positive social progress would result.

This belief in the possibility of human progress according to discernible natural laws forms the foundation for Gilman's life and work. At seventeen she set for herself what would be her life's work: "to help humanity" (Gilman 1935/1990, 36). To her this meant to discover the natural laws by which society evolves and to convince people to follow them so that society would advance. In her autobiography, *The Living of Charlotte Perkins Gilman*, she writes:

> I figured it out that the business of mankind was to carry out the evolution of the human race, according to the laws of nature, adding the conscious direction, the telic force, proper to our kind—we are the only creatures that can assist evolution. . . . (Gilman 1935/1990, 42)

Beginning around the turn of the century, scholars began rejecting social evolutionary theory because of its inability to represent the complexities of both society and mind. Thinkers such as John Dewey, Thorstein Veblen, and William James moved on to develop theories that were more rooted in human experience and more subject to revision and change over time, rejecting the "grand design" theories that social evolutionists shared.[3] Gilman, however, never wavered from her world view and remained convinced that society could be radically improved if it would only follow social evolutionary laws.

A large part of the reason why Gilman never rejected social evolutionary theories lies, in my opinion, in her unusual intellectual development and position. Because Gilman's mother was forced to rely on her family for their food and shelter, they moved constantly from the home of one relative to another. In her autobiography, Gilman states that they moved eighteen times in nineteen years, primarily between Providence, Rhode Island; Hartford, Connecticut; and Springfield, Massachusetts. This resulted in an erratic education. Gilman calculated that her formal education consisted of four years spread out among seven institutions (Gilman 1935/1990, 8, 18, 27). Gilman received no higher education whatsoever, and no scholarly training. In fact, she had no interest in standard academic pursuits. Her career and writings were focused on conveying information and ways of thinking to ordinary people—as a true reformer, to change the world. Because of this, Gilman paid no attention to placing her writings and thought within a scholarly tradition. In fact, she had very little regard for the past and its traditions—she was a visionary and a reformer, focusing on a better future and how society could achieve it. She was strongly independent and relied on her own insights. She did, however, refer to other thinkers of her time to corroborate her arguments, particularly Lester Ward, Edward A. Ross, Richard Ely, and Thorstein Veblen. Their writings often provided her with the more scholarly evidence she needed to defend her views; she borrowed especially from Ward much of the evidence in botany and zoology that is scattered throughout her writings.

But the fact that these outdated social theories form the framework for her thinking does not cancel out the great contribution that her insights made, both to the thinking of her day and to current thinking on these issues. Gilman's great contribution lies in the fact that she went beyond the conventional norms of her day (many of which we still struggle with today) and focused her keen vision on social categories in a fresh way. She focused her analysis on *groups* in society—primarily men, women, and children—rather than on individuals, and analyzed their relative place and role in society in general. This focus on groups was especially powerful because two of the groups she focused on—women and children—had long been seen primarily in private, individualized terms. The power of her insights enabled her to develop a new and bold perspective on children's place in society and the status of women and their traditional roles and duties that is still challenging and valuable today. As historian Ann Lane states in her analysis of Gilman's life and thought:

> Even today . . . her work stands as a major theoretical contribution to feminist thought. She offered a perspective on major issues of gender with which we still grapple: the origins of women's subjugation; the struggle to achieve both autonomy and intimacy in human relationships; the central role of work as a definition of self; new strategies for rearing and educating future generations to create a humane and nurturing environment. (Lane 1991, 3–4)

Gilman's Feminist Insights

Gilman's feminist insights are most powerfully articulated in her first and most significant book, *Women and Economics* (1898/1966). Gilman begins the book by analyzing the current status of women in society in terms of her social evolutionary perspective, concluding that the present state of affairs concerning women and their domain hinders social progress. Gilman's central argument revolves around what we know today as the "separate spheres" perspective. She describes how duties and responsibilities that are related to being human, and thus belong to all of us as human beings, have been split into "masculine" and "feminine" in society, so that maintaining and caring for the private world of husband, home, and children and the qualities associated with these activities have come to be seen as essentially feminine, while activities in the public world of politics, business, art, science, and education and their associated qualities have come to be seen as essentially masculine.

Gilman argues that this splitting of human life and work into separate spheres is unnatural and harms both men and women because it limits each sex's experience and understanding of the world. But its most serious negative consequence, according to Gilman, is that by limiting each sex in this way, it limits the contribution that each sex can make to society, since both men and women are prevented from developing into full human beings who possess both "masculine" and "feminine" qualities.

Gilman recognized that fundamental changes would have to occur in society if it was to allow both men and women to develop as full human beings. She argued that as long as women remained dependent on men economically, isolated in the home, and divorced from the public world of work, they would never achieve equal humanness with men. She called for an end to the exclusion of women from public work and argued for woman's right to be economically independent and perform satisfying human work outside the home.

Gilman argued that since child-rearing and the household industries of cooking, cleaning, and laundry are actually human tasks and not related solely to women by biology, they could best be performed if they were organized as all human work is organized, which means, according to Gilman, being socialized, organized, and specialized. On the other side of this equation, she argued that men needed to be involved in the human aspects of the traditional feminine role so that they could develop as full human beings as well. Gilman argued that the human responsibilities currently performed by women in their homes should be recognized as responsibilities of the society as a whole.

Gilman developed and presented her alternative vision of society—in which the values of collaboration, cooperation, and mutual respect were central, and in which men and women worked together on an equal footing—in her three utopian novels, *Moving the Mountain* (1911), *Herland* (1915), and *With Her In Ourland* (1916). Of these three, *Herland* is by far Gilman's best work, the most powerful and most developed vision of a better society. It can also be read as a description of her educational philosophy in practice, and I will discuss this work shortly to illustrate her ideas about the role of education in society and pedagogy.

This brief overview of Gilman's feminist insights reveals how much thought she gave to social problems related to what we term today "gender roles." The current movement among some men to cultivate and value more "feminine" or nurturing traits involves a recognition of what men have lost through the genderization of certain tasks and traits in our society. Gilman discussed these losses throughout her writings and extended that discussion to what society as a whole loses in this process. Gilman's assertion that it is damaging for women to be forced to remain isolated in their individual homes, economically dependent on their husbands, and cut off from the public world of work, found powerful expression in the 1960s women's movement, and continues today. The power of Gilman's feminist insights makes *Women and Economics* a book that should be required reading in courses focusing on social issues, showing the historical roots of more recent classics such as *The Feminine Mystique.*

Gilman's Social Theory and Three Conceptions of the Role of Education in Society

Gilman's social thought is extensive and is heavily connected with her social evolutionary thought. In order to keep our focus on the role of education in her thought, I will organize my discussion in this section around three different conceptions of the role of education in society that are found in Gilman's writings. I will show that these three conceptions represent three different levels of power and importance in Gilman's educational philosophy.

Education as Social Nourishment

The first conception of the role of education in society is the conception of education as social nourishment. This conception is developed most fully in Gilman's book *Human Work* (1904). Because it is completely embedded in her social evolutionary perspective, there is nothing in this conception that is novel or unique. But we must briefly discuss it because it clearly presents Gilman's belief in the primacy of the group, a belief that is woven throughout all her writings.

To Gilman, humanness resides in social relations; it is not an attribute of individuals apart from their membership in society: "'We' are human, 'I' am an animal, save as 'I,' being part of Society, embody and represent it," Gilman writes (Gilman 1904, 60). Being part of the social whole is not a static state, but a dynamic, active state in which one is constantly interacting with other members of society in a web of intricate inter-dependencies. Gilman, like other social evolutionists of her day, compared society to the human body, using the term "the social organism." Just as the cells in an organism, the members of society perform specialized functions and in turn benefit from all other members' functioning. This performance of social functions is what Gilman defines as human work. Human work is distinguished from other labors because it serves social ends rather than simply individual ends. Gilman illustrates this point:

> Teaching as an activity is not predicable of individuals. It is a power to transmit the social gain in intelligence and knowledge among the social constituents. . . . Teaching is a social function; a very elaborate and long developed social function. The teacher is an extreme instance of the social functionary. Other than as a social functionary he does not exist. (Gilman 1904, 90)

There is a reciprocal relation between the individual and society: As a member of society, the individual must perform his/her social function to meet the social organism's needs, but then the organism must ensure that the individual's needs are met through the social functioning of other members of society. "The teacher, teaching, cannot support himself. His time, his strength, his enormously specialised [sic] skill, are spent in teaching, and the society which made him and which needs him, necessarily supports him," Gilman explains (Gilman 1904, 90).

Gilman uses the term "social nourishment" to describe the support that must be provided to individual members of society. To Gilman, social nourishment includes basic "animal" necessities such as proper food, shelter, and clothing, as well as "social" necessities such as communication with other people and the stimulation of new ideas and places. Gilman states that proper social nourishment is a *right* of all members of society: "The individual has a right to those things necessary for him to best serve Society. That is, the carpenter has a right to his tools, and the musician to his instrument, both to their special education, and they and all men to the food, shelter, clothing, and other things *necessary to their best social service . . .* " (Gilman 1904, 307). In this reciprocal relation, this right has a corresponding duty, as Gilman describes: "To assume right functional relation to Society, to one another . . . simply to find and hold our proper place in the Work in which and by which we all live" (Gilman 1904, 368–69).

One of the central features of Gilman's view is that the greater part of social nourishment is needed in youth, as a social "investment" in future work. Gilman points out that before the individual can properly produce, certain things must be given to him/her, one of which is a proper education. "In free education," she writes, "we do supply the young . . . with both energy and direction, so that he grows up better able to work and to work rightly . . . " (Gilman 1904, 284). Since the welfare of society rests with the workers, and its future with the young, "a conscientious and aroused society, seeing how unjustly neglected have been its most valuable constituents, cannot do too much to bring to them, and to their children, all the social nourishment they can absorb, i.e. to provide the best possible educational environment for the children who need it most" (Gilman 1904, 375).

It is interesting to note here that Gilman espouses a social position akin to what we term "equity" arguments today—she does not advocate that each child be treated equally, or given equal resources, but, rather, that children be given all they can absorb and that the best educational environments be provided to the children who need it most.

Thus, in Gilman's social philosophy the rights and duties of the individual do not reside in his/her status as an individual human being, but are all predicated on his/her status as a member of society. Thus, the society always has primacy over the individual: the work that one is to perform is for society's benefit, and one's rights to social nourishment accrue only because of the role one plays in meeting society's needs. It is interesting to note here that Gilman makes no status distinctions among the kinds of work that are performed; her writings clearly indicate that she felt that finding the work one is suited for and performing that work put people on an equal footing.[4]

Analysis

This conception of education as social nourishment, because it is directly based on social evolutionist theory, is the most conventional and weakest of the three conceptions of education I have identified in Gilman's writings. It has the least to offer us today, since its basis has been discredited as a viable theory of society. There are also validity problems with its central assumption (a central tenet of social evolutionary thought) that what is best for society is what is best for the individual. In other words, it is a deterministic theory, since it assumes that there is one right function for each individual to perform, that right function is best for society, and the individual's main task is to find that function and fulfill it. Thus, the purpose of one's life is already set, and the individual's job is to discover and then fulfill it.

What happens to the individuals who don't discover it? Or who discover it late in life and so did not receive the proper training to fulfill it? For example, what if someone's proper function is as a doctor, but he or she did not realize this and studied instead to be a musician? In Gilman's theory, this is where education plays a vital role—it would have to be the mechanism whereby children discover their right functional relation and are then given the proper training to fulfill it. What about those who might discover it but refuse to fulfill it? In this view, such an act would be breaking a fundamental social law, and those committing it might even be cast as criminals. Why would not fulfilling your proper function be so serious an act? Because this view of education and society is based on the belief that society is progressing toward a better version of itself if it follows the natural laws. Therefore, if someone refuses to follow the natural laws and assume his/her right functional relation, this person is hindering society's progress. Although Gilman does not extend her thinking to this point, it follows from her theory that following one's proper function will bring happiness and fulfillment, and not following it will bring unhappiness and lack of fulfillment, because the individual is a "member" of an organic society who lives and breathes with him or her. Thus, to be in opposition with the larger organism would cause pain and discomfort; indeed, in the bodily sense, it often causes death of the cell involved. Thus, this view of society does not have validity unless one accepts a deterministic view of humanity.

There are two aspects of this theory that I believe have merit: (1) the value placed on children and their proper care and upbringing and (2) the fact that this value extends to all children, since all children are part of the social organism. These two aspects of Gilman's theory allow her to stand much of typical nineteenth-century American social thought on its head, as it were. In particular, by framing education as social nourishment in this way she is able to reframe education as a nurturing activity and to place it in the public sphere, because it is the social organism as a whole that is responsible for the nourishment. This socializes and legitimizes the care, upbringing, and education of children and allows women, as the primary nurturers of her day, into the public realm. Thus, it provides support for two of the most powerful insights Gilman contributed to American thought: breaking women out of the prison of individual homes and families and breaking children out of the same isolation as individual "possessions." It brings women into the public realm with something of value to contribute, and it brings children into the public realm and extends responsibility for their care, nurturance, education, and general welfare to all of society.

In basing this conception on social evolutionary thought, in our language the current "fad" of her time, Gilman uses a conventional foundation and framework to support these two original and radical insights. While the underlying framework has not withstood the test of time, her radical insights still have much to offer educators today.

Education as Social Parentage

In this second conception of the role of education in society, Gilman narrows her focus from the most general level of the social organism to a socialized parental relationship between children and society. She states, "The true relation of the State to the child includes the parental relation . . . " (Gilman 1900, 278). And Gilman clearly indicates that by "the state" she means "the collective parents, who constitute society" (Gilman 1900, 279). She writes:

> The civilized human parent lives as part of an elaborate society,—a State; and, as a member of the State, he holds a new relation to his child—she holds a new relation to her child: they—and they are the State—hold a new relation to their children. (Gilman 1900, 279)

This new relation is "social parentage" (the title of her final chapter in *Concerning Children* [1900], her book devoted to the care and education of young children). With this concept, Gilman socializes our traditional understanding of the duties and responsibilities that parents have for their children's welfare and growth by extending that same relationship throughout society so that all adults stand in this relation to all children. She states, "Civilised [sic] society is responsible for civilised [sic] childhood" (Gilman 1900, 290).

Education is one of the primary responsibilities of social parentage, particularly the education of young children. Gilman sees children primarily in social terms as society's means of continuation and, most especially, improvement. "The surest, quickest way to improve humanity is to improve the stock, the people themselves; and all experience shows that the time to improve people is while they are young," she writes in *Concerning Children* (Gilman 1900, 6). But because we have such a limited and narrow view of education, we don't see the need: "The truth is we never think of education in connection with babyhood, the term being in our minds inextricably confused with school-houses and books," Gilman writes, when, in reality, "a child is being educated in every waking hour by the conditions in which he is placed and the persons who are with him" (Gilman 1900, 135).

In her writings, Gilman stresses the importance of educating young children (that is, children from birth to age six). She explains why it is that we have neglected this responsibility: "The one main cause of our unfairness to children is that we consider them wholly in a personal light" (Gilman 1900, 118). Again, Gilman's powerful focus on groups enables her to see this fact so clearly. "Our whole attitude toward the child is too intensely personal," she states (Gilman 1898/1966, 289). We speak of "my child," or "Mrs. Smith's little Mary," almost implying that children are private "possessions" of particular adults.

As long as we see children in this personal light, we do not see their needs as a group. "But the moment we begin to address ourselves to the needs of children as a class, the result is different" (Gilman 1900, 118). It is not until they reach age six that society acknowledges its responsibility to educate children through the provision of free public education. But before that age, children have no status in society—they are isolated and hidden in their homes, often raised by nurses or maids (Gilman 1898/1966, 270–94). This means, for Gilman, that society wastes six of the most important years of the development of its own future and the improvement of the race. In fact, Gilman sees our social responsibility for young children to be the same as, if not greater than, that for older children: "The baby has as good a right to his share of our educational funds, private and public, as the older child; and his education is more important" (Gilman 1900, 138; see also 127).

In stressing the social responsibility of education and the inclusion of young children in the educational process, Gilman had to argue against the belief that individual parents were solely, and only, responsible for their own young children. She argues that in an interdependent, complex society such as ours, this individualistic approach to children's welfare is archaic. She blames some of this archaic approach on our outdated beliefs about sexual roles, seeing mothers in individualistic terms and thus seeing the care and education of their children in individualistic terms. In this way her feminist insights contribute to her educational theory.

Analysis

Although Gilman connects this conception of the role of education in society to her social evolutionary framework in her writings, it is not actually related to social evolutionary thought. Instead, it takes our conventional understanding of the parent–child relation and socializes it, broadening it to the larger society. The central function in this conception is parenting—which involves the activities of nurturing, caring for, providing for, and educating children.

This is indeed a radical vision of society. Imagine a society explicitly structured around caring for all its children. Immediately, we see that excellent health care and education for all children would be paramount values, as would expert care for their physical and psychological needs and growth.

Gilman's powerful insight here into viewing children as a class existing in the public realm pulls them out from behind the veil, as it were, of individual private homes and families, and exposes how poorly treated they are in our private and individualized society. If we actually felt as parents do about all children, radical changes would occur. Clearly, our present society is light years away from this point. If children's needs were primary, how differently we would judge our behavior and lives. Budget battles over defense spending might be put aside in favor of early childhood education; child abuse and incest would simply not be tolerated. In short, individual children would not be left to their fate to withstand the particular vagaries of their birth or legal families.

As with the idea of education as social nourishment, this conception of education enables Gilman to reframe education as a *nurturing* activity and to place it in the public sphere, in this case because nurturing is a common and accepted relation between parents and children. It requires us to recast our traditional notions of children, parents, and families. And this conception has great value in its radical reframing of some central social roles. Unfortunately, Gilman did not flesh out this vision of society any further.

Education as Social Motherhood

Gilman's conception of education as "social motherhood" is the most developed and most powerful of her three conceptions of the role of education in society. The concept of "social motherhood" is one of the central tenets of Gilman's social philosophy.

In fact, in studying her writings about social motherhood, this concept emerges as the required *key* to social progress. Gilman often uses the term "human motherhood" as well; they are interchangeable since, as we have seen, she identifies the human with the social. I will use both terms as well, as I follow Gilman's development of this concept. Gilman grounds her concept of social motherhood in her evolutionary schema, identifying two functions of human motherhood:

> To leave in the world a creature better than its parent. This is the purpose of right motherhood.
>
> In the human race this purpose is served by two processes: first, by the simple individual function of reproduction, of which all care and nursing are but an extension; and second, by the complex social functions of education. (Gilman 1898/1966, 179)

Gilman goes on to connect education to motherhood:

> This [education] was primarily a maternal process, and therefore individual; but it has long since become a racial rather than an individual function, and bears no relation to sex or other personal limitation. . . . Human functions are race-functions, social functions; and education is one of them. (Gilman 1898/1966, 179–80)

Gilman makes a clear distinction between motherhood as an individual function and as a social function. She states: "Simply to bear children is a personal matter. . . . Education is collective, human, a social function" (Gilman 1898/1966, 283).

Gilman's Utopian Vision of Social Motherhood

Gilman paints a vivid portrayal of her conception of social motherhood in her utopian novel *Herland.* Herland is a country that has been isolated from the rest of the world due to a cataclysmic disaster centuries ago, in which all the men were killed. The women who survived somehow developed the power of asexual reproduction. In this country of all women and girl-children, Gilman has the freedom to develop a utopian society without the genderization of traits and activities so prevalent in our society. As Ann Lane, biographer and editor of Gilman's work, describes *Herland:*

> *Herland* soars. Gilman romps through the game of what is feminine and what is masculine . . . what is culturally learned and what is biologically determined male-female behavior. Her belief in the power of humans to alter their societies and to control nature in their own interest is carried out literally in *Herland.* (Lane 1979, xiii–xiv)

In *Herland* Gilman is able to actualize her social philosophy and her conception of education as social motherhood. Herlandian society is based on the central value of social motherhood, and education is one of its primary functions. In Herland, motherhood is the primary social category. Whether or not a particular woman bears a child, she stands in the mother–child relation to all children, and a woman who has borne a child stands in the same relation to all other children. As a Herlandian states: "We each have a million children to love and serve—*our* children" (Gilman 1915/1979, 71). The central focus of social motherhood, as in Gilman's theoretical writing, is the improvement of the race in all ways possible. As a Herlandian explains:

> The children in this country are the one center and focus of all our thoughts. Every step of our advance is always considered in its effect on them—on the race. You see, we are *Mothers*. (Gilman 1915/1979, 66)

This concern to improve the race is a societywide value and is approached rationally. Gilman describes Herland as a country where these intelligent, resourceful women have put all of their scientific knowledge and their clear minds to work on the best way to improve the race, and have devised highly effective child-rearing and educational practices to this end. A Herlandian states: "We are at work, slowly and carefully, developing our whole people along these lines. It is glorious work—splendid! To see the thousands of babies improving, showing stronger clearer minds, sweeter dispositions, higher capacities . . . " (Gilman 1915/1979, 105–6). Thus, motherhood in Herland is not an instinctual, emotional, personal activity, but a rational, social activity.

Transforming Education into a Human Activity

In her theoretical writings, Gilman's concept of social motherhood enables her to transform education into a human activity. By showing that "the origin of education is maternal" (Gilman 1911, 143), Gilman is able to argue that the influence of motherhood should be allowed back into the educational process. In her book *The Man-Made World* (1911), Gilman argues that men have dominated the educational process for centuries. In so doing, they have bestowed their "male" qualities on the educational system. Gilman identifies these as desire, combat, and self-expression. In her characteristic social evolutionary scheme, men possess these qualities because they were necessary for the performance of the male's natural reproductive functions. The male's desire spurs him to seek out the female, self-expression enables him to attract her, and combat spurs him to fight off his rivals for the female (Gilman 1911, 9–13, 28–30). In contrast, Gilman identifies the "female" qualities as nurturance, education, and industry, which were necessary for the performance of the female's natural reproductive functions. Nurturance impels the female to nurse, protect, and safeguard the well-being of the young; education impels her to teach them how to survive; and industry impels her to work to provide food and shelter for them (Gilman 1911, 36, 143–53, 190). To Gilman, these three male and three female qualities are the only sex-related qualities we possess as humans, and are our inheritance from our evolutionary past. All other qualities belong to us as humans, not as males or females.

But because men have dominated social functions in our "androcentric," or male-dominated, culture, Gilman argues that their sex-related qualities have come to be seen mistakenly as human qualities and have become socialized as elements of all sorts of social institutions: competitive sports, capitalism in business and industry, and individualistic artistic expression, for example. Women's qualities, on the other hand, remained individualized just as women remained isolated in their individual homes, and thus came to be seen as "feminine" rather than human. Nurturance, for example, is seen as a private female attribute, part of the private world of home and family, whereas competitiveness is seen as a human attribute, part of the public world of work and organized social structures (Gilman 1911, 17–25).

Gilman goes on to argue that a different process occurred regarding women's tasks and duties. In the course of our evolution, some of the tasks associated with the female qualities of nurturance, education, and industry, such as providing food and shelter for the child and family, and the education of older children (from age six on), were taken over by men. Because their work was socialized, specialized, and organized, men were able to perform these tasks more efficiently. In contrast, the tasks that remained women's responsibility remained unspecialized and individualized, mirroring women's place in society, and came to be seen as feminine functions rather than as human activities (Gilman 1900, 284–85).

To Gilman, we have progressed so much further in educating older children than we have with our younger children precisely because the former received the beneficial influences of men's advanced social development. But this beneficial element has a corresponding deleterious element. According to Gilman, any aspect of life that is dominated by only half of humanity is going to be excessively influenced by the sex-related qualities of that group. Thus, the educational system contains deleterious aspects of excessive male influence springing from their sex-related qualities: the sole incentive of self-interest and excessive competitiveness (Gilman 1911, 151).

By describing how the public institution of education—which up until now, Gilman argues, was seen in solely male terms—is really an outgrowth of social motherhood, Gilman has the basis for arguing that the traditionally "female" qualities and responsibilities have a proper and natural place in education. She could base her case for this on the fact that, after all, the educational function grew out of motherhood. And it is precisely the maternal qualities that Gilman wishes to bring into education. She explains:

> To feminize education would be to make it more motherly. The mother does not rear her children by a system of prizes to be longed for and pursued; nor does she set them to compete with one another, giving to the conquering child what he needs, and to the vanquished, blame and deprivation. . . . Motherhood does all it knows to give to each child what is most needed, to teach all to their fullest capacity, to affectionately and efficiently develop the whole of them. (Gilman 1911, 152)

These female qualities, Gilman argues, are a part of the human experience, and are the complement to male qualities; their absence from the educational process makes it unbalanced. Since education is a human function, this imbalance hinders social progress. She states: "Our educational system is thwarted and hindered . . . by an over-weaning masculization" (Gilman 1911, 155–56). Thus, the feminization of education is actually the humanization of education because it would mean that both aspects of the human experience would be part of the educational process.

Gilman sees the humanization of education as following the same lines as the humanization of society: allowing women—with their experiences, qualities, and responsibilities—into all human activities. This would involve institutional changes in the teaching staff (women teachers and the expression of maternal qualities should be encouraged in education), in the treatment of male and female students (both should be supported to develop both male and female qualities and be taught to perform both tasks and responsibilities), and in the process of teaching and learning (competition, for example, would cease to be the only motivating force, and cooperation would be stressed). Further, social institutions and society in general would change fundamentally, as society took seriously its responsibility to fulfill the child care and home care duties traditionally associated with women.

Humanizing Individuals and Society

But Gilman does more than advocate for the humanization of the educational process and society in general. She also argues for the humanization of all the individual members of society. "The advance of civilization calls for human qualities, in both men and women," Gilman states (Gilman 1911, 155). This is a more radical step. Whereas her theory of humanizing education involves the notion of balancing male with female qualities in the educational institution, her idea of humanizing people involves developing human qualities in each individual person. This is a more difficult undertaking, and Gilman realizes that it cannot occur without the accompanying institutional changes of humanizing education.

But she also recognizes that the development of human qualities cannot take place in a vacuum; she understands the link between school and society. She discusses the difficulty of this educational endeavor, because it goes against so many aspects of our behavior and beliefs. She is very aware of the differential socialization of children based on sex that is part and parcel of her culture. She states: "From the time our children are born, we use every means known to accentuate sex-distinction in both boy and girl" (Gilman 1898/1966, 51).

Gilman believes that this type of gender socialization sacrifices humanness for an excessive sex-distinction. She thinks that her proposal that education develop human qualities in all children, accompanied by her structural changes, would lead to "A Human World" much superior to the present one. She recognizes that this world would be predicated on such a different view of people that its social relations and structure are impossible to completely foresee. "We can make no safe assumption," she writes, "as to what, if any, distinction there will be in the free human work of men and women, until we have seen generation after generation grow up under absolutely equal conditions" (Gilman 1911, 250). She does, however, offer a picture of a transformed education:

> That every child on earth shall have right conditions to make the best growth possible to it; that every citizen, from birth to death, shall have a chance to learn all he or she can assimilate, to develop every power that is in them—for the common good;—this will be the aim of education, under human management. (Gilman 1911, 254)

Analysis

This conception of the role of education in society as social motherhood is the most original and powerful of Gilman's three conceptions of the role of education in society for two reasons. First, because it socializes motherhood, making its qualities and responsibilities valuable and necessary to society as whole. Second, because it connects motherhood to a basic, ongoing, rational social function carried out in the public realm, and in bringing motherhood into this realm, brings women along with it.

Martin has analyzed Gilman's philosophy of education as portrayed in *Herland*, focusing specifically on the ideal of the educated woman found in Herland and the place and preparation for the "tasks, functions, institutions, and traits of character that philosophy, as part of our culture, has associated with women—" what are commonly referred to today as the reproductive processes of society (Martin 1985). I will draw on Martin's discussion in my analysis of Gilman's concept of social motherhood.

First, the conception of education as social motherhood socializes motherhood. It brings what was (and is) traditionally seen as a private function into the public realm and, in addition, makes it the responsibility of all members of society, not only those who are themselves mothers. In bringing motherhood into the public realm, the functions of motherhood gain status, since the private functions traditionally associated with individual women in their homes have commonly held lower status. It also changes our understandings of what motherhood is, if we think of all adult members of society standing in relation to children in this way, including men and women without children. What does it mean to say that men are in a relation of motherhood to children? It means that men should have the same affective qualities of nurturing, care, and concern for children that we associate with mothers. In this way, Gilman brings into the public realm many gender-related qualities. Indeed, one of Gilman's central arguments throughout her work is the necessity of bringing women's gender-related traits and qualities into the public realm and allowing and expecting men to develop and exhibit them as well, thus enabling men to become more human by possessing the full range of human traits and qualities. As I will discuss shortly, the reverse of this process is involved as well, in which women are expected to develop and exhibit traits and qualities traditionally associated with men.

Second, the conception of education as social motherhood connects motherhood to a basic, ongoing, and rational activity in the public realm and brings women into the public realm. If education is a function of social motherhood, then the qualities we commonly associate with education—planning; theoretical and practical knowledge; judgment; broad perspective; and social, policy, financial, psychological, and other issues involved in educating children—all become related to motherhood and, by extension, to women (being those traditionally associated with motherhood). This fits well with Gilman's feminist arguments to allow women to develop their intellect and become professionals in their own right, working outside the home and earning their own pay at professions that are socialized, specialized, and organized.

In this way, education as an activity will be changed, and, on a larger scale, society as a whole will be changed. Gilman is very aware of the changes that will be involved in bringing women and the "feminine" traits and functions into the public realm. As Martin points out, Gilman's chapter on education in her book *The Man-Made World* (1911) "reveals her unwillingness to send women out of the home into an unreconstructed world" (Martin 1985, 163). As Martin points out, Gilman does not argue to bring women and their traditional functions and gender-related traits and qualities into the public realm in order to create a world "in which women are assimilated into male roles in a male world" (Martin 1985, 163). On the contrary, Gilman believed that when women and these traits and functions are brought into the public realm, that realm would necessarily change, and she was in favor of the type of radical change that would result from men becoming more "feminine" and women becoming more "masculine." However, as Martin points out, Gilman was unaware of "the problems that arise when both sexes are expected to acquire traits genderized in favor of one." Martin continues:

> It is one thing for girls to grow up to be fleet, fearless, agile, calm, wise, and self-assured in a society that considers these traits not so much human as masculine. It is another thing altogether for the ideal of mother love to be held up for boys in a society that considers nurturance and caring to be feminine traits. (Martin 1985, 166)

Thus, although Gilman was aware of the radical nature of the social changes her proposal involved, she underestimated the difficulty of implementing such a radical educational proposal. Martin points out two other flaws in Gilman's conception of education as social motherhood: Gilman's portrayal of mother love does not include emotion, and her vision lacks a place for intimacy, sexuality, and passion. It seems to me that Gilman was so intent on showing motherhood as a rational activity that she neglected these important aspects of human life.

Although Gilman's vision of mother love is flawed, her vision of social motherhood as the primary value and organizing structure of a society is still powerful and contributes much to our understanding of society, women's place in it, and education and its relation to it. The power of her vision is that it connects reason and rationality with motherhood and with women in a fundamental way, and it brings motherhood and, therefore, women into the public realm by making education a function of social motherhood. This means that all the processes we traditionally associate with motherhood—the care and nurturance of children from birth (actually, even before birth through prenatal care)—become public social responsibilities and virtues.

Gilman's Pedagogical Theory

As we have seen, Gilman's social theory of education enables her to bring women and young children out from behind the veil of private homes into the public world. It only seems natural, then, that she focuses her attention on young children's education in her pedagogical theory. In fact, this is one of the most distinctive and original features of Gilman's pedagogical theory. Gilman believed that these early years are actually the most important educationally because of her idea of the nature of knowledge and her psychological views. The most comprehensive statement of her psychological views is found in her work, *Our Brains and What Ails Them*, serialized in her journal, the *Forerunner*, in 1912. Here Gilman discusses the reasons why she believes we have not advanced further in increasing our intelligence and improving our methods of education and presents her own plan in these areas. She describes the focus of her study as "mental mechanics," stating: "The brain is here discussed as an organ, and our mental exercise as being dependent on the health and proper exercise of that organ" (Gilman 1912a, 22).

Gilman describes the activity of the brain in terms of basic "brain functions": receiving and retaining impressions; collating and coordinating these impressions, with each other and with memories and imagination; making judgments based on these impressions; and planning actions based on these judgments. In addition, Gilman identifies three basic faculties of the brain: memory, imagination, and judgment. These three faculties enable the brain to perform its two highest functions: "to Decide and to Do" (Gilman 1912b, 166). To Gilman, action is intimately connected with brain function. "The main use of our brain is to manage conduct," Gilman writes (Gilman 1912a, 26).

Action and managing conduct are central because, as an evolutionary product, the brain is influenced by its environment and naturally works to adapt to it. To Gilman, there are two environments: the external (the outside world) and the internal (our ideas, memories, and thoughts). The external environment is a particularly strong influence in young children's learning because their internal environments are not yet formed and so cannot offset the influence of the external environment. This means, further, that the young child's everyday learning has a powerful effect on his/her future because this internal environment, once formed, will have a great influence on everything else he/she learns and does. Gilman sees the young child's brain as a fresh and vital force. It has not yet learned bad habits of thought and behavior, accumulated large amounts of useless information, or fixed various beliefs as true based on tradition, ignorance, or authority. Because all is new to the young child, he/she is learning every day. She states:

> Here is little Albert being educated. He is not going to school yet. He is "not old enough" . . . but he is old enough to be learning the a,b,c of life at the hands of those with whom he chances to be. A child learns every day. That cannot be helped. What he learns, and how, we can largely dictate; but we cannot keep his brain shut until he gets to school, and then open it for three or four hours a day only. (Gilman 1900, 77)

To rephrase Gilman's point, we do not think of the young child's activities as learning or realize that the child is being educated by these activities because we confuse learning and education with the social institution of schooling.

Child Culture

"The education of a child consists in every impression received by the growing brain, not merely those received when we are instructing it" (Gilman 1900, 237). Gilman argues that we should engage in "child culture," in which we design the young child's external environment to nurture proper learning and education. Gilman argues that at present we neglect the most important factor in young children's education by paying no attention to their external environments. Gilman points out that the young child's typical environment is the private home, which is designed for adults and for adult industries and activities and is thus uncomfortable and dangerous to young children:

> From the pins on the carpet, which baby puts in his mouth, the stairs
> he falls down, the windows he falls out of and the fire he falls into
> . . . "the home" is full of danger to the child. (Gilman 1900, 129)

Gilman next analyzes the effects of the people in the young child's environment. The child's primary caretaker is either the mother or, if the family is well off, a servant. Gilman finds both of these caretakers lacking in the ability to provide proper education for the young child. The servant does not have the education, background, or standing in the household to be an appropriate educator. The typical mother, while she may possess devotion, passionate tenderness, and "the lasting love, the ceaseless service, the ingenuity and courage" (Gilman 1911, 152, 160) of maternal feeling, does not have the requirements of a competent child educator, because these feelings are not enough to ensure the development of children into beneficial members of a complex, civilized society. "In all other human work we have the benefit of the accumulated progressive experience of the ages," Gilman writes. "Only the culture of babies—most important of all work—is left to that eternal amateur—the mother" (Gilman 1913b, 262). In other words, most mothers begin learning how to care for children when they have them, and so are amateurs, at least at first. But even if they are knowledgeable about child-care, they are not experts in child culture. Gilman believes that the education of young children should be conducted by specialized experts in that field. As for every professional, Gilman identifies three requirements of a competent child educator: talent, training, and experience. She writes:

> The old assumption is that the interests of the child are best served by
> the continuous and exclusive devotion of the individual mother.
>   The new assumption is that the interests of the child are best
> served by the additional love and care, teaching and experience, of
> other persons, specialists in child culture. (Gilman 1913a, 37)

However, this does not mean that the mother's place is subverted by the trained infant educator. We only think that because "we persist in confounding mother and teacher," Gilman writes. "The mother's place is her own, and always will be. Nothing can take it from her" (Gilman 1900, 135). Instead, the mother will work with the infant educator, adding her particular knowledge of her child to the infant educator's expertise and observation of the child.

Baby-Gardens

Gilman has a clear and powerful vision of where these infant educators will educate young children in a proper environment: what she calls "baby-gardens." These are special places designed for young children, where they will be cared for and taught in the company of other young children for part of each day. She gives a vivid description of these institutions:

> A room really designed for babies to play in need have no "furniture" save a padded seat along the wall for the "grown-ups" to sit on, a seat with little ropes along the edge for the toddlers to pull up and walk by. The floor should be smooth and even, antiseptically clean, and not hard enough to bump severely. A baby must fall, but we need not provide cobblestones for his first attempts. Large soft ropes, running across here and there, within reach of the eager, strong little hands, would strengthen arms and chest, and help in walking. A shallow pool of water, heated to suitable temperature, with the careful trainer always at hand, would delight, occupy, and educate for daily hours. A place of clean, warm sand, another of clay, with a few simple tools,—these four things—water, sand, clay, and ropes to climb on—would fill the days of happy little children without further "toys." These are simple, safe, primitive pleasures, all helpful to growth and a means of gradual education. (Gilman 1900, 129–30)

Gilman asserts that caring for and educating young children in baby-gardens is no different than six-year-olds attending school for part of the day, and that any worry that this would break the bond between mother and child is as unfounded as it is with mothers and school-age children. Gilman insists that her plan would result in "a far quieter and more peaceful life than is possible for the heavily loved and violently cared for baby in the busy household; and the impressions it did meet would be planned and maintained with an intelligent appreciation of its mental powers." Gilman continues, once again reassuring mothers: "The mother would not be excluded, but supplemented, as she is now, by the teacher and the school" (Gilman 1898/1966, 287).

Gilman continues this comparison between baby-gardens and schools for older children by arguing that society has the same responsibility for the provision of baby-gardens that it has for free public education for older children. Gilman envisions a system of baby-gardens that would rest on the same basis as our educational system for older children: public institutions for all and private institutions for those who prefer. "The baby has as good a right to his share of our educational funds, private and public, as the older child; and his education is more important," Gilman writes (Gilman 1900, 138).

Another important feature of the baby-garden is that education there is social. As we have seen, Gilman sees the social aspect of our lives as the primary basis for our humanity. Thus, she feels strongly that providing young children with a social environment with their peers and trained child educators is necessary to their proper social development.

Curriculum

Once Gilman has established the need for baby-gardens staffed with trained child educators, she describes the type of curriculum these child educators would follow. The curriculum would be based on the brain's natural sequence of development and so would focus on developing the intimate connection between knowledge and action. In developing a plan for this type of action-oriented curriculum, Gilman states that we must first give up a common child-rearing practice that militates against this type of learning: the practice of exacting blind obedience from children by training them to "mind." Gilman explains that an action-oriented curriculum requires that children learn to connect their action with its natural consequences. Understanding this connection enables us to follow the brain's natural sequence of learning: impressions are received, compared, and judged, and a plan of action is created and then carried out. The child can then recognize and judge the consequences of his/her action. But the practice of "minding" stops this natural sequence:

> We have systematically checked in our children acts which were the natural consequence of their observation and inference; and enforced acts which, to the child's mind, had no reason. Thus we have trained a world of people to the habit of action without understanding, and also understanding without acting. (Gilman 1900, 51–52)

Not only do children lose their initiative to pursue their own acts, but they also become habituated to acting from another person's wishes and thus become susceptible to manipulation and control.

Instead of this type of training, the child's training should be based on connecting act and consequence. Gilman provides the following example. Suppose you are playing with your child and she is rude to you. You should enforce "a just and accurate retaliation" (Gilman 1900, 88). Stop playing with her immediately, put her down, and leave her alone. After a series of these episodes, the child will understand that rudeness results in being left alone. Thus, she will see the connection between her act and its consequences. This new knowledge also provides power: she also knows how to avoid being left alone by avoiding being rude. In this way the child "learns to modify his conduct to a desired end, which is the lesson of life" (Gilman 1900, 88). This type of training avoids the ill-feeling of a personal assault that many common types of punishment create in the child through hitting, screaming, or other threatening behavior.

The purpose of this type of discipline is the development of the habit of thoughtful behavior. Gilman states:

> Habits work in all directions; and a habit of thoughtful behavior is as easy to form, really easier, than a habit of obedience,—easier, because it would be the natural function of the brain to govern behavior if we did not so laboriously contradict it. (Gilman 1900, 55)

How is this habit to be formed? Gilman proposes the use of graduated exercises suitable to the child's developmental level. These exercises should serve to reinforce the child's dawning understanding of the connection between knowledge and action, and in this way will connect mind and behavior.

In addition to developing this habit, Gilman advocates for developing the habit of logical thinking through carefully planned, repetitive, graduated exercises. She believes that the search for consistency and connection among our ideas is a natural tendency that must be developed: "It is the logical tendency, the power to 'put two and two together' . . . that holds our acts in sequence and makes human society possible" (Gilman 1900, 58).

How shall this education be accomplished? Gilman advocates a natural, unconscious education that is tailored to each individual child's abilities and needs. This curriculum is natural and unconscious to the child, but very conscious and planned to the child educator. She states:

> The progressive education of a child should be, as far as possible, unconscious . . . [in] a beautiful and delicately adjusted environment . . . in which line and colour and sound and touch are all made avenues of easy unconscious learning . . . In the baby-garden the baby will learn many things, and never know it. (Gilman 1900, 144–45)

In the baby-gardens, the child's "natural faculties are allowed to develop in order and to their full extent" (Gilman 1900, 146). This is accomplished because the child educators observe each child closely and develop activities to meet each child's learning needs. Gilman writes:

> Each child has been under careful observation and record from the very first. His special interests, his preferred methods, his powers and weaknesses, are watched and worked with carefully as he grows. If power of attention was weak at first, he is given special work to develope [sic] it. . . . (Gilman 1900, 147–48)

Gilman then describes the content of this unconscious education:

> So he gradually learns that common stock of human knowledge which it is well for us all to share,—the story of the building of the earth, the budding of the plant, the birth of the animal, the beautiful unfolding of the human race, from savagery to civilisation [sic]. He learns the rudiments of the five great handicrafts, and can work a little in whit, in metal, in clay, in cloth, and in stone. He learns the beginnings of the sciences, with experiment and story, and finds new wonders to lead him on, no matter how far he goes,—an unending fascination. (Gilman 1900, 146–47)

It follows from Gilman's idea of unconscious education that assessment and motivation in education would change. Gilman criticizes the current system of education, which has "made a battlefield of the college and the school" (Gilman 1916b, 247), basing education on a competitive system "which sets one against the another and finds pleasure not in learning . . . but in getting ahead of one's fellows" (Gilman 1911, 151). Gilman argues that education has been dominated by a view of life as combat, whereas in fact growth, not combat, is the "true theory of life" (Gilman 1916a, 14).

Gilman's Pedagogical Theory in Practice: *Herland*

A vivid and comprehensive portrayal of Gilman's pedagogical theory in practice can be found in *Herland.* Growth is the fundamental principle of life in Herlandian society, and all Herlandians respect this process in their children. Since Herlandian society recognizes its primary responsibility for the education of all children from birth, the entire country has been scientifically designed as an educational environment for children. The children freely travel the land, safe because of its special design, inspired to learn from their environment by their natural curiosity. Always with the children are numbers of specially trained teachers, ready to answer questions and lead each child on to a deeper knowledge of the subject. Each child's educational program utilizes the child's own interest and learning patterns and is unconscious to the child, although highly conscious to the group of educators who indirectly guide the child, always leaving her free to act on her own ideas and judgments. In this way the natural connection between knowledge and action is maintained, and as it is strengthened, the child's ability to manage her conduct increases. By following this method, educators develop habits of thoughtful behavior and judicious reasoning in young children, so that they may grow into self-regulating, independently thinking adults who will further advance Herlandian society.

Gilman's Educational Philosophy in Her Day

Gilman's pedagogical theory shares much in common with the progressive education movement that was growing in influence in the last decade of the nineteenth century, when she was writing *Concerning Children*. Since John Dewey is commonly acknowledged as the "interpreter and synthesizer" of the progressive education movement (Cremin 1964, 234), I will briefly outline the similarities in their theories.[5]

Dewey and Gilman both advocated a natural, unconscious form of learning in a child-centered curriculum. Both were interested in designing controlled learning environments for children that would allow them to act on their natural impulses and experience the consequences in order to learn the connection between actions and their consequences. This view of learning is a pragmatic, utilitarian view that stresses action: not only in learning, but in problem solving. To both Dewey and Gilman, thought is essentially oriented toward action. In addition, both view the development of proper habits of thought as essential, so that children are able to receive and manipulate the impressions they receive, coordinate them, make judgments, and plan and carry out a course of action to attain their goals. Gilman and Dewey both believe that the development of these habits of thought is necessary to provide children with the power to direct their actions to attain their goals. Again, the purpose of thought is effective action.

Neither Dewey nor Gilman invented all these beliefs about thought and action and learning. Various threads of these theories can be traced back to the educational philosophies of John Locke (1632–1704), Jean Jacques Rousseau (1712–1778), Friedrich Froebel (1796–1852), and Johann Pestalozzi (1796–1827). Many of these ideas were tried in various forms and with various degrees of success in the infant school movement in the first half of the nineteenth century and the kindergarten movement in the second half of the nineteenth century.[6] Thus, these ideas were in general circulation in the late nineteenth century, and both Dewey and Gilman were able to weave these threads together into the fabric of a coherent educational philosophy.

Where Dewey and Gilman differ is in their social philosophies of education. According to Dewey, the tremendous changes in society brought about by industrialization and urbanization had fundamentally changed the way that educational processes were carried on in society. The family, the church, and the community were no longer able to perform their traditional educational functions because of these changes. Thus, Dewey argued, the school must take on these responsibilities. In this way Dewey rejected the separation of school from life. But even further, Dewey argued that the school should be seen as an embryonic community that should sift out the negative factors of contemporary social life and represent a better vision of a democratic society for its members. In this way the school becomes both a critique of present social life and an approximation of an ideal democratic society. He believed that the school's most fundamental objective was to educate all children for their role in the democratic system.

Gilman did not share Dewey's interest in democracy. She shared his concern for the need for unity and order in the rapidly changing American society, but her answer lay in her form of collectivism, the social whole being primary and individuals finding and fulfilling their proper place within it. This is not to say that she did not believe in democracy; rather, she did not see it as the central feature in her vision of society. She was most interested in developing a collectivist society based on mutual interdependence and an ethic of social service as described in *Human Work* and portrayed in *Herland*. Gilman saw the development of independently thinking, socially sensitive adults as the means of achieving this society. It could be said that Dewey and Gilman share much in their ideals of the educated adult, but that they see this adult functioning within different social structures.

Since Gilman's pedagogical theory is so similar to Dewey's, the question arises as to why his educational thought had such a great and lasting impact on generations, while hers quickly faded into obscurity. I think there are four answers to this question. First, Dewey was a respected educator and professor who in the course of his academic career influenced hundreds of his students, readers, and colleagues. He was trained in the academic tradition, and his works became part of the canon. Gilman, on the other hand, had no academic training or position. She was an outsider to this world, a self-professed social reformer. She did not engage the academic tradition or the academy in her writings and speeches, which were aimed at the concerned public. Second, Dewey's educational philosophy is much more developed and accessible than Gilman's. Dewey wrote over twenty books related to his educational philosophy; Gilman wrote one book devoted to educating young children—the remainder of her educational theories are interwoven throughout her other books. Part of my project in this chapter is to bring her educational theory together and analyze it as a whole.

Third, Dewey's underlying social theories were more modern and able to incorporate the complexities and pluralities of twentieth-century American life, while Gilman's were not. Gilman's social theories are based on and developed within the framework of social evolutionism; Dewey's thought is most often classified in the progressive tradition, which succeeded social evolutionism as the dominant world view around the turn of the century. This is particularly interesting when one notes that Dewey was born one year before Gilman, and yet his thought is characteristic of a later tradition. As we have seen, Gilman never wavered from her social evolutionary theoretical framework, even in the face of compelling evidence to the contrary.[7] Thus, when one considers that Gilman's educational theory was couched in this outdated framework, it is understandable that it fell into obscurity.

The fourth and final reason has been supplied by Jane Roland Martin in her groundbreaking work on the status of women and the traits, tasks, and responsibilities traditionally associated with women in educational philosophy. Martin argues that, as has been demonstrated in many fields, such as psychology, history, and sociology, "the disciplines exclude women from their subject matter" (Martin 1982, 133). She writes that women

> are excluded both as the subjects and objects of educational thought from the standard texts and anthologies: as subjects, their philosophical works on education are ignored; as objects, works by men about their education and also their role as educators of the young are largely neglected. (Martin 1982, 134)

It is easy to see how Gilman met this fate: both because she was a woman, and because her theories focus on women and young children, subjects not considered to be part of the "educational realm," as Martin calls it, the public world of school that has been delimited as the appropriate area of study for educational philosophers.[8]

What Gilman's Philosophy of Education Contributes to Education Today

What does Gilman's philosophy of education have to contribute to our understanding of the challenges in education today? In my opinion, many of Gilman's central insights are just as relevant today. For example, she argues that many of our public institutions are excessively individualistic and competitive. This is a criticism frequently raised about our society today. Further, new methods of assessment, such as portfolio assessment, are being introduced in schools across the country. One goal of these alternative assessment tools is to reduce the emphasis on competition in schools. Her revelations about the negative effects of what we call today genderized traits are still discussed in numerous books and scholarly articles, and many of us feel the effects of this gender socialization in our everyday lives. Many women worry about being too "aggressive" at work, or earning more than their husband or boyfriend; many men feel trapped within the narrow confines of the unemotional, workaholic husband and provider. Parents worry about raising their girls to be self-confident and assertive and their boys to be caring and compassionate, while their daughters beg for Barbie dolls and their sons demand the latest in high-tech toy weaponry.

Unfortunately, we can also see how little progress our society has made in the area of the care and education of young children since Gilman published *Concerning Children* almost one hundred years ago. Our society still does not take responsibility for the care and nurturance of young children, leaving them to enjoy or suffer from the vagaries of the life situation into which they are born or legally placed. The way we view children in our society is similar to the notion of private property; we think conception or adoption confers a type of ownership, which extends to the right of parents or guardians to decide the type of medical treatment, upbringing, education, physical environment, and nutrition that "their" children will have. This results in terrible suffering and stunted lives for a huge number of children.

According to the Children's Defense Fund, 14.6 million children live in poverty, and the younger children are, the poorer they are. One in every four children under six is poor, as are 27 percent of children under three (Sherman 1994, xvi). Poverty brings with it, among other problems, increased risk for abuse and neglect, inadequate nutrition and health care, substandard education, high dropout rates, and a high risk of death at an early age (Edelman 1994, xvi–xvii).

Further, we still do not consider the upbringing of young children to be educational or valuable, and it is certainly not valued as highly as the education of older children. In fact, our child care workers are paid considerably less than most other occupations, often minimum wage, and the pay scale for educators typically increases with the age of their students. Gilman wanted to turn this hierarchy on its head, arguing that the earliest education is the most important because it is the foundation for all else, and arguing that those who taught the youngest children should receive the highest pay and prestige.

Gilman can accurately be described as a radical feminist because she saw to the root of these societal problems. Her ability to look under the taken-for-granted assumptions about women and children allowed her to see them as a class or group—a sizable portion of society—and to analyze their relation to society. While women's opportunities and rights have increased dramatically since Gilman lived, their work in the home is still devalued, their primary role as caretakers of home and family is still individualized and assumed, and their needs as a class or group are still neglected: they do not have the right to paid maternity leave, adequate health care, adequate day care, or equal health insurance or medical research dollars. Gilman shows that there is a way to see the rights and needs of women and children as a class without being blinded by the "veil" of individual family units. She does this because she focuses on the societal level, seeing the necessary contributions that women do, and children will, make to society. These contributions give women and children a public status and ensuing public rights, and confer on society a public responsibility to meet their needs and recognize their contributions.

Although Gilman couched all her ideas about the status of women and children in society within her social evolutionary theories, her radical insights are still valid today. While today we know how limiting the social evolutionary theory is, for Gilman it was empowering, because it gave her an acceptable sociological/theoretical framework in which to place her views on women, children, genderization, and education. It gave her an acceptable reason for why things were the way they were, and she was able to fit her vision of a good society and the proper role of women within it into this theoretical framework. It is a compelling tool, because the primary notion of progressive social evolutionary theory was that society could advance only if it followed certain rules. Gilman believed that she had uncovered those rules, and this imbued her writings and speeches with the considerable power of her conviction that she was helping to improve society.

But Gilman was also a typical nineteenth-century reformer, and her nonconformist views in these areas did not carry over into other areas. Her writings show her to be racist, classist, and xenophobic. She mirrored the opinions of most White, upper-class nineteenth-century women about the poor and working class, immigrants, and minorities. In my description and analysis I have taken her writings to truly mean all children and all members of our society; that may not have been her intent. Although she never stated or wrote that some members of society should have different types of education or futures because of their income, race, class, or ethnicity, her prejudices may mean that when she wrote about "all of society" she was thinking of "all White nonimmigrant, nonpoor members of society." However, the reality that she was a product of her times and that her thinking was limited by her prejudices does not change the fact that her insights apply just as correctly to all members of our complex and diverse modern society.

Conclusion

In conclusion, Gilman believed that human life was fundamentally social and that we all derived our humanity from our relation to society. She believed that the collective good was concomitant with individual good. The purpose of human life in general, and each of us in particular, was to advance ourselves and thus advance society. She felt that she had uncovered the natural laws that, if followed, would allow us to advance toward a better future. Within this framework, the role of education in society is to support all members in society so that they can find and perform their proper duties. Her conception of education as social motherhood is her most powerful insight into the social aspect of education. It allows her to bring the personal nurturing qualities and responsibilities of motherhood, and along with them women themselves, into the public realm. In this way education and society will be humanized because of the addition of this half of humanity's experiences, traits, and tasks. In turn, women will be humanized because they will be allowed out of their private, isolated homes and into the public realm, where they will acquire the experiences, traits, and tasks of the public realm.

Many of Gilman's theories were prevalent during her lifetime. She shared her belief in social progress with other progressive social evolutionists, she shared her pedagogical theories with the progressive education movement, and she shared some of her ideas about the importance of early childhood education with the kindergarten and infant schools movement. She shared many of her feminist convictions with some fellow suffragists and feminists. In one sense, Gilman is a exquisitely developed product of her time, a synthesizing of many aspects of the social thought of her time into one person. But Gilman is more than the sum of these theories and movements. She added to these ideas as well. Her radical insights into the basis of gender roles and gender socialization, the outdated traditions and unproved myths that they are based on, the harm that they perpetrate on all members of society—men, women, and children—as well as on society itself, cut deep into the taken-for-granted fabric of nineteenth-century social life. And in cutting through this fabric, as it were, she opened up new possibilities and ways of seeing the world. Men could become more nurturing, women more analytical. Children could be viewed as valuable to society, to be educated and nurtured. Even more radical, all children are viewed this way, not only our own—the poor, the unwashed, the uneducated—just the same as our own (although in Gilman's theoretical world there would be no poor, unwashed, or uneducated children). In the years since she wrote her first books, bits and pieces of her theories have been tried, but always some other parts have been left unexamined. Unfortunately, we have never had the chance to see how her theories as a whole would work in actual practice. It certainly would be an interesting experiment.

Notes

[1]Gilman called herself a "humanist," not a feminist, because she wanted to improve the lives of both men and women and because her ultimate goal was to improve humanity, not only women's lives and status. (Gilman 1913a, 36). Today, she is known as a feminist because her vision of social progress contained incisive insights into the status of women and children in society and the harm that the separate spheres of ideology cause society.

[2]See Carol Farley Kessler, *Charlotte Perkins Gilman: Her Progress toward Utopia* (Syracuse: Syracuse University Press, 1995); Joanne B. Karpinski, *Critical Essays on Charlotte Perkins Gilman* (New York: G. K. Hall, 1992); Larry Ceplair, *Charlotte Perkins Gilman: A Nonfiction*

Reader (New York: Columbia University Press, 1991); Polly Wynn Allen, *Building Domestic Liberty: Charlotte Perkins Gilman's Architectural Feminism* (Amherst: University of Massachusetts Press, 1988); Gary Scharnhorst, *Charlotte Perkins Gilman: A Bibliography* (Metuchen, NJ: Scarecrow Press, 1985); Ann Palmeri, "Charlotte Perkins Gilman: Forerunner of a Feminist Social Science," in *Discovering Reality: Feminist Perspectives on Epistemology, Metaphysics, Methodology, and Philosophy of Science*, edited by Sandra Harding and Merrill B. Hintikka (Boston: d. Reidel, 1983); Dolores Hayden, "Domestic Evolution or Domestic Revolution," Chapter 9 of *The Grand Domestic Revolution: A History of Feminist Designs for American Homes, Neighborhoods, and Cities* (Cambridge: MIT Press, 1981); Carol Ruth Berkin, "Private Woman, Public Woman: The Contradictions of Charlotte Perkins Gilman," in *Women of America: A History*, edited by Carol Ruth Berkin and Mery Beth Norton (Boston: Houghton Mifflin, 1979); Lois N. Magner, "Women and the Scientific Idiom: Textual Episodes from Wollstonecraft, Fuller, Gilman, and Firestone," *Signs* 4 (Autumn 1978): 61–80.

[3] See Richard Hofstadter, *Social Darwinism in American Thought* (Boston: Beacon Press, 1955), Chapter 7; Albion W. Small, "Fifty Years of Sociology in the U.S. (1865–1915)," *American Journal of Sociology* 21 (May 1916): 721–864; John C. Burnham, *Lester Frank Ward in American Thought* (Washington DC: Annals of American Sociology, Public Affairs Press, 1956 1–17.)

[4] This was in keeping with Gilman's political views, which can best be described as collectivist, communitarian, and non-Marxian socialist. See Gilman 1935, 131, 198; Lane 1991, 184–85, 230–31; Hill 1980, 167–75, 283–94.

[5] My very brief outline of Dewey's views is based on John Dewey, *Democracy and Education* (New York: The Free Press, 1944). See in particular, 11, 20–22, 52–53, 74–77, 83–87, 152–57.

[6] For a fuller discussion of these philosophers and movements in relation to Gilman's views, see Karen E. Maloney, "The Theory of Education of Charlotte Perkins Gilman: A Critical Analysis," Ed.D. diss. Harvard University Graduate School of Education, 1985.

[7] Jill Conway discusses this point in "Stereotypes of Femininity in a Theory of Sexual Evolution," *Victorian Studies* 14 (1970): 47–62. It is interesting to note that the same fate of obscurity befell Lester Frank Ward, from whom Gilman borrowed many of her examples from botany and zoology in her writings. See John C. Burnham, *Lester Frank Ward in American Thought* (Washington, DC: Annals of American Sociology, Public Affairs Press, 1956).

[8] For a full discussion of Martin's views on this issue, see her book, *Changing the Educational Landscape: Philosophy, Women, and Curriculum* (New York: Routledge, 1994).

References

Cremin, L. 1964. *The Transformation of the School: Progressivism in American Education, 1876–1957*. New York: Vintage Books.

Degler, C. N. 1956. Charlotte Perkins Gilman and the Theory and Practice of Feminism. *American Quarterly* 8 (Spring): 21–39.

Edelman, M. W. 1994. Introduction to *Wasting America's Future: The Children's Defense Fund Report on the Costs of Child Poverty*. Boston: Beacon Press.

Gilman, C. P. [1898] 1966. *Women and Economics: A Study of the Economic Relation Between Men and Woman as a Factor in Social Evolution*. Reprint. New York: Harper and Row.

———. 1900. *Concerning Children*. Boston: Small, Maynard and Co.

———. 1904. *Human Work*. New York: McLure, Phillips and Co.

_____ . 1911. *The Man-Made World or, Our Androcentric Culture.* New York: Charlton Corp.

_____ . 1912a. Our Brains and What Ails Them: Ch 1 Introductory *Forerunner* 3 (January): 22–26.

_____ . 1912b. Our Brains and What Ails Them: Ch. 6 The Newspaper and the Modern Mind *Forerunner* 3 (June): 161–67.

_____ . 1913a. On Ellen Key and the Woman Movement. *Forerunner* 4 (February): 35–38.

_____ . 1913b. Education for Motherhood. *Forerunner* 4 (September): 259–62.

_____ . [1915] 1979. *Herland.* New York: Pantheon Books.

_____ . 1916a. Growth and Combat, Thesis *Forerunner* 7 (January): 13–14.

_____ . 1916b. Growth and Combat, Ch. 9 Influence on Education. *Forerunner* 7 (September): 246–51.

_____ . [1935] 1990. *The Living of Charlotte Perkins Gilman: An Autobiography.* Reprint. Madison: The University of Wisconsin Press.

Hill, M. A. 1980. *Charlotte Perkins Gilman: The Making of a Radical Feminist, 1860–1886.* Philadelphia: Temple University Press.

Lane, A. J. 1979. Introduction to *Herland.* New York: Pantheon Books.

_____ . 1991. *To Herland and Beyond: The Life and Work of Charlotte Perkins Gilman.* New York: Meridian/Penguin.

Martin, J. R. 1982. Excluding Women from the Educational Realm. *Harvard Educational Review* 52: 133–48.

_____ . 1985. *Reclaiming a Conversation: The Ideal of the Educated Woman.* New Haven, CT: Yale University Press.

Sherman, A. 1994. *Wasting America's Future: The Children's Defense Fund Report on the Costs of Child Poverty.* Boston: Beacon Press.

READING

Our Relations and Theirs

Charlotte Perkins Gilman

An excerpt from *Herland*

Well, here is the Herland child facing life—as Ellador tried to show it to me. From the first memory, they knew Peace, Beauty, Order, Safety, Love, Wisdom, Justice, Patience, and Plenty. By "plenty" I mean that the babies grew up in an environment which met their needs, just as young fawns might grow up in dewy forest glades and brook-fed meadows. And they enjoyed it as frankly and utterly as the fawns would.

They found themselves in a big bright lovely world, full of the most interesting and enchanting things to learn about and to do. The people everywhere were friendly and polite. No Herland child ever met the overbearing rudeness we so commonly show to children. They were People, too, from the first; the most precious part of the nation.

In each step of the rich experience of living, they found the instance they were studying widen out into contact with an endless range of common interests. The things they learned were *related,* from the first; related to one another, and to the national prosperity.

"It was a butterfly that made me a forester," said Ellador. "I was about eleven years old, and I found a big purple-and-green butterfly on a low flower. I caught it, very carefully, by the closed wings, as I had been told to do, and carried it to the nearest insect teacher"—I made a note there to ask her what on earth an insect teacher was—"to ask her its name. She took it from me with a little cry of delight. 'Oh, you blessed child,' she said. 'Do you like obernuts?' Of course I liked obernuts, and said so. It is our best food-nut, you know. 'This is a female of the obernut moth,' she told me. 'They are almost gone. We have been trying to exterminate them for centuries. If you had not caught this one, it might have laid eggs enough to raise worms enough to destroy thousands of our nut trees—thousands of bushels of nuts—and make years and years of trouble for us.'

"Everybody congratulated me. The children all over the country were told to watch for that moth, if there were any more. I was shown the history of the creature, and an account of the damage it used to do and of how long and hard our foremothers had worked to save that tree for us. I grew a foot, it seemed to me, and determined then and there to be a forester."

This is but an instance; she showed me many. The big difference was that whereas our children grow up in private homes and families, with every effort made to protect and seclude them from a dangerous world, here they grew up in a wide, friendly world, and knew it for theirs, from the first.

Their child-literature was a wonderful thing. I could have spent years following the delicate subtleties, the smooth simplicities with which they had bent that great art to the service of the child mind.

We have two life cycles: the man's and the woman's. To the man there is growth, struggle, conquest, the establishment of his family, and as much further success in gain or ambition as he can achieve.

To the woman, growth, the securing of a husband, the subordinate activities of family life, and afterward such "social" or charitable interests as her position allows.

Here was but one cycle, and that a large one.

The child entered upon a broad open field of life, in which motherhood was the one great personal contribution to the national life, and all the rest the individual share in their common activities. Every girl I talked to, at any age above babyhood, had her cheerful determination as to what she was going to be when she grew up.

What Terry meant by saying they had no "modesty" was that this great life-view had no shady places; they had a high sense of personal decorum, but no shame—no knowledge of anything to be ashamed of.

Even their shortcomings and misdeeds in childhood never were presented to them as sins; merely as errors and misplays—as in a game. Some of them, who were palpably less agreeable than others or who had a real weakness or fault, were treated with cheerful allowance, as a friendly group at whist would treat a poor player.

Their religion, you see, was maternal; and their ethics, based on the full perception of evolution, showed the principle of growth and the beauty of wise culture. They had no theory of the essential opposition of good and evil; life to them was growth; their pleasure was in growing, and their duty also.

With this background, with their sublimated mother-love, expressed in terms of widest social activity, every phase of their work was modified by its effect on the national growth. The language itself they had deliberately clarified, simplified, made easy and beautiful, for the sake of the children.

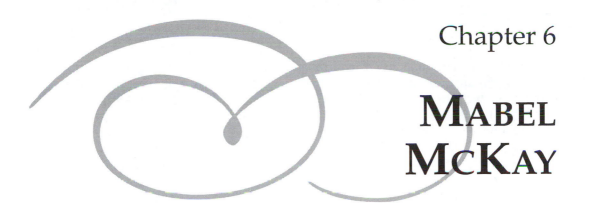

Chapter 6

MABEL McKAY

Learning to Weave and to Dream—Native American Educational Practices

By Renae Bredin

Introduction

> Best of all they told me the hummah-hah stories, about an earlier time when animals and humans shared a common language. In the old days, the Pueblo people had educated their children in this manner; adults took time out to talk to and teach young people. Everyone was a teacher, and every activity had the potential to teach the child. (Silko 1996, 63)

It is in the telling of stories that people learn. Sometimes the stories are not so good, and sometimes the stories are powerful and strong. This chapter is a storytelling, a way of talking about learning from Mabel McKay (1907–1996), Pomo Dreamer, healer, and basketweaver, and from Greg Sarris, college professor and elected chief of the Coast Miwok tribal group, who knew Mabel McKay and wrote down her story.

The questions posed in this book on women who have pioneered educational thought are the kinds of questions that may be difficult to answer in the context of American Indian educational philosophies and practices. The individualist notion of a single pioneer forging a new path is set in contradistinction to American Indian contextual and communal based world views. By lifting Mabel McKay out of the community as an individual educator, I do some violence to the spirit and practice of learning in which she is embedded. But, perhaps by a conscious self-reflexivity, a constant effort to understand how one might speak of a culture as an outsider, I might mitigate some of the consequences of that inevitable violence and appropriation.

The first problem to be addressed is to determine just which educational practices are to be discussed in relation to American Indians. Post-contact education of Native American children has generally consisted of either off-reservation boarding schools that children were forced to attend, and in which they were culturally reprogrammed to become as White as possible, or Bureau of Indian Affairs schools that functioned in similar ways, but on the local level. Very early in Indian–White relations, the French settlers participated in reciprocal education exchange agreements with Northeastern tribal groups, sending their own sons to be educated by indigenous families, and bringing the sons of the Indians to be educated in Western European language and culture.[1] The British did not participate in this project of mutual understanding, creating the atmosphere that prevails even today. "The English . . . saw the education of Indian children as a unilateral process in which they designated themselves as the superior race burdened with the responsibility of rescuing the sons of the forests from savagery and transforming them into cultured albeit subservient members of the Empire" (Deloria 1982, 59). The Mormon Church's Indian placement program, in which American Indian children leave their families to spend the school year in the homes of church members, continues in this tradition.

These colonial practices have had their lasting, negative effects on American Indian education. But there is another, parallel world in which culture, language, tradition, and competencies have been taught, a world of tribal educational practices characterized by several elements that emphasize the learning process as communal, informal, experiential, sacred, and grounded in oral traditions and storytelling.[2] For our purposes here, the pioneering work that Mabel McKay has done as teacher to and for Greg Sarris is to reassert these tribal educational practices in the face of continuing internal colonization. And so, as I tell you the story of Mabel and Greg and how they have taught and learned with each other, the larger questions of this book will be raised and addressed, but perhaps in ways those of us schooled by Western systems of objectivism will find difficult to recognize.

Biographical Sketch

Learning from the Voice

> Mabel didn't know too much. She didn't ask. "You listen to me," the voice was saying. "I'll teach you. You don't tell nobody what I'm telling you. You don't ask them questions about it. You're being fixed to be a doctor." "What's a doctor?" Mabel asked. "You'll know when the time comes." (Sarris 1994, 22)

Mabel McKay

Mabel McKay was born in Nice, Lake County, California, in 1907, to Daisy Hansen and Yanta Boone, then raised by her grandmother, Sarah Taylor. Sarah's brother, Richard, brought the Dream religion (Bole Maru) to Lolsel, near Clear Lake, California, bringing people together "to hear his Dreams" and dream and dance themselves: "Dreaming new dances and songs, sacred activities that would keep them alive after the white people had taken everything but their souls" (Sarris 1994, 8). McKay grew up in the midst of shifting social relations between White men, White women, and Pomo women in the Lake County area. Disease, public policy, and increased immigration to the area had effectively reduced the number of Pomo men living and working in the area and had created, then reduced, the number of domestic jobs available to Pomo women between 1850 and 1940 (Patterson 1995, 141–43). Mabel's grandmother did laundry, cleaned houses, and worked in the fields, mostly for White people, all the while caring for her granddaughter after Daisy left and Sarah's husband had died.

At a very early age, Mabel began to learn about her calling as a healer, a doctor, not in the classrooms of White teachers, not even in some stereotypical shaman/apprentice discourse, but in her dreams. She dreamed of ugly things, poisonous, bloody, deadly. The spirit or voice inside of her talked to her, teaching her about sucking out diseases and fixing her voice for singing. The spirit taught her how to weave the baskets that would make her famous, which are collected at the Smithsonian Institution in Washington, D.C. But Mabel learned to weave in order to heal:

"Spirit show me everything. Each basket has Dream" . . . "I have rules for that," the spirit said. " . . . Your throat has been fixed for singing and sucking out the diseases I've been teaching you about . . . " "Well, how am I to suck?" Mabel asked. "You'll know when you get to that point. You will have a basket to spit out the disease. All your baskets will come from me. Like I told you. Watch how things turn out." The spirit explained each of the songs that Mabel could hear and sing clearly now. "This is your setting-down song, for when you're calling me. This song is for putting the sickness to sleep. You will have many more songs." (Sarris 1994, 31–38)

Freud taught Western European White people that we could learn things about ourselves from our dreams. But the voice Mabel is listening to here in her dreams is not a dislocated Freudian jigsaw puzzle waiting to be untangled. This voice in Mabel's dream is clear, precise, and here to teach her a craft and a calling. As a dreamer, Mabel will learn about doctoring, weaving, poison, and power. She has privileged access to the sacred, to knowledge that can only be conferred by spirit guides. The Spirit also guided Mabel during her healing work:

Once, while she was singing over a woman from Colusa, she found herself unable to extract the pain in the woman's chest. Her hand had located the pain, what the spirit described as a tiny spotted fish, but she was unable to pull it up, out of the woman. "Now you have to use your mouth," the spirit said as Mabel sang. "How am I going to use my mouth?" she asked. The spirit said: "Your throat has been fixed for many years. Now it's ready to use. And that basket you completed a while back, that spitting-out-sickness-basket at your side, it's ready too. It's hungry. You must feed it with your spit. Now, you are ready. The song has put that little fish to sleep. Take it out with your mouth . . . " And Mabel took the fish into her throat and coughed it out into the basket. The Colusa woman was healed that way. (Sarris 1994, 94)

This is not what you were expecting to read, is it? You were thinking that Mabel McKay perhaps invented some method for teaching people about Mother Earth and how to respect her, or how to bridge two cultures, and that this method might be something you could replicate in some small way. But these are precisely the expectations that Mabel McKay spent her life as a teacher overturning. It is in her reversal of expectations that Mabel McKay succeeds as a pioneering American Indian teacher.

I first learned about and from Mabel McKay by reading the stories she had told to Greg Sarris, a mixed blood Filipino, Jewish, Miwok/Pomo Indian, and a scholar and thinker who had grown up around McKay and her community, mostly on the fringes. He has written her stories in a number of places, particularly in his book *Mabel McKay: Weaving the Dream* (Sarris 1994). Mabel asked him to write down her story, her life, and Greg, in need of a doctoral dissertation for his Ph.D. in English, agreed (Sarris 1994 1, 53). This years-long book project, which finally was not Sarris' dissertation, is our main source of information about Mabel McKay and the stories of her life and her teachings. Sarris tells us how difficult it was to capture Mabel in words:

> I kept wondering how I was going to write about Mabel's life. She was baffling, even for me. Certainly the facts of her life were interesting and warranted a story. World-renowned Pomo basketmaker with permanent collections in the Smithsonian and countless other museums. The last Dreamer and sucking doctor among the Pomo peoples. The last living member of the Long Valley Cache Creek Pomo tribe. The astute interlocutor famous for her uncanny talk that left people's minds spinning. The facts were easy. The life was not. (Sarris 1994, 3)

Sarris tells the story of first finding McKay as he "hung out" around Santa Rosa, California. Having been adopted at birth by George and Mary Sarris, Greg knew little about where he had come from. "I didn't know anything. Sometimes I wondered if I was Mexican. Maybe Indian. Black possibly" (Sarris 1994, 47). Mostly on his own because of his ambiguous familial status, he followed McKay's adopted son, Marshall, home and met Mabel:

> My Indian friends told me that Mabel and Essie Parrish were Indian doctors . . . I wasn't interested in spells and such things then. I was respectful of Mabel, and appreciated her kindness and caring. And the fact that I had to stop my crazy talking, my fears and insecurities when I was around her. She always seemed at least one step ahead of me, and in her presence, where I was quiet, I felt peaceful, relaxed, even as she kept me alert, on my toes. She talked, told me stories I would hear over and over again. The stories seemed wild, unusual at times, but sitting there at the kitchen table, even at the age of fifteen or sixteen, I knew what it was like to have a mother who cared enough to tell you stories. (Sarris 1994, 49)

Greg and Mabel continued in this vein for many years, Mabel talking and telling stories, Greg listening and asking questions, Mabel telling more stories, or retelling stories, Greg asking for clarification, Mabel telling stories.

In the final pages of Sarris's fine book about Mabel McKay's life and work, he has this to say about what he understands Mabel McKay was trying to teach him:

> I sat back in my chair. I felt my feet on the ground. I saw clearly. Things came together. It wasn't just her story she had wanted me to know. While trying to help her, while trying to trace her story, I traced my own . . . Her story, the story, our story. Like the tiny basket in my shirt pocket, different threads, sedge and redbud, woven over one willow rod into a design that went round and round, endless. (Sarris 1994, 164–65)

This is a weaving of stories, identities, and processes, threading together layers of knowledge that, unlike Western systems of knowledge, is not observable, quantifiable, or replicable. "Things come together" for Sarris as he makes the connections between Mabel's stories and his own and the context in which they occur. When Sarris wonders aloud why McKay never told him what was happening, McKay's daughter Violet reminds him, "'Because . . . you wouldn't believe. You had to wait and see how it turned out" (Sarris 1994, 165). Stories are never about one thing only. They function on many levels. The same story might have different uses, given the context of the telling, the listeners, and the intent of the storyteller. Every teller innovates in telling stories that have been told by others and in retelling stories they have themselves told before.

This book, *Mabel McKay: Weaving the Dream*, this set of stories Sarris writes, begins as a collaboration to tell McKay's story for the non-Indian world of scholars, anthropologists, and museum curators who want to know about the last of the great Pomo weavers and healers. But it becomes the story of Sarris learning not only about his own identity, but also about the purpose and meaning of life and his role in society, Indian and non-Indian alike. While McKay learns from the Dream world, Sarris learns from her stories about the Dream world and about the world she and Sarris share.

Overview of McKay's Thought

Turning the Auditorium Upside Down

I believe that I have warned you that you will not necessarily hear what you expect to hear in this story of American Indian teaching practices. Those of you familiar with Carlos Castenada and his teacher Don Juan may imagine that this relationship between McKay and Sarris is somehow like that other one of shaman/apprentice (a relationship more about White notions of Indians than about Indians themselves), a kind of one-on-one ritual training into dreaming, weaving, and doctoring. But McKay is not Don Juan (even Don Juan is not really Don Juan). Sarris opens *Weaving the Dream* with a story about a trip to Stanford University, where Mabel is lecturing, answering questions from an auditorium of students and faculty:

> The scene was typical. Mabel lecturing, answering questions from an auditorium of students and faculty who wanted to know about her baskets and her life as a medicine woman . . .
>
> "You're an Indian doctor," a young woman with bright red hair spoke from the middle of the room. "What do you do for poison oak?"
>
> "Calamine lotion," Mabel answered. She was matter-of-fact. The student sank into her chair. (Sarris 1994, 1)

This young woman expects Mabel the Pomo medicine woman to offer some mysterious, exotic secret Indian remedy. Instead, McKay answers with the obvious, what anyone (read: White) might do, use calamine. McKay is teaching this auditorium full of non-Indians about themselves and their world view by overturning their assumptions about Indians, without a lecture or any direct statement about this young woman's assumptions. Sarris describes the scene:

> There it was. Quintessential Mabel. Nothing new. Same stories and questions. Same answers. This small Indian woman, over eighty years old, with coifed black hair and modish glasses, this little Indian woman in a mauve-colored summer dress adorned on the shoulder with a corsage of imitation African violets, had turned a Stanford auditorium upside down. (Sarris 1994, 3)

In fact, McKay was often a guest lecturer at local colleges and universities and an invited speaker at state fairs and museums. "She kept weaving and regularly taught classes near Davis . . . [and] traveled to museums and universities to talk" (Sarris 1994, 131). As a teacher, McKay crisscrossed the boundaries of institutional educational practices and interpersonal, experiential learning.

This crisscrossing of the objectivist distinction between experience and intellectualizing is crucial to our understanding of McKay as a model practitioner of indigenous educational pedagogy. Sarris recounts McKay's story of the community of women she encounters shortly after her second marriage. She found herself living with the Sulphur Bank people in the Ukiah Valley of Northern California, near Clear Lake, her home. She didn't know anyone except her new husband. But she found her way, as she was weaving her incredibly delicate baskets, mostly for people who had ordered them because of her great skill as a basketweaver. In a reciprocal exchange of both information and goodwill, the women of Sulphur Bank showed her the best places to dig sedge roots and to find redbud for her baskets:

> In exchange for the women's generosity, Mabel put up great dinners, and gave each of the women a miniature basket for her health and protection. She explained her basketweaving rules—no drinking or menstruating when you weave—and provided they followed the rules, she showed them how to trim sedge roots just so and how to use willows picked at certain times of year so that the baskets would be watertight. (Sarris 1994, 89)

The communal nature of this relationship among the women of Sulphur Bank, including McKay, resists the models of learning in current use among non-Indian, American institutions, models such as the banking concept of education, in which the teacher knows things, deposits that knowledge in the student repository, and then withdraws exactly what had been deposited, nothing more.[3]

However, before lapsing into some idyllic rapture about unspoiled indigenous communal living that would immediately solve the contemporary problems of teaching and learning models, if we could only "return," listen to how Sarris goes on to describe the informal teacher/student relationship that prevailed. Even as he makes clear the reciprocal nature of this relationship, Sarris also identifies the authority with which McKay moves through the group when it comes to her expertise:

> Aside from the brief lectures she had given each day at the State Fair in Sacramento about the materials she used in her basketry, this was her first experience teaching. She sat with the women, checking their work and making suggestions. "I remember my grandmother used to say the same thing," one of the women said after Mabel showed her how to gently bend a willow rod. (Sarris 1994, 89)

In turn, the Sulphur Bank women taught her how to make chili and stews, bake mud hens from the lake, and the Sulphur Bank language. While there is reciprocity, the one who knows, whether it is about baskets or baking, goes about checking and correcting, making suggestions. Mabel's teaching is now part of another woman's story about her grandmother, a teacher who also suggested and corrected. The distinction from non-Indian practices here is contextual. McKay is providing a different model for authority, which is not quite the same as abandoning authority. Most teachers attempt to include hands-on experiences for their students, but within the context of non-Indian institutions, those experiences are more anomalous than common.[4] Gregory Cajete asserts the relationship between experience and theory in *Look to the Mountain*.

> The real situation provides the stage for most Indigenous learning and teaching. Overt intellectualization is kept to a minimum in favor of direct experience and learning by doing. Teaching through a real situation expands the realm of learning beyond speculation and allows the students to judge the truth of a teaching for themselves. (Cajete 1994, 224)

But how does this notion of learning through direct action fit the model of storytelling as the primary source of teaching and learning between Mabel and Greg? Isn't listening to stories a passive behavior; isn't the listener just listening, doing nothing? Here again, Western assumptions about listening are in play. For the storyteller in a tribal context, or in other cultural contexts for that matter, listening to a story, hearing a story, being part of a storytelling moment, is about actively participating in the process. Good listeners respond, add, agree, disagree, ask questions, and then take up the story in other contexts, retelling and innovating for the next listeners. The chain of stories from the Dream, to Mabel, with Sarah, written down by Greg, all include innovations for the moment. Mabel doesn't tell Greg stories over and over in the same place at the same time and with the same purpose or context. Greg doesn't just listen, he asks questions, drives the car, and talks back, all the while making interpretations and applications, learning his own story in the process. "I must begin to understand it as a story for me, not only as a story that positions me in certain ways, but also as a story that can inform me about that position" (Sarris 1994, 83).

"Mi Qu Bake 'Eh Mau Ama Diche Me"
"This Story Is for You"[5]

So here I am, giving you a gloss of what I have read about Mabel McKay's teaching strategies as observed, experienced, and recorded by Greg Sarris. But who am I to be telling you these things? I am not Pomo or Miwok, or even tribal. I have been taught how to learn in predominantly non-Indian institutions. And I have not learned experientially from McKay. I have read, and then read some more. In "Reading Narrated American Indian Lives: Elizabeth Colson's Autobiographies of Three Pomo Women," Sarris cautions that "in losing sight of my presence as a reader I will not see how my critical work is tied historically and politically to a real world" (Sarris 1993, 88). It is crucial, in the face of a history of colonization and appropriation of Native American art, spirituality, storytelling, culture, language, and tradition, that I too, embed my critical work in a historical, political matrix. I tell you these stories as a reader, not an actor, nor as a reporter.

This transaction is a kind of "cross-cultural project" (Green 1992, 83), one in which I am learning to use the most traditional strategies of "literate" institutional education—read the material, then take the test. But, again, Sarris offers a position in which I, as reader, and by association you, as reader, might participate in his dialogue with McKay. My own work, and my own teaching, have been transformed by what I have read by Sarris, both about McKay and about how one speaks of a culture as an outsider.

In Sarris' stories, I am drawn into a world view not my own, but certainly one that has informed U.S. cultural practices for centuries (without credit). What underlies the assumptions in the uses of storytelling is what I might constitute as a tribal under-standing of knowledge as contextual, inseparable from experience, and implicit in sacred/everyday life. In "Education and Imperialism," Vine Deloria, Jr. (1982) contrasts tribal and non-tribal assumptions about knowledge:

> Content and applicability are simultaneous and identical. Indians were practical; whites wanted to instruct in abstractions. Indians wanted to produce useful people; whites wanted to transmit a body of information regardless of its immediate usefulness . . . we are not talking particularly about prejudice but about a preconceived notion of what constitutes useful information and knowledge. (58–59)

For Deloria, the emphasis in indigenous practices is on "the value of the individual human personality rather than the objective body of knowledge which must be consumed" (1982, 60). The transmission of contextualized, experiential, sacred knowledge is intimately linked to the individual, and individuals are intimately linked through storytelling. Leslie Marmon Silko, in describing a particular world view based in Pueblo Indian culture, says, "The oral narrative, or story, became the medium through which the complex of Pueblo knowledge and belief was maintained" (1996, 30). Storytelling is everyday, experiential learning through the organizing principle of narrative. And so, for me, the cultural outsider, Sarris writing the stories becomes Sarris' storytelling, because he doesn't *tell* me, the reader, what constitutes American Indian teaching practices, but tells me stories *about* someone who teaches. Sarris doesn't understand abstract meaning through the stories with which McKay answers his questions, but he learns a whole field of perception.

In "Higher Education in the Fourth World," Ray Barnhardt identifies a key element of traditional teaching practices as the "emphasis on orality over literacy as the primary means for codifying and transmitting knowledge" (1991, 25). Mabel's strategies are fully grounded in orality—storytelling, reciprocity, ritual singing. Her partnership in learning with Greg is experiential and oral, not in the conventional mode of "a one-way inculcation of knowledge from teacher to student" (Barnhardt 1991, 25).

Barnhardt goes on to describe the "highly personalized relationship between teachers and students" and the importance of elders as a "source of valuable knowledge and expertise" (1991, 24–25):

> There is a preference for creating opportunities for students to learn in a setting where the teacher acts more in the role of tutor/facilitator than as a repository of knowledge that should be passed on to students. In this way, teaching and learning are considered reciprocal and symbiotic processes in which knowledge and skills grow out of a mutual exchange and shared experience, and in which all participants are teachers as well as learners. (Barnhardt 1991, 25)

In "Storytelling in the Classroom: Crossing Vexed Chasms," Sarris again directs our understanding of storytelling as a potent pedagogical strategy. In this article, published first in *College English*, then later in his own collection of essays titled *Keeping Slug Woman Alive: A Holistic Approach to American Indian Texts*, he describes his experiences in using oral storytelling practices successfully in Native and non-Native classrooms, including a college freshman writing course. By using stories that the students tell as texts for learning critical thinking skills, as well as basic writing techniques, Sarris draws on the cultural and personal experiences with which those students are familiar:

> The three stories I have related illustrate, I hope, the potential for storytelling to empower and engage culturally diverse students while providing, in turn, a context for a strong sense of critical thinking for all of us, students and teachers alike, such that the nature of our shared reality and our relationship to it is made more visible and less intimidating. The potential is just that and no more; my stories are models of and not necessarily models for using storytelling to foster critical discourse. But it is interesting to me how even these three stories always prompt more stories. (Sarris 1993, 168)

Ah, here's the solution to the problems of current educational practice. Tell stories, and in the stories we will all learn. Again, before lapsing into that idyllic rapture about unspoiled indigenous communal living offering the magic bullet to classroom practices, listen to what Sarris adds as a footnote at the end of his article. "And in many classroom situations storytelling may be inappropriate. Lest there be any doubt, I am not suggesting here or elsewhere that storytelling is the best or only way for students to respond to texts or to the teacher or to one another" (1993, 168). Mabel lectures at the local community college and tells stories to Greg, and Greg tells stories and has students tell stories in a summer classroom, but Greg also reads papers at academic conferences. Within any given context, not either/or, but both/and strategies make up their enactment of indigenous teaching practices.

Dreaming First

> Another time Mabel spoke to a group of Stanford medical students who wanted to know about "ethnic medicine" and how to work cooperatively with native healers. She prayed and sang a song, all of which lasted about five minutes, then sat down and talked about the dictates of her spirit and her audience. "OK," she said, "now who can tell me what I just said?" The students and their professors were quiet, stunned. "Ain't nobody got a word for me?" she asked finally and laughed. "I thought you wanted to know about healers." (Sarris 1994, 113)

Gregory Cajete shows us just where this crosscultural misunderstanding might be located—in the "mindset of objectivism." Cajete's recent *Look to the Mountain: an Ecology of Indigenous Education* is one of the first full-length studies defining indigenous pedagogy. He offers a foundation for the analysis of this story about Mabel and the group of non-Indian medical students. "Objectivist research [about Indian education] has contributed a dimension of insight, but it has substantial limitations in the multi-dimensional, holistic, and relational reality of the education of Indian people" (1994, 20). These students are unprepared for a lesson grounded not in objectivist reality, but embedded in a complex Cajete describes as the "affective elements—the subjective experience and observations, the communal relationships, the artistic and mythical dimensions, the ritual and ceremony, the sacred ecology, the psychological and spiritual orientations" (1994, 20) of relationally based indigenous educational practices.

Think back to the ways we have seen Mabel McKay approach teaching moments: telling stories, overturning conventions, exchanging, singing a healing ritual to teach—reasserting, in other words, what Cajete (1994) is marking as a relational set of indigenous practices:

> Traditional American Indian education historically occurred in a holistic social context that developed the importance of each individual as a contributing member of the social group. Tribal education

sustained a wholesome life process. It was an educational process that unfolded through mutual, reciprocal relationships between one's social group and the natural world. This relationship involved all dimensions of one's being, while providing both personal development and technical skills through *participation* in community life. It was essentially a communally integrated expression of environmental education. (Cajete 1994, 26)

Mother McKay

Within such a holistic context, the question of the role and place of women in society and education becomes both preeminent and radically immaterial. Gender relations within most tribal communities, including the Pomo,[6] operate under assumptions similar to indigenous educational strategies—balance, community, experience. Non-Indian Western world views are more commonly grounded in a dual system of dominance and subordination, with roles assigned based on gender rather than experience, ability, or community good. While it is clear that only Mabel could teach Greg what he learns, and that Mabel's presence as an elder woman was an integral part of the lessons she teaches to the college students and the women of Sulphur Bank, her strategies are not necessarily or only a woman's strategies. She participates in a community of teachers and learners, even though those teachers and learners are not only Kashaya Pomo, and she participates in ways that are culturally contextualized, in both Indian and non-Indian settings and systems.

The historical and ethnographic literature *about* Native American women is replete with misinformation about their lives and their places within tribal groups, a theme Rayna Green has identified as the "Pocahontas perplex."[7] The desire for the Indian princess and the hatred of the Indian squaw are the racist binary oppositions in which American Indian women have been narratively and culturally trapped by non-Indian outsiders. But this binary reveals more about non-Indian cultural conditions than about women's roles in specific tribal groups. Indigenous women operate across a range of social systems in tribally specific contexts along a broad continuum of roles and ranks, historically and presently.

Marjane Ambler reports in *Tribal College* that a number of women are currently filling leadership roles in tribal colleges. Roughly 39 percent of the presidents of tribal colleges are women, and they serve in a number of other administrative capacities. While she asserts the reluctance of these women to be identified as feminist if that meant "putting down Indian men," these women are working to provide role models for younger women. "'A lot of the divisions you find in non-Indian societies don't apply in Indian societies, perhaps because there is more respect for the individual in Indian society'" (Ambler 1992, 10).

Again, lest we find ourselves lapsing into that idyllic rapture about unspoiled indigenous communal living where men and women live in balance, Rayna Green reminds us that the coming of the Europeans produced an altered state of affairs in which "the roles of women in Indian societies were 'deliberately undermined' because they conflicted with the patriarchal, European way of looking at power and authority" (quoted in Ambler 1992, 12). In many pre-contact tribal groups, women held positions of some power: ". . . the peoples who practiced female-centered religions not only revered their women and treated them with respect but also placed a great deal of responsibility in their hands" (Green 1992, 23). Contemporary American Indian men and women operate in a complex web of traditional and post-contact gender relations. How can we know or understand the gender relations that prevail among the Pomo and which circulate around and between Mabel McKay and Greg Sarris?

As in the differences between objectivism and relational thinking, cultural misunderstandings might lead us to read McKay as the nurturing mother earth figure or New Age medicine woman. By turning our attention to the model of indigenous practices we have been learning from McKay, we can ameliorate, if not fully circumvent, this misunderstanding in relation to her gender.

Conclusion

Slender Relations

If we return to our earlier assertions of reciprocity, storytelling, experience, and community as important elements of indigenous teaching practices, we can see some similarities between these ideas and what Frances A. Maher and Mary Kay Thompson Tetreault call "feminist pedagogies" (1994, 9). Teaching approaches marked by relevance, the individual learner's relation to the material, a redefined community of learners, interactivity, the contextualization of women's lives, and the validation of the stories of the student learners are linked to, but not necessarily the same as, the indigenous model Cajete and others have drawn. Maher and Tetreault are reporting on a particular set of teaching practices associated with theories of women's lives and social relations by feminist thinkers, theories such as Nancy Chodorow's pioneering work on women as relational and reciprocal in their thinking, as well as work by Mary Belenky and her colleagues in *Women's Ways of Knowing*, who "articulated a concept of 'connected knowing' based largely on experiential and relational modes of thought" (Maher and Tetreault 1994, 3). The construction of a particularly feminine way of thinking and knowing, a mythic community of women thinking alike, offers yet another space of idyllic rapture about a community of women to which we might return. But this community is a carefully constructed category, one that fails to encompass the differences across categories of women.

But this set of teaching practices is also directly linked to yet another model of teaching, that of Paulo Freire's radical pedagogy, which advocates the relational over the objectivist as a liberatory "pedagogy of the oppressed." Freire offers a model of teacher/student relations that attempts to overturn traditional arrangements of power, with the student and teacher in dialogue, working through critical assessments of concrete contradictions. There must be discerned "an indivisible solidarity between the world and the people and admits of no dichotomy between them . . . thinking which does not separate itself from action . . . " (Freire 1995, 73). As in the contextualized, relational assumptions implicit in indigenous strategies, dialogue, or a form of communal storytelling, is the way that action directed at transforming structures of oppression will be made possible. Here we see a link from Freire's pedagogy of the oppressed to feminist pedagogy, the notion that relations of power are overturned to further social change through a restructuring of Western European educational practices.

And it is here that I would like to make what will of necessity remain a slender connection between indigenous education and current feminist pedagogical theorizing. As Rayna Green asserts, "given the hostile climate on reservations for discussion of any theory applied to Indians, I doubt feminist theory of any stripe would be well received" (1980, 264). However, these connections between Freirian, feminist, and indigenous pedagogical practices offer a location for unraveling gendered cultural misunderstandings. McKay's affinity with the nonauthoritarian model, Freire's link to a feminist model of power relations and radical liberatory teaching, and feminist interventions into McKay's (and Sarris') silence about gender, converge in the space of the stories, those that Mabel tells Greg, and that I then tell you.

Which is the story I am telling you. In reading about Mabel and Greg, and in trying to understand what might constitute a Native American practice of teaching that is distinct from Western EuroAmerican models, I am working to undo my own culturally bound notions and my own set of teaching practices, a work that intersects at the boundaries of feminism, radical pedagogy, and indigenous education. And in my story, which is about Greg and Mabel, I hope that you too have learned something about your own set of boundaries and understandings, perhaps even reexamined what it is you think might be the qualities and dispositions you, as educator, student, and lifelong learner might develop. "And as the old people say, 'If you can remember the stories, you will be all right. Just remember the stories'" (Silko 1996, 58).

Notes

[1]Vine Deloria, Jr., delineates the history of White-Indian relations and educational practices in "Education and Imperialism" (1982). See also Jorge Noriega's "American Indian Education in the United States: Indoctrination for Subordination to Colonialism" (1992).

[2]See Cajete (1994), Medicine (1982), Wendt (1995), Barnhardt (1991), and Charleston (1994) for careful descriptions of indigenous educational practices.

[3]Paulo Freire (1995), in his groundbreaking work on radical pedagogy, defines and debunks the banking model of education: "Implicit in the banking concept is the assumption of a dichotomy between human beings and the world: a person is merely *in* the world, not *with* the world or with others; the individual is spectator, not re-creator" (56).

[4]In non-indigenous settings, hands-on practice is often detached and decontextualized. For example, my ten-year-old daughter was recently asked to bring in a stalk of celery—the teacher would provide water and food coloring. This lesson in the way a plant gets food has been repeated in every grade since kindergarten. Her teacher identifies this isolated, repetitive demonstration as a "hands-on" experience. My daughter describes it as "boring."

On the other hand, in a recent edition of *The NAPS Journal* from the Native American Preparatory School in New Mexico, Susan Abbott describes a "hands-on" experience: "For example, in Socorro, I had an Adopt-An-Ag program, where students adopted a piece of agriculture and did soil and water testing on it." The difference in scope, quality, and inter-relationships is too clear to comment upon.

[5]Greg Sarris (1993), *Keeping Slug Woman Alive: a Holistic Approach to American Indian Texts*, (81).

[6]In "The Interaction of Culture and Sex Roles in the Schools," Bea Medicine (1982) cautions that there is no "Indian" woman, but multiple roles and cultures among some 200 indigenous groups (29).

[7]See Rayna Green and Vine Deloria, Jr., for complete discussions on the problem of the Pocahontas stereotype.

References

Ambler, M. 1992. Women Leaders in Indian Education. *Tribal College* 3(4): 10–14.

Barnhardt, R. 1991. Higher Education in the Fourth World. *Tribal College* 3(2): 11–23.

Cajete, G. A. 1994. *Look to the Mountain: an Ecology of Indigenous Education.* Durango, CO: Kivaki Press.

Charleston, G. M. 1994. Toward True Native Education: a Treaty of 1992. *Journal of American Indian Education* 33: 8–56.

Deloria, V., Jr. 1982. Education and Imperialism. *Integrateducation* 19(1–2): 58–63.

Freire, P. 1995. *Pedagogy of the Oppressed.* New York: Continuum.

Green, Rayna. 1980. Native American Woman. *Signs* 62:248–67.

_____ . 1992. W*omen in American Indian Society.* New York: Chelsea House.

Maher, F. A., and M. K.Thompson Tetreault 1994. *The FeministClassroom: An Inside Look at How Professors and Students are Transforming Higher Education for a Diverse Society.* New York: Harper Collins.

McDonald, D. 1989. "Stuck in the Horizon:" a Special Report on the Education of Native Americans. *Education Week* (2 August): 1–7.

Medicine, B. 1982. The Interaction of Culture and Sex Roles in the Schools. *Integrateducation* 19(1–2): 28–37.

The NAPS Journal. 1996. Native American Preparatory School, Inc. (Fall).

Noriega, J. 1992. American Indian Education in the United States: Indoctrination for Subordination to Colonialism. In *The State of Native America: Genocide, Colonization, and Resistance,* ed. A. M. Jaimes, 371–402. Boston: South End Press.

Patterson, V. 1995. Evolving Gender Roles in Pomo Society. In *Women and Power in Native North America,* ed. L. F. Klein and L. A. Ackerman. Norman, OK: University of Oklahoma Press.

Sarris, G. 1993. *Keeping Slug Woman Alive: A Holistic Approach to American Indian Texts.* Berkeley: University of California Press.

_____ . 1994. *Mabel McKay: Weaving the Dream.* Berkeley: University of California Press.

Silko, L. M. 1996. *Yellow Woman and a Beauty of the Spirit: Essays on Native American Life Today.* New York: Simon and Schuster.

Swearingen, C. J. 1986. Oral Hermeneutics During the Transition to lLiteracy: The Contemporary debate. *Cultural Anthropology* 1: 139–56.

Wendt, K., comp. 1995. Ahkwesahsne Science & Math Pilot Project. *Pathways: The Ontario Journal of Outdoor Education* 8(3): 14–19.

READING

Sarah Taylor's Granddaughter

Greg Sarris

An excerpt from *Mabel McKay: Weaving the Dream*

The scene was typical. Mabel lecturing, answering questions from an auditorium of students and faculty who wanted to know about her baskets and her life as a medicine woman. As always, she was puzzling, maddening. But that morning I studied her carefully, as if I might see or understand something about her for the first time. She had asked me to write her life story, and after knowing her for over thirty years and with stacks of notes and miles of tape, I still didn't know how.

"You're an Indian doctor," a young woman with bright red hair spoke from the middle of the room. "What do you do for poison oak?"

"Calamine lotion," Mabel answered. She was matter-of-fact. The student sank into her chair.

A distinguished-looking man in gray tweed raised his hand. Mabel looked down from the podium to the front row where he was sitting.

"Mabel, how old were you when you started weaving baskets?"

Mabel adjusted her modish square glasses. "Bout six, I guess."

"When did you reach perfection?"

Mabel didn't understand the professor's question and looked to where I was sitting, behind a display table showing her baskets.

"When did your baskets start to be good?" I ventured. "When did you start selling them?"

Mabel looked back at the man. "Bout nineteen, eighteen maybe."

"Was it your grandmother who taught you this art?"

"It's no such a thing art. It's spirit. My grandma never taught me nothing about the baskets. Only the spirit trained me." She waited for another question from the man, then added, " I only follow my Dream. That's how I learn."

The young woman from the middle of the room shot up again. Clearly, she was perplexed. "I mean, Mabel, do you use herbs and plants to treat people?"

"Sometimes."

"Do you talk to them? Do they talk to you?"

"Well, if I'm going to use them I have to talk, pray."

The woman paused, then asked, "Do plants talk to each other?"

"I suppose."

"What do they say?"

Mabel laughed out loud, then caught her breath and said, "I don't know. Why would I be listening?"

At that point the professor who had sponsored Mabel's visit announced that time was up and that people could look at Mabel's baskets on their way out. He reiterated the fact that Mabel was an Indian with a different world view, reminding the audience of her story earlier about meeting the Kashaya Pomo medicine woman Essie Parrish in Dream twenty years before she met her in person. The professor, an earnest man in his mid-forties, turned to Mabel. "You must have recognized Essie Parrish when you first saw her in person, didn't you, Mabel?"

Mabel, who was fussing to detach the microphone from her neck, looked and said, "Yes, but she cut her hair a little."

There it was. Quintessential Mabel. Nothing new. Same stories and questions. Same answers. This small Indian woman, over eighty years old, with coifed black hair and modish glasses, this little Indian woman in a mauve-colored summer dress adorned on the shoulder with a corsage of imitation African violets, had turned a Stanford auditorium upside down. No one cracked her.

On the way back to the Rumsey Reservation that day, I kept wondering how I was going to write about Mabel's life. She was baffling, even for me. Certainly the facts of her life were interesting and warranted a story. World-renowned Pomo basketmaker with permanent collections in the Smithsonian and countless other museums. The last Dreamer and sucking doctor among the Pomo peoples. The last living member of the Long Valley Cache Creek Pomo tribe. The astute interlocutor famous for her uncanny talk that left people's minds spinning. The facts were easy. The life was not.

Chapter 7

JANE ROLAND MARTIN

Women, Schools, and Cultural Wealth

Introduction

In 1980, a year's fellowship from the Bunting Institute of Radcliffe College to do basic research on women and education radically changed the direction of the work I had been doing in the philosophy of education since earning my Ph.D. in 1961. The first stage of what I now think of as my life's work began with my discovery that when one lifts the veil of ignorance and sees women as both the subjects and objects of educational thought, not only the academic discipline of the philosophy of education but also what may be called our culture's educational ideology are revealed as deeply flawed. I examined this insight in *Reclaiming a Conversation: The Ideal of the Educated Woman* (1985).[1]

The second stage of my post-1980 research was devoted to answering a question that *Reclaiming a Conversation* left unanswered. In the concluding chapter of that book I wrote that we need to rethink the education of both sexes in a way that honors both the productive and the reproductive processes of society. In *The Schoolhome: Rethinking Schools for Changing Families* (1992),[2] I outlined the solution I developed over a period of years to the problem of how schools can and should give the reproductive processes of society their due.

As *Reclaiming a Conversation* left a key question open, so did *The Schoolhome*. What I have begun to see as a third stage of my ongoing research program in the

Jane Roland Martin

philosophy of education began as an attempt to solve the problem of how school can shoulder and share some of home's traditional educational tasks without becoming hopelessly overburdened. Making explicit the themes of "cultural wealth" and "multiple educational agency" that were implicit in *The Schoolhome,* in this chapter I will sketch in the new perspective on education that I am even now in the process of developing.[3]

Part I: Bringing Women into Educational Thought

The question on my mind when I began my study of women and education in 1980 was the very straightforward one: What is the place of women in educational thought? Within a matter of weeks I had my answer. Whether one was thinking of women as the subjects or the objects of educational thought, for all intents and purposes we had no place at all: as subjects, women's philosophical works on education were ignored; as objects, works by women and men about women's education and their role as educators of the young were largely neglected. Moreover, the very definition of education and the educational realm adopted implicitly by the standard texts in philosophy of education, and made explicit by contemporary analytic philosophers of education, excludes women.

Had I embarked on this research project ten or fifteen years earlier than I in fact did, I might well have abandoned the effort then and there. But by 1980 a flourishing body of new scholarship on women had alerted me to the fact that at least two of the greatest educational thinkers in the history of the West—Plato and Rousseau—had discussed women's education in major treatises. It also led me to suspect that, across the centuries, women as well as men had put forward well-developed theories of education. I thus realized that the problem I discerned was not that in three thousand years of Western educational thought nothing important had ever been said by or about women. Rather, the dominant texts in the field had disregarded works written by women while allowing the subject of female education to drop out of the picture altogether.

Launching my study of women and education at a time when the exclusion of women's lives, experiences, and achievements from the theories and narratives of psychology, history, literature, and critical studies of the fine arts had already been documented, I was prepared for the discovery of our absence from the texts and anthologies of educational philosophy. My subsequent findings of androcentric bias in the prevailing analyses and interpretations of the philosophy of education were not unexpected either. What I did not foresee at the outset was that my research question would soon shift from the somewhat wistful, "Where are the women?" to the theoretically far more interesting, "What happens to educational thought when women are brought into it?"

Recovering Rousseau's Fundamental Insight

When in 1980 I sat down to write a paper about Rousseau, little did I dream that it would be a case study of the transformative potential of scholarship on women (Martin 1981b). As I pored over his great pedagogical novel, *Émile,* and immersed myself in feminist commentaries on Rousseau's recommendations regarding the education of the girl Sophie, I began to understand just how deeply dependent on his philosophy of girls' education was Rousseau's philosophy of boys' education. Then, sitting at my desk one afternoon, I was electrified by the thought that when Sophie is brought into the equation, the standard interpretation of Rousseau's philosophy of education is proven wrong.

Here then was my first inkling that once one acknowledges the presence of girls and women in the educational landscape one begins to see just how incomplete and, indeed, ill-judged are the academy's standard renderings of educational history and philosophy. This hypothesis was confirmed a short while later when I discovered that I had only to take the education of women seriously for the concept of the educated person formulated by the highly respected British philosopher R. S. Peters to become suspect (Martin 1981c). My conjecture about the transformative potential of the study of the education of girls and women gained additional support when, upon examining the accepted philosophical analyses of teaching, of liberal education, and of education itself, I found that they would also have to be reconsidered (Martin 1982).

With hindsight, the reason why the study of women has profound consequences for educational thought is not difficult to discern. In fact, however, it took me some time to realize that, because of the way the culture constructs gender, we women carry a lot of "baggage." By this I mean that, in the past, Western culture attributed to us—and quite possibly still does attribute to us—the body of knowledge, the network of skills, and the various sets of tasks, duties, and traits that the culture associates with the institutions of home and family and with the "reproductive processes"[4] of society that are housed therein. So that when women go unseen in the educational landscape, this constellation of knowledge, skills, and activities is also rendered invisible.

When women are missing from educational thought, philosophical theories and analyses of education can ignore the "cultural wealth"[5] that society associates with us. The disappearance from view of "the world of the private home," to use Virginia Woolf's apt phrase (Woolf 1938, 78), and the cultural wealth it has traditionally preserved and transmitted, is very serious. Perhaps its worst consequence is that it encourages theorists to mistake one of education's functions for education itself.

Despite his evident misogyny—or possibly because of it—Rousseau is the philosopher who draws attention to this error of reducing education's social role to one of its parts. He may not have been the first to see the mistake, but he is the one who so clearly spelled out the need for a philosophy of education that encompasses life in the world of the private home as well as in the public world of politics and the professions. He did so because he pictured himself in conversation with Plato: "Read Plato's *Republic.* It is not at all a political work, as think those who judge books only by their titles. It is the most beautiful educational treatise ever written" (Rousseau 1762/1979, 40). In Rousseau's eyes, Plato's beautiful treatise had only one flaw: "That noble genius had planned everything, foreseen everything," he says in *Émile*, yet he forgot that it is "the good son, the good husband, and the good father who make the good citizen" (Rousseau 1762/1979, 362).

As is well known, in *The Republic* Plato has Socrates perform an experiment in imagination. Thinking away existing conditions, he and his friends then construct the "Just State." In Book V of *The Republic*, Socrates then argues that women as well as men can be rulers of the "Just State" and, on the grounds that identical roles require identical education, he makes the radical proposal that the female guardians of the state be given the same education as their male counterparts, indeed that the two sexes be educated together (Plato 1974, 113–19). In Book V of *Émile*, Rousseau embraced *The Republic*'s assumption that the function of education is to prepare people to carry out their predestined societal roles, but he replaced the Platonic vision of a society in which men and women rule together for the common good with one in which the two sexes are assigned very different tasks and functions. Thus, the education Rousseau designed for the boy Émile was intended to produce the type of citizen described in Rousseau's, *The Social Contract:* a rational self-governing individual whose judgments are objective and whose beliefs are formed independently of others. The education he designed for the girl Sophie, on the other hand, was intended to produce a traditional wife/mother: a woman who would bear and raise many children, govern her husband's household, oversee his garden, act as his hostess, care for his reputation, and, above all, please him.

To understand fully Rousseau's reasons for prescribing for Sophie the education he did, one needs to know that in *Émile V* hr was addressing what he took to be two fundamental mistakes contained in *The Republic* V. In the latter, Plato abolished the institutions of private marriage, home, family, and child rearing for the guardians of the Just State. There he also argued that sex—or gender, as we would now say—is a difference that makes no difference in determining whether a person is suited by nature to rule, and hence makes no difference in determining a person's education. Against Plato, Rousseau maintained that private marriage, home, family, and child-rearing are essential ingredients of the ideal state and that the activities and tasks associated with these belong to women. Treating gender as the difference that makes all the difference, Rousseau divided everything according to sex: societal tasks, the knowledge and skill he considered essential to their performance, and the personal qualities and traits of character he associated with them.

Émile was published in 1762. In 1792 British feminist theorist Mary Wollstonecraft entered the conversation.[6] Just as Rousseau perceived what was missing in Plato's philosophy of education, Wollstonecraft pointed to the flaw in Rousseau's. Rejecting Rousseau's account of women's nature and education, in *A Vindication of the Rights of Woman* she argued that Sophie's education does not prepare her to be rational or self-governing, characteristics she believed were essential for a good wife and mother.

Wollstonecraft's critique of Sophie's education and character has been echoed throughout history by many of those most concerned with the education of women. Yet compelling as it was—and still is—her appropriation for her daughters of the educational goals Rousseau posited for Émile is based on the questionable assumption that the educational ideal that he held up for Émile is the proper and complete one for both sexes.

In fact, although Rousseau's Sophie is passive and full of guile, she is also the one with the patience, gentleness, zeal, and affection necessary for raising children. Furthermore, she is the one with the tenderness and care "required to maintain the union of the whole family" (Rousseau 1762/1979, 361) and the one who is willing and able to make the lives of her loved ones agreeable and sweet (Rousseau 1762/1979, 365).

Rousseau's fundamental insight in *Émile* was that the plausibility of Émile's education is due to the existence of Sophie and the fact that Émile and Sophie are united in partnership. This insight is lost to view when Sophie disappears from the history of educational thought, for it is in Book V of *Émile* that Rousseau made clear the crucial role she is to play in Émile's life and in the larger society. In Rousseau's philosophy, Sophie has full responsibility for carrying out the reproductive processes of child rearing and maintaining home and family for Émile, and is to be educated in the qualities necessary for doing so. Equally important, the man Émile, even when educated according to plan, is not and cannot be a complete moral person. Only in partnership, said Rousseau, can Sophie and Émile be completely moral, and, even then, neither individual alone is a complete moral person; rather, the *union* of Sophie and Émile constitutes a complete moral entity.

Toward a Gender-Sensitive Philosophy of Education

It is as easy for today's readers of *Émile* to overlook Sophie's virtues and be dazzled by Émile's as it was for Wollstonecraft, for Rousseau tended to concentrate on what she correctly diagnosed as Sophie's vices. However, once the educations of Sophie and Émile are considered in relation to that of Plato's guardians, one can see just how problematic it is to extend to women the educational ideal Rousseau held up for males without first transforming it. Rousseau modeled the ideal guiding Émile's education on Plato's ideal for the guardians of his Just State. Granted, Plato himself extended this ideal to both sexes, but in the Just State, whatever reproductive processes the guardians require—for example, child rearing—will be carried on by others. It is at least arguable, therefore, that Plato's guardians do not need to possess Sophie's virtues—although in the final analysis this argument fails to convince (Martin 1985).

Unlike most commentators on Plato, Rousseau read Book V of *The Republic* carefully and took its social programs concerning women, children, and the family seriously. He understood that Plato's philosophy of education is incomplete in that it specifies the education of those responsible for defending and ruling the state but is silent about the education of those who would carry out society's reproductive processes. Rousseau knew that, having rejected Plato's social program, he could not embrace Plato's philosophy of education without modifying it significantly; he realized he would have to make sure that in his own philosophy someone was educated to perform the tasks and functions to be carried on in Émile's home. In principle, Rousseau could have chosen Émile for this role or he could have rejected a sex-based division of labor altogether. Not surprisingly, however, he chose Sophie for it. Having done so, and having designed Sophie's education accordingly, he felt free to retain for Émile the educational ideal Plato held up for his male and female guardians. Just as Plato had removed all responsibility for carrying on the reproductive processes of society from the guardians' lives, so Rousseau removed it from Émile's.

One need not embrace Sophie and the gender-based division of labor in which her education is grounded in order to benefit from Rousseau's conversation with Plato. The main lesson I learned from my readings of *Émile* is that unless men and women want to drop out of their lives responsibility for society's reproductive processes, they must acknowledge that the educational ideal Plato holds up for his guardians of both sexes is as incomplete as the one Rousseau holds up for Émile. I hasten to add that recognition of Rousseau's insight does not entail an endorsement of his prescriptions for a patriarchal society in which only males can be citizens or for a patriarchal family in which wives must endure their husbands' wrongs without complaining. It does not require one to support a two-track educational system and a division of labor based on sex or gender. It does, however, require that we take Sophie's virtues seriously and seek ways of incorporating them into the ideals we develop to guide the education of the women and men who should today be sharing responsibility for the reproductive processes of society.

Fortunately, it is not necessary to choose between two flawed educational ideals: one bound explicitly to gender, as Rousseau's is; the other bound implicitly to gender, as Plato's is. Another possibility is open to us: joining Rousseau's insight that traits and gender are connected to Plato's insight that roles and gender are not fixed by nature, we can opt for a gender-sensitive ideal. Taking gender into account when it makes a difference and ignoring it when it does not, such an ideal allows us to build—into curricula, instructional methods, and learning environments—ways of dealing with trait genderization and with the many and various other gender-related phenomena that impinge on education today.

In acknowledging the difference of sex without making us prisoners of gender, a gender-sensitive ideal allows one to continue the Platonic project of building into the education of girls and women traits genderized in favor of boys and men; or, to put it more accurately in relation to our own society, genderized in favor of White, middle-class males. It also enables us to undertake the new and even more revolutionary project of building into everyone's education traits genderized in favor of females. It must be understood that Sophie's virtues tend to be evaluated positively in females, but negatively in males.

We should, then, anticipate that boys and men will encounter problems in acquiring them, just as girls and women encounter problems acquiring Émile's virtues. We should also anticipate problems in their being incorporated into an ideal guiding education, for the very fact that they are Sophie's virtues will very likely make them suspect in the eyes of many. I say "incorporated" rather than "included" because I believe that Sophie's virtues cannot simply be "added on" to Émile's. On the contrary, in the process of expanding our governing educational ideal, both Sophie's and Émile's virtues will be transformed (cf. Martin 1992, 108ff.). Be this as it may, if our philosophy of education is to be complete, it must take seriously those virtues of Sophie that are related to the successful performance of the reproductive processes of society. Indeed, it must be acknowledged that if men and women are to be complete people, regardless of their gender, they must acquire Sophie's virtues as well as Émile's—or some appropriate transformation thereof.

The Education-Gender System

Falsely identifying preparation for participation in the productive processes of society—or, as I now prefer to say, for life in the so-called public world of work, politics, and the professions—as the one and only task of education instead of merely one of education's tasks, educational philosophers have ended up defining their field of study in relation to the "sphere" of society that has traditionally been considered men's preserve. Needless to say, they have done this without making their ideological commitments explicit; indeed, for the most part without even being aware that they have ideological commitments. But this is only half the story, for the phrase "educational thought" is fundamentally ambiguous. Although I did not immediately realize this, after 1980 my research program underwent two shifts of question, not one. Initially there was the move to the question of how my research on women affected educational thought in the narrow, academic sense of the term. Eventually, however, my question became, "When women are brought into educational thought and the workings of gender are closely examined, what happens to the culture's fundamental, albeit tacit, assumptions about education? How are they affected?"

Although the two senses of "educational thought" are closely related, they need to be distinguished if only because a philosopher can so easily misread the culture.

My first intimation that the academic theories and analyses I had been criticizing from a feminist perspective might not be mere figments of a philosophical imagination, but reconstructions of fundamental cultural assumptions, came when in 1982 I read Richard Rodriguez's educational autobiography, *Hunger of Memory*. Writing as a layman about his own educational journey, Rodriguez presented a picture of what it was to become an educated person in the United States that uncannily matched Anglo-American philosophy of education's accepted academic rendering. Rodriguez's teachers aimed exclusively at preparing him for membership in the public world. In fact, the education he described did not merely overlook the knowledge and skills, attitudes and values, virtues and other dispositions required for life in private homes and families; it actively encouraged him to turn his back on that other "world."

Absorbed as I still was in documenting the transformational potential of the study of women in relation to the paradigms of the academy, I filed away for later use the idea that my own research might also shed light on the culture's educational ideology. It was not long, however, before my work began focusing directly on that phenomenon.

My change in focus after completing *Reclaiming a Conversation* was occasioned by my growing interest in the relationship between school and home. This preoccupation was fueled in the first place by my discovery that although the eighteenth-century Swiss educational thinker Johann Friedrich Pestalozzi had extolled the educational skills and talents of mothers, the texts and anthologies in my field ignored this portion of his work. However, I had also become increasingly concerned about the violence in U.S. society and its effects on the children: vast numbers of children of both sexes and of all classes and races in the United States were—and still are—daily experiencing violence in just about every aspect of their lives and more and more of them were—and still are—themselves behaving violently at earlier and earlier ages. As if this were not bad enough, no one in positions of responsibility seemed to see the violence as an educational issue—not philosophers, not statesmen, not politicians, not even school officials. Agreeing with Pestalozzi that home has a curriculum and that mothers are its main teachers, I was quite bewildered by the silences on the subject. Becoming daily more certain that the great changes in the nature and structure of the private home and family that were then taking place in the United States had serious implications for education, I wondered why the nation itself was ignoring the issue.

As an analytic philosopher I was accustomed to reading and critiquing the texts of the academy but I soon discovered that when the subject was school and home, this established procedure was of little use. Scholars had long ago buried Pestalozzi's praise of mothers as teachers, John Dewey's insights into home's educative role, and Maria Montessori's idea of school as a surrogate home. Nor had my contemporaries produced any theories of their own on these subjects. If I wanted to understand why even education's critics and reformers behaved as if neither the violence in society nor the social transformation of home and family was any of their business, I would have to study the culture's patterns of thought about education rather than the writings of scholars.

Ultimately this exercise in cultural archaeology led to the unearthing of a complex set of tacit cultural assumptions about education; as it happens, a set riddled with contradictions. For example—and I should make it clear that I am speaking now primarily, although not exclusively, about the United States—the culture takes it for granted that home and school are partners in the education of a nation's youth. How do I know this? Only by attributing this implicit belief to the culture can one explain the dominant conception of schooling as preparation for membership in the public world of work, politics, and the professions. For this narrow view of school only makes sense in relation to the corresponding assumption that home has a domestic curriculum that equips children for life in the world of the private home.[7] Yet as even the briefest survey of English usage shows, the very same culture that presupposes home's educational contributions denies home's status as an educator. From a linguistic standpoint, mothers do not "teach" their children: they *rear* them, they *raise* them, they *foster* their growth, they *nurture* their development. In the same spirit, home and family are said to *socialize,* not "educate," children. Moreover, the term "curriculum" is not normally used in relation to the private home; indeed, the very idea that home has a curriculum is considered to be an absurdity.

In both thought and action, the culture posits a division of educational labor between home and school while at the very same time denying that home performs such work. In other words, the culture simultaneously considers home an educator of its young and refuses home that designation. If one keeps the women in our educational landscape in view, one can see that the culture is now operating according to an outdated and incredibly gendered ideology of education. Indeed, Western culture's dominant educational practices and ideology of education represent what may be called an "education-gender system." Implicitly dividing social reality into the world of the private home and the world of work, commerce, politics, and the professions, just about all of us—parents, politicians, school teachers and administrators, and just plain citizens—take it for granted that the function of education is to transform children who have heretofore lived their lives in the one place into members of the other. Assuming that the private home is a natural institution and that, accordingly, membership in it is a given rather than something one must achieve, we see no reason to prepare people to carry out the tasks and activities associated with it. Perceiving the public world as a human creation and membership in it as something at which one can succeed or fail and therefore as problematic, we make the business of education preparation for carrying out the tasks and activities associated with it.

Now this in itself does not make an educational system gendered. That quality is conferred on our system by the fact that, culturally speaking, the two worlds are gender-coded. Given that the one is considered men's domain and the other is considered women's, and that education's ideology and practices are predicated on this dichotomy, gender becomes a basic dimension of the whole system.

To illustrate: The assumption we all make that becoming educated is a process of acquiring new ways of thinking, feeling, and acting might appear to be gender-neutral. Yet it is, in fact, gender-bound and biased. If the educational system is to be "rational," these new ways must be functional—or at least they must be thought to be functional—in relation to life in the public world. But this, in turn, is to say that they must be functional in a world that, historically speaking, was a male preserve and to this day reflects this fact. Furthermore, there is no need at all for the newly acquired ways of thinking, feeling, and acting to be—or to be considered—functional in relation to the world of the private home, a world whose inhabitants are presumed to be female. On the contrary, since these two worlds are culturally represented as polar opposites, there is no way that preparation for life in the one could foster ways of thinking, feeling, and acting that are functional in the other.

Woolf said in *Three Guineas* that life in the world across the bridge from the private home is competitive and that the people there must be pugnacious and possessive in order to succeed. We in the West signify our agreement with her by assuming that the qualities or traits of love, nurturance, and the 3Cs of care, concern, and connection that are culturally associated with the private home—and, of course, with women—run counter to education's raison d'être. Indeed, in the United States we take these to be such obstacles to the achievement of the objective of preparing children for life in the public world that we make one of primary school's main tasks that of casting off the attitudes and values, the patterns of thought and action associated with home, women, and domesticity.

It is surely no accident that the reports on the condition of American education published in the 1980s gave home the silent treatment. Viewing children as travelers to the public world, they saw school as the place children stop en route in order to acquire the knowledge, skills, attitudes, and values that they presumably will need when they reach their destination—a kind of wayside inn. Once children enter school they do not go home again in this unexamined scenario; not ever, not even as adults. The authors of these volumes totally forgot that life is lived in both places and so, at least in the United States, do almost all of education's theorists and practitioners, critics, and reformers.

It is downright irrational to persist in assigning school a function that is defined in relation to, and relies on, home's educational agency while at the same time denying the existence of that very agency. It is also the height of folly to assign what we take to be our one and only acknowledged educational agent the single task of preparing children for life in the public sphere, although even as adults they will continue to dwell in private homes. In addition, in view of the great changes home has undergone in recent decades and of the importance to both the individual and society of the "cultural wealth" that home has been charged with transmitting, to equate education with schooling yet continue to endorse a function for school that is premised on home's carrying out an opposite but equally important function, is shortsighted in the extreme.

The fact is that the breakdown in the latter part of this century of Western culture's patriarchal home and family and of the old gender-based division of labor makes obsolete the old gendered definition of school's function. The social system that denied women entry into the world of work, politics, and professions had numerous problems, not the least of which was the subordination of women. Nonetheless, if one accepted its premises, it provided a plausible rationale for the way home and school divided up their educational responsibilities. Except in the very poorest families, mothers stayed home to do, and to teach their daughters to stay home and do, the domestic work that boys in school relied on as they mastered the knowledge, skills, attitudes, and values required by society's economic and political work; work whose execution the fathers and uncles who actually engaged in these occupations counted on. Now things have changed. Briefly put, the people culturally assigned responsibility for preserving and transmitting the domestic portion of our cultural wealth are often too busy to do this job well. Today, girls accompany boys to school and women from all walks of life enter the public world.

If society's domestic work was limited to what goes by the name of "housework," it might not matter that because of the historic changes in home, family, and gender roles the cultural wealth in home's keep is now at risk. But the domestic work to which I refer simultaneously infuses domestic environments with Sophie's virtues—the 3Cs of care, concern, and connection to others—and instructs the next generation in them. Were there a third sex that could be prevailed upon to transmit what psychologist Carol Gilligan has called the ethic of care (Gilligan 1982; cf Noddings 1984), it might not be so misguided of us to allow school to persist in its old function. But unless one wants to count the electronic media as such, and I see no grounds for doing so, there is none in the offing.

Part II: Bringing Domesticity into School and World

At the turn of this century—in 1899, to be exact—John Dewey started off a series of lectures in Chicago with a description of the changes in American society wrought by the Industrial Revolution. "It is radical conditions which have changed, and only an equally radical change in education suffices," he said (Dewey 1956, 12). One of those radical conditions was the removal of manufacture from the household into factories and shops. It was Dewey's genius to see that the work that in the relatively recent past had been done at home had genuine educational benefits and to perceive that these had become endangered. It was his great insight that some other educational agent could and should take over what had previously been one of home's responsibilities.

I draw attention to Dewey's analysis because in the United States at the turn of the twenty-first century, home and family have once more been transformed. The critical factor now is the removal of parents from the household. With many homes headed by a single parent, usually a mother, and most families in need of two salaries just to maintain a home, for many hours each day there is simply no one at home. Of course, if nothing more were at stake than a child's misgivings at being home alone or a mother's exhaustion after working a double shift, educators might be justified in ignoring our changed reality.[8] But, to put it starkly, there is now a great *domestic vacuum* in the lives of children—children from all walks of life. The question is, then: "What radical changes in school will suffice?"

A Moral Equivalent of Home: the Schoolhome

In the United States as in other industrialized societies, home has traditionally been the agency responsible for turning infants who "are barely human and utterly unsocialized," into "full-fledged members of the culture" (Ortner 1974, 77–78, 79–80). Sherry Ortner's words bring to mind the "Wild Boy" of Aveyron. Until he emerged from the woods, Victor had no exposure to the curriculum that inducts our young into human culture; not even to wearing clothes, eating food other than nuts and potatoes, hearing sounds, sleeping in a bed, distinguishing between hot and cold, walking rather than running (Lane 1979). He had to be taught the things that people other than parents of the very young and teachers of differently abled children assume human beings instinctively know.

Shattering the illusion that what is called "second nature" is innate, Victor's case dramatically illustrates that what we adults learned at home as young children is far more basic than the school studies we call our basics. We consider reading, writing, and arithmetic essential—hence basic—components of education because of their roles in preparing young people for membership in the public world; specifically, for enabling them to be citizens in a democracy and economically self-sufficient individuals. In addition, we take the 3Rs to be fundamental because of the part they play in initiating our young into history, literature, philosophy, and the arts—"high" culture or Culture with a capital "C." Bring home's educational role into the picture, however, and one realizes that these three goals—achieving economic viability, becoming a good citizen, and acquiring high culture—only make sense for people who have already learned the basic mores of society.

Now there are some today who discern the great domestic vacuum in children's lives, blame it on women, and would have us turn back the clock to a presumed golden age when mothers stayed home and took care of their young. These social analysts are simply oblivious to the present demands of economic necessity. They are also loath to acknowledge that it is not women's exodus from the private home each day that creates a vacuum in our children's lives. It is the exodus of *both* sexes. Had men not left the house when the Industrial Revolution removed work from the home—or had fathers not continued to leave the house each morning after their children were born—women's departure would not have the ramifications for children that it does.

The question is not, "Whom can we blame?" It is, "What are we as a nation, a culture, a society going to do about our children? In a widely read essay entitled "A Moral Equivalent of War" written in 1910, William James introduced the concept of moral equivalency into our language. Given the great domestic vacuum in the United States today, the concept of *a moral equivalent of home* is as germane as James's moral equivalent of war ever was. Indeed, of the many things we can and should do for our children, perhaps the most important is to establish a moral equivalent of home for them.

To avoid misunderstanding, let me say that I am *not* proposing that home be abolished. When James spoke of a moral equivalent of war, he had in mind a substitute for war that would preserve those martial virtues that he considered the "higher" aspects of militarism (James 1910/1970). When I speak of a moral equivalent of home, I have in mind the *sharing of responsibility* for those educative functions of home that are now at risk of extinction. Who or what will do the sharing? In accordance with Dewey's insight and in light of school's universality, its ubiquitousness, and its claims on a child's time, there is no institution so appropriate for this task as school.

Thinking of school as a special kind of production site—a factory that turns out workers for the nation's public and private sectors—government officials, business leaders, granting agencies, and educational administrators focus today on standards. In an age when the lives of all too many children bring to mind Dickens' novels, it is perhaps to be expected that young children in school are pictured as raw material, teachers as workers who process their students before sending them on to the next station on the assembly line, and curriculum as the machinery that over the span of twelve or so years forges the nation's young into marketable products. However, this conception of schooling totally ignores the needs and conditions of children, their parents, and the nation itself at the end of the twentieth century.

At the very least, children need to love and be loved. They need to feel safe and secure and at ease with themselves and others. They need to experience intimacy and affection. They need to be perceived as unique individuals and to be treated as such. The factory model of schooling presupposes that such conditions have already been met when children arrive in school; that school's raw materials—the children—have, so to speak, been "preprocessed." Resting on the unspoken assumption that home is school's partner in the educational process, the model takes it for granted that it is home's job to fulfill these basic needs. Thus, the production line picture derives its plausibility from the premise that school does not need to be a loving place, the classroom does not need to have an affectionate atmosphere, and teachers do not need to treasure the individuality of students because school's silent partner will take care of all this.

One consequence of the great domestic vacuum that exists in children's lives today is that we can no longer depend on home to do the preprocessing. Speaking generally, it cannot be counted on to have the time or the energy to transmit the love; the 3Cs of care, concern, and connection; and the knowledge, skills, attitudes, and values that enable each individual born into this society to become a member of culture in the broadest sense of that term. If for no other reason, then, the factory model of schooling is untenable. To be sure, one can irrationally cling to it. Insisting that school's raw materials are so defective that they cannot possibly be turned into acceptable end products, one can blame and penalize the victims of home's latest transformation instead of insisting that school respond to their plight. The nation's children will be far better served, however, if we change our conception of school. The nation also stands to gain from a new idea of school, for its continued well-being ultimately depends on the well-being of the next generation and of its successors.

The recent transformation of home and family belies the very model of schooling that our political and educational leaders tacitly accept. A conception of school as a moral equivalent of home is, on the other hand, as responsive to end of twentieth-century conditions as the factory model is insensible to them. Thus, I propose that we as a nation set ourselves the goal of turning our school*houses* into school*homes*.

Instead of focusing our gaze on abstract norms, standardized tests, generalized rates of success, and uniform outcomes, the idea of the *Schoolhome* directs action to actual educational practice. Of course a schoolhome will teach the 3Rs. But it will give equal emphasis to the 3Cs of care, concern, and connection—not by designating formal courses in these but by being a domestic environment characterized by safety, security, nurturance, and love. In a schoolhome, classroom climate, school routines and rituals, teachers' modes of teaching, and children's ways of learning are all guided by a spirit of family-like affection. And so is the relationship between teacher and student, and between the students themselves. Of course the inhabitants of a schoolhome will learn science and literature, history and math. But they will also learn to make domesticity their business. Feeling that they belong in the schoolhome and, at the same time, that the Schoolhome belongs to them, the children will take pride in their physical environment while happily contributing their own labor to its upkeep. Perhaps even more important, with their teachers' help, the pupils in a schoolhome will countenance no violence, be it corporal punishment or teacher sarcasm, the bullying of one child by others or the terrorization of an entire class, or the use of hostile language about whole races or the denigration of one sex.

Now I realize that America's private homes never were idyllic sanctuaries, and that at present they, like our streets, are sites of violence. When I propose that our schools be home-like, however, I have in mind ideal, not dysfunctional, homes. Thus, in recommending that school be a moral equivalent of home, I assume a home that is warm and loving, and neither physically nor psychologically abusive; and a family that believes in and strives for the equality of the sexes.

Yet is home an appropriate metaphor for school in a nation whose population is as diverse as ours? It is, *provided* we recognize that one century after Dewey's Chicago lecture the question has become, "How can we create a moral equivalent of home in which children of *all* races, classes, and ethnicities feel at home?"

A New Curricular Paradigm

To make all our children feel at home in school, it is not enough to turn our schoolhouses into safe and loving places. The school curriculum must also be transformed. Those today who criticize this country's schools and make recommendations for their improvement pay little attention to the changed composition of the nation's population. I call them "Restorationists" because, seemingly impervious to the pressing need our nation now has for a new inclusionary curriculum that will serve all our children, they want to restore the old outmoded one. Looking back with longing at the curriculum of their youth, they would reinstate a course of study designed for an earlier age and a different people.

It scarcely needs saying that a more inclusive curriculum is not necessarily a better one. Yet in a society in the process of changing color, as the United States is, can courses in African philosophy be considered frivolous? In a nation with a history of slavery and a continuing record of racial division and inequality, are the study of Black history and literature and the inclusion of slave narratives on the reading lists of American history and literature courses the irrelevancies they are described as? In a land in which rape is rampant, the victims of child sexual abuse are most often girls, and women are subjected to sexual harassment at home, at school, and at work, is it sensible to say that courses that represent and analyze women's history, lives, and experiences are parochial and take too subjective a point of view? If school is to make all U.S. children feel at home in both school and society, curriculum space must be reserved for the works, experiences, and societal practices of women as well as men, poor people as well as the middle classes, and ethnic, racial, and other minorities. But even more than this is required.

Protesting a school curriculum very like that which the Restorationists would piece back together—one whose subjects of study represent abstract bodies of knowledge divorced from the activities of everyday life—Dewey called upon us to educate "the whole child." I, in turn, ask that we educate *all* our children in our *whole* heritage so that they will learn to live in the world together.[9] Because that whole heritage includes ways of living as well as forms of knowing, societal activities and practices as well as literary and artistic achievement, we need more than a curriculum that honors diversity. We need a new curricular paradigm: one that does not ignore the disciplines of knowledge but reveals their proper place in the general scheme of things as just one part of a person's education; one that integrates thought and action, reason and emotion, education and life; one that does not divorce persons from their social and natural contexts; one that embraces individual autonomy as but one of many values (cf Martin 1985).

Unfortunately, even when this nation's heritage is defined multiculturally, it is all too easy for school to instruct children *about* it without ever teaching them *to be* active and constructive participants in living—let alone how to make the world a better place for themselves and their progeny. This is especially so when school's business is thought to be the development of children's minds, not their bodies; their thinking and reasoning skills, not their emotional capacities or active propensities. Yet a nation that cannot count on home to perform its traditional educative functions dare not settle for so narrow a definition of school's tasks.

I need hardly say that the vision of a school curriculum I am putting forward stands in stark contrast to that of the Restorationists. The one they advocate consists of the standard disciplines of knowledge—the natural sciences, the social and behavioral sciences, the humanities—along with the 3Rs, the tools considered essential to learning them. But to base the curriculum of our nation's schools on these studies is quite simply to teach our young *about* life: to turn out observers *of* it, not participants *in* it.

We need to ask ourselves if the United States at the turn of the twenty-first century is well served by a population of onlookers. In the best of cases, education for spectatorship teaches students to lead divided lives. Instructing them to apply their intelligence in observing the world, it teaches them by default, if not design, to be unthinking doers. Mindless imitation is, however, the easiest path for someone to follow who has not been trained to bring intelligence to bear on living. In the worst of cases, then, an education for spectatorship consigns students to the nasty, brutish, and short life that the philosopher Thomas Hobbes long ago attributed to the state of nature.

It is sheer folly to expect our young to live and work together at home and in the world if they have never, ever learned to do so. Yet the Restorationists would devote little or no curriculum space to the enormous range of ways of acting and forms of living that the young of any nation need to learn. In the schoolhome, mind and body, thought and action, reason and emotion are all educated. Furthermore, if the occupations that children pursue there are well-chosen, they will integrate these elements in such a way that they in turn can be integrated into the lives those young people lead both in school and in the world.

When school is a surrogate home, children of all ages and both sexes not only engage in the domestic activities that ground their everyday lives there—the planning, cooking, and serving of meals or the cleaning, maintaining, and repairing of the physical plant. They participate in one or more of the integrative forms of life that stands at the very center of the curriculum.

Let me briefly list the integrative potential of two such activities—theater and newspaper. To begin with, theater and newspaper spin webs of theoretical knowledge in which students can be "caught." One thinks immediately of language, literature, and social studies, but these forms of living also give rise to serious ethical and legal questions. Moreover, for those who engage in them, mathematical, scientific, and technical knowledge looms large. Furthermore, besides spinning webs of knowledge, however, theater and newspaper spin webs of skills such as reading, writing, speaking, listening, drawing, designing, and building. In so doing, they connect mind and body, thought and action. By reaching out to every human emotion, they also join both head and hand to heart.

The webs of knowledge and skill that theater and newspaper weave, and the integration of thought and action, reason and emotion that they effect might in themselves justify placing these activities at the center of curriculum. Their integrative claims are enhanced, however, by the fact that social interdependence is built into them from the start. Through the demands of the shared task as well as the realization that everyone's efforts not only count but are vitally important, participants become bonded to one another. These two activities have the added integrative advantage that their products—the plays performed, the newspapers published—can be designed to speak to everyone's experience and to be seen or read by everyone. Tying the inhabitants together with invisible threads spun by shared emotions that derive from common experiences, they can thus weave young people of different races, classes, ethnicities, physical abilities, and sexual orientations into their own web of connection.

Since there are numerous activities that can be integrative in these several different ways, the decision as to which ones to make the linchpins of any particular schoolhome curriculum must, I think, be based on local considerations, not the least of which are the interests and talents of both the teaching staff and the students. This, of course, means that as local conditions change, so perhaps will the choice of multiple integrative activities.

I also want to stress that although theater and newspaper—or, for that matter, farming and building a historical museum—easily lend themselves to vocationalism and professionalism, these are *not* the interests that the schoolhome represents. Its concern is that the children in its care receive an education for living and working together in the world. Thus, the schoolhome is *not* a training ground for actors, architects, or journalists. Its students put on plays, raise crops, and put out newspapers *not* to win competitions or add to their resumes. The best student actor by Broadway or Hollywood standards does *not* necessarily play the lead; the best feature writer or cartoonist does *not* necessarily get published. Rather, the schoolhome is a moral equivalent of home, where this nation's children can develop into constructive, contributing members of culture and society, into individuals who want to live in a world composed of people very different from themselves and who have practiced doing so. As I envision it, the schoolhome is also a place that possesses and projects a larger point of view: that of this nation itself as a moral equivalent of home and, ultimately, of the whole world of nations and of the planet Earth as such.

The Domestic Tranquillity Clause Writ Large

No matter how badly American society needs schools that are moral equivalents of home; no matter how important it is that we transmit this nation's whole cultural heritage to the next generation; no matter how essential it may be to teach them the 3Cs—without a remapping of home, school, and world, the requisite reforms do not stand a chance. So long as our culture believes that the function of school is to equip children for life in the public world of work, politics, and the professions and accepts as norms what Woolf considered flaws in the men who worked there—the possessiveness, jealousy, pugnacity, and greed that she feared would contaminate women—the schoolhome will be called counterproductive. So long as the logical geography of education remains the same, the schoolhome's efforts to remember domesticity will be perceived as dysfunctional.

Does this mean that the idea of the schoolhome is doomed to die aborning? Has school no choice but to dissociate itself from home? There is another option: remapping the public world. Instead of renouncing the schoolhome because its values, attitudes, and patterns of behavior conflict with those on the other side of the bridge, we can try to make the values, attitudes, and patterns of behavior that belong to the public world conform to those of the schoolhome.

In the United States there is a historical precedent for doing just this. Although it is seldom remembered, one of the objectives the founding fathers intended the Constitution to serve was to ensure domestic tranquillity. Historians seem to agree that the inclusion of domestic tranquillity on the list of ends that the United States Constitution hoped to ensure was, in large part, a response to the fear of insurrection occasioned by Shays' Rebellion. Still, the framers' language is not merely academic. Had they spoken of "civic" tranquillity, we might justifiably conclude that their interest was simply in ensuring governmental stability. In contrast, use of the term "domestic" cast the new nation in a special light. If England had once been home to the colonists, they were now to consider the United States of America their home.

Two centuries after Shays' Rebellion, another kind of domestic intranquillity—an *antisocial* form that seems to have been relatively unproblematic for them—is a far greater danger today than insurrection. Tearing the social fabric as surely as rebellion unties civic bonds, domestic violence writ large and small violates the very rights of life, liberty, and the pursuit of happiness that the United States Constitution was meant to protect.

If ever there was a time to remember the domestic tranquillity clause of the United States Constitution, it is now. If ever there was cause for increasing *our* vision of the domestic to match that of the framers while enlarging *their* understanding of tranquillity to meet present realities, we have it.

Yet even if the United States judicial system was inclined to give due weight to the domestic tranquillity clause of the Constitution, we would be remiss to view one of the most important issues of our age as primarily a matter of law. A conception of the nation as home, of public space as a place of safety and security, of the relationship among citizens as one of harmony and shared goals rather than antagonistic claims: all this constitutes a reorientation of thought, feeling, and action. For this new perspective, and for the knowledge and skill that must accompany it, we must look to education.

When education is viewed as preparation for membership in the public or civic "sphere," as it now is, then all education reduces to civic education. Civic education in the limited sense of citizenship or patriotic education or education about one's country's form of government then becomes one among many elements of civic education broadly understood. Similarly, when the civic "sphere" is seen as a domestic domain, as I am recommending it should be, domestic education in the limited sense of home economics becomes one among many elements of domestic education writ large.

In other words, when our perception of the civic changes, so must our vision of education. Insofar as an expanded domestic realm promises to supplant an ethic of violence and violation with one of safety and security, peace and love, our new vision will reorient educational theory and practice. One who makes the ensuring of domestic tranquillity one of the central aims of education claims for young people a very special quality and kind of moral instruction, and for society a very special kind and quality of moral life. This new vision does not simply infuse formal programs in moral education with goals and objectives derived from our interest in ensuring domestic tranquillity, however. It requires that *all* aspects of our educational endeavor be made consistent with, and reflective of, this end.

What does this bode for the nation's schools, and for our colleges and universities as well? At the very least it bodes a commitment to the safety—the bodily and psychological integrity—of students and to education in the 3Cs of care, concern, and connection. It bodes, therefore, a shift away from teaching methods and classroom practices that, shunning these virtues, inhibit collaboration and cooperation, as well as a rejection of the privileged status now bestowed on education for spectatorship. Equally important, it bodes a greater subject matter inclusiveness that, along with an increased respect for difference and diversity, transmits an appreciation of domesticity itself.

As school now conducts our young from the domestic into the civic or public realm, it teaches them to devalue that place called home and the things associated with it. Its lessons, constituting a hidden curriculum in anti-domesticity, are conveyed as much by the silences of the curriculum as by the explicit derogation of the domestic. If we are to ensure domestic tranquillity, school's complicity in transmitting a hidden curriculum in anti-domesticity must be acknowledged. Because U.S. society has assigned responsibility for carrying out the tasks and activities of the private home on the basis of gender, the by now well-documented silences about—and the negative portrayals of—women are implicated, too. Because its prejudices have placed African Americans closer to nature than to culture, the silences about and negative portrayals of Black men, as well as women of all races, are also implicated. The connections between education's implicit denigration of women and African Americans, on the one hand, and the domestic on the other are seldom if ever acknowledged. Nevertheless, the strands of these three hidden curricula are interwoven.

It is essential to raise to consciousness school's hidden curricula about race and gender if the harm done by the present hidden curriculum in anti-domesticity is to be redressed (cf Martin 1976). All of us have absorbed the lessons of this latter curriculum so well, however, that its eradication will not be accomplished easily. Nor, for that matter, will it be easy to persuade educators in the various fields of knowledge to give study of the domestic the legitimacy that is its due, for they themselves tend to devalue the domestic. Nevertheless, to ensure domestic tranquillity both in our private homes and the larger society we must teach our students and ourselves to revalue domesticity so that domesticity will become everyone's business.

But the claims of domesticity do not end at this nation's borders. For good reason the founders made the new nation the site of the domestic. Some two hundred years later we must reclaim their insight without accepting the domestic boundaries they took for granted. Today a domestic/public split separating our *home*land from other lands is as fraught with danger as was the fragmentation of states inherent in the Articles of Confederation the founding fathers saw fit to reject. In an age in which not merely the nation, indeed not merely the human species, but *all* life is at risk, the earth itself must be seen for what it is—our home. "We have inherited a large house," Martin Luther King once said, "a great 'world house' in which we . . . must learn somehow to live with each other in peace." (Eck n.d., 20) The domestic tranquillity we seek in our private homes and need desperately to extend to our national home must be projected onto the whole world and ultimately onto the whole planet, and these projections must then be turned back onto all facets of education.

Part III: Bringing a Cultural Wealth Perspective into Education

To say that the gendered division of educational functions between home and school no longer makes sense is not to say that in the coming century home should abdicate its educational role. Rather, school and home need to work together to pass down to future generations the cultural wealth that used to be, and is still considered by many to be, home's and only home's responsibility. But will school still *be* school if it takes on new functions and shoulders responsibility for transmitting different portions of our cultural wealth? Education in general and schooling in particular are as subject to change, as much a part of the societal flux, as everything else. Thus, to suppose that school has some immutable task or function that it and only it must carry out, or that it has custody of one and only one small portion of our heritage, is to attribute to school an essential nature it does not possess. Yes, school can add new functions and become a guardian of different forms of cultural wealth. It can also shed or share old functions and time-honored custodial duties without losing its identity.

In bestowing broader responsibilities on school in the twenty-first century, do I place too great a burden on it? Not if one joins together the broad concept of cultural wealth that was implicit in *The Schoolhome* and a concept of multiple educational agency. Then, even as school takes on the new functions the times require, it can share some of its present functions with other educational agents: vocational education with industry—something that is now done in many Western societies; science, social studies, and art education with museums—something one sees glimmerings of in our own society; music education with symphony orchestras and opera companies; physical education with health professions; and so on.

Defining the Wealth

It was only after I began to develop the cultural wealth perspective on education I present here that I noticed that Dewey's *Democracy and Education* begins with a discussion of cultural transmission. "Society exists through a process of transmission quite as much as biological life," wrote Dewey on page three of his magnum opus on education (Dewey 1961, 3). Saying "the fact that some are born as some die, makes possible through transmission of ideas and practices the constant reweaving of the social fabric." He added that the renewal cannot be taken for granted: "Unless pains are taken to see that genuine and thorough transmission takes place, the most civilized group will relapse into barbarism and then into savagery" (Dewey 1961, 3–4). Dewey's 1916 treatise also opens with an acknowledgement that school is but one method thereof. Indeed, after affirming the importance of school to this process, he issued a caveat: "but it is only one means, and compared with other agencies, a relatively superficial means" (Dewey 1961, 4).

The truth is, however, that as one turns the pages of *Democracy and Education*, the cultural standpoint of the first chapter gives way to an individualistic perspective. I do not mean that Dewey espoused a philosophy of radical individualism, let alone that his philosophy abstracted individuals from their political and social contexts. On the contrary, *Democracy and Education* contains a philosophy of education for a democratic society, one in which individual human beings are thoroughly social creatures and community plays a central role. My point is simply that, his opening remarks notwithstanding, Dewey's main concern in *Democracy and Education* was the growth and development of individuals. In addition, despite his acknowledgment of school's limitations, Dewey allowed school to take over his text.

Struck by Dewey's insight into the relationship of home and school, in *The Schoolhome* I stressed the fact that these two institutions are partners in the educational enterprise. When, shortly after that book's publication, I began to think more generally about the preservation and transmission of the culture's wealth, my conception of educational agency began to expand. Let me explain by drawing an analogy to Adam Smith's discussion of economic wealth.

When, in 1776, Adam Smith inquired into the wealth of nations, he was as concerned with its nature as its causes. "That wealth consists in money, or in gold and silver, is a popular notion which naturally arises from the double function of money, as the instrument of commerce and as a measure of value" he said in Volume I of his treatise on the topic (Smith 1776/1976, 450). Indeed, the definition of wealth as money was so commonplace in his day that, in Smith's view, even David Hume had not sufficiently questioned it when studying mercantilism, Europe's then dominant economic system. "It would be too ridiculous to go about seriously to prove, that wealth does not consist in money, or in gold and silver; but in what money purchases, and is valuable for purchasing," Smith wrote in *An Inquiry into the Nature and Causes of the Wealth of Nations* (Smith 1776/1976, 459). And he added: "Money, no doubt, makes always a part of the national capital; but it has already been shown that it generally makes but a small part, and always the most unprofitable part of it" (Smith 1776/1976, 459).

The subject of Smith's *Inquiry* was economic wealth. Although I did not have the concept of cultural wealth in mind when I wrote *The Schoolhome*, that book can be read as a treatise on this subject—provided one understands the notion of cultural wealth broadly.

That cultural wealth consists entirely of "high" culture—or perhaps more accurately of the "higher" learning—is as popular a notion in the United States at the end of the twentieth century as the confusion of money, or gold and silver, with wealth was in eighteenth-century England. If that earlier false equation was due to money's double role, possibly ours arises from a similar duality. Granted, one cannot say that the attainment of the knowledge of art, literature, history, philosophy, or the behavioral and the natural sciences is a measure of an individual's value in the United States today. Anti-intellectualism is too strong a current in the society. Yet it is fair to call the acquisition of the higher learning the main measure of value within the educational sphere. And, similarly, as money was the instrument of the commerce of Smith's day, the higher learning is the instrument of the education of our own.

It has rightly been said that Smith democratized the concept of a nation's wealth by broadening the definition to include not just the wealth of kings, or even the wealth of the merchant class, but the goods that *all* people in a society consume (Heilbroner 1953, 45). In rejecting the narrow definition of cultural wealth as high culture or the higher learning, I take similar action. Of course, high culture is a part of our cultural wealth. But there is far more to a culture's wealth than the acknowledged classics of art, music, and literature; more even than philosophy and economics, history, science, and psychology.

Culture in the broadest sense of the term includes not just artistic and scholarly products. It encompasses the institutions and practices, rites and rituals, beliefs and skills, attitudes and values, world views and localized modes of thinking and acting of *all* members of society over the *whole* range of contexts. Not everything in a cuture's stock counts as wealth, of course, for the term "wealth" carries with it a poitive assessment. But it is a far cry from acknowledging that a culture's stock consists in liabilities as well as assets to the assumption that high culture or the higher learning exhausts its riches.

The sense of culture—and by extension cultural wealth—that I have in mind is akin to the anthropologist's. When anthropologists study cultures, they do not dream of limiting their sights to some small esoteric subset of practices and accomplishments. Anthropological definitions of culture as "all learned behavior"—or, alternately, as "the whole range of human activities which are learned and not instinctive" (Herskovits 1952, 21; Beattie 1964, 20)—encompass whatever might correspond to our own conceptions of high, popular, and material culture and they embrace countless other items as well. An old farmer's know-how, an artisan's craft, a mother's daily lessons to her offspring in the 3Cs of care, concern, and connection are all, therefore, grist for an anthropologist's mill. As cultural assets, these also fall squarely in the category of cultural wealth.

The price of an arbitrary reduction of cultural wealth to high culture is enormous, for it effectively cuts off future generations from huge portions of cultural wealth. But now suppose that the definition of cultural wealth is every bit as broad as it needs to be.[10] Slavery, war, child abuse, wife beating, the torture of political prisoners are not natural phenomena; they are learned, not innate. But then, according to a broad definition of culture, they are cultural practices. Must we therefore consider these a part of a culture's *wealth?* Not at all. *Representations of* immoral achievements and evil practices—whether historical, psychological, sociological, philosophical studies; or fictional, artistic, photographic, theatrical portrayals—can all belong to the wealth of cultures, although whether or not they do must be determined on a case-to-case basis. This wealth does not include the human atrocities themselves, however.

Think of the Nazi concentration camps and the uses to which they were put. They were creations of culture, not nature: of that there can be no doubt. Yet by no stretch of the imagination do they constitute part of the wealth of cultures. In contrast to the concentration camps themselves, however, the artifacts of the camps, the photographs of victims and perpetrators, and the scale models in the Holocaust Memorial Museum in Washington, D.C., can certainly be said to increase cultural wealth. Providing the underpinnings for a coherent narrative about a culture's depravities, they enable visitors to connect to the victims of a particular story. Similarly, in the United States, the African burial grounds now being extensively unearthed, studied, and protected beneath New York City provide us with invaluable information into the rituals, beliefs, and practices of those men, women, and children enslaved during the eighteenth and nineteenth centuries in that geographic area. They, too, are a form of our cultural wealth and they enable us to understand anew the victims of another story.

The good and the bad, assets and liabilities alike, constitute a culture's *stock* from which source its cultural wealth is drawn. A culture's wealth, in other words, is only that portion of cultural stock that is deemed valuable.

It is a measure of how deeply ingrained in our collective consciousness is the equation between culture and high culture that no one considers absurd a definition of culture that mistakes a part for the whole. Yet it verges on the ridiculous that we take pride in being a literate culture, worry that literacy rates may have declined, yet do not count the 3Rs themselves as items of cultural wealth. It is equally inconsistent that we call the existence of moral codes one of the marks of civilization, yet define cultural wealth so that the 3Cs of care, concern, and connection do not belong to it. And it makes little sense that religious doctrines, political practices, medical treatments, engineering skills—indeed the whole range of human occupations—tend to be excluded from this category.

The problem with our own or any reductive definition of cultural wealth is that this culture's stock, like any culture's, is broadly based. No single type of thing can possibly exhaust its wealth because so many types constitute its stock. Were cultural wealth a purely theoretical construct having no practical application, an exclusionary rendering of it would be of little consequence. Education's mandate to transmit the cultural heritage anchors this concept in everyday affairs, however. After all, what is a culture's heritage if it is not its wealth? Of course, in the name of transmitting that heritage a culture may, in spite of its good intentions, hand down cultural liabilities to its young—for instance, the practices of child abuse and war—as well as assets. Yet surely the object is to pass on to them whatever cultural stock is perceived to be of value. And just as certainly, insofar as cultural wealth is identified with high culture, a nation or society will be ignoring the greater part of its wealth.

Still and all, a broad definition of cultural wealth appears to have one fatal flaw, namely that of assigning high value to trivial pursuits. In actuality, however, rather than commit this cardinal sin, a democratic definition leaves open the question of the relative value of the various items of wealth just as it is neutral on the issue of which parts of the wealth should be handed down. In excluding apparently trivial pursuits from the category of cultural wealth *by definition,* we deny ourselves the opportunity to discover their educational possibilities. We also run the risk that the knowhow someone might some day be able to adapt to new purposes will become extinct.

A reductive definition of cultural wealth does more damage than this, however. It is a dangerous policy to restrict the wealth of cultures to high culture, because no single institution of a society is the conservator of a culture's whole wealth. Suppose a portion of the whole were being squandered by one of the custodians; or, less melodramatically, that for reasons beyond anyone's control, its guardian could no longer preserve and nurture it. If the assets were not considered to belong to the culture's wealth, their loss would not even be noticed. If noticed, their disappearance would cause no alarm. On the other hand, if the items appeared on an inventory of cultural wealth, they would sooner or later be missed, whereupon decisions could be made about whether a new form of guardianship was required.

The supposition is not purely hypothetical. The guardianship of the old farmer's know how that Wendell Berry described in his essays on farming (Berry 1987, 152–61) was once a family matter but, for complex economic, technological, and sociological reasons quite beyond the control of any one individual or family grouping, the self-appointed caretaker of this portion of our wealth has for some time been unable to carry out its responsibilities. The fact that we are only dimly aware of this historic trend and quite unmoved by it is an alarming confirmation of the desperate need for a panoramic view of the contents of cultural wealth.

The inability of home and family to be effective transmitters of the 3Cs and the ethics of care represents another case in point. Since we do not count such virtues as belonging to our cultural wealth, it does not occur to most of us that home and family have traditionally been considered their custodians. Nor do we stop to think that if these assets are no longer being adequately conserved or successfully handed down, new guardians may have to be appointed.

Multiple Educational Agency

I do not want to paint too grim a picture of cultural loss. There are many wonderful instances of good conduct toward America's past—some as prosaic as cookbooks, others as uncommon as the living museums at Williamsburg, Virginia, and Sturbridge, Massachusetts. Museums and libraries, opera companies and ballet corps, recording companies and publishing houses, historical societies and book clubs: these and countless other institutional forms have been created to recover, protect, and nurture cultural assets. Some of the custodial arrangements serve simply as warehouses for keeping old stock. Others put tools, diaries, household goods, musical scores, and other artifacts on display. Some treat practices and artifacts alike as rusty relics. Transmitting as they preserve, others put the relics into a form in which they can be studied and understood. On occasion, they even provide opportunities for something more.

In addition to institutions such as museums that have been specifically designed to protect and preserve the wealth, ones like school, home, church, neighborhood, and workplace do so in the course of transmitting it to the next generation. Preservation and transmission may be theoretically distinct processes, the one directed to the protection of assets for the next generation and the other to handing the stock over, passing it down to them, yet these two functions are often so intimately connected in practical life as to be virtually indistinguishable. Keep a set of documents in an archives long enough for the next generation to take physical possession of it and it will, in effect, have been transmitted to them. Teach your skills to your sons and daughters and your know how will be preserved.

Try now to imagine Adam Smith proposing his broad definition of the wealth of nations and at the same time giving tacit consent to the old mercantile system. The discrepancy between the traditional ways of thinking and acting and his new, enlarged vision of a nation's wealth would have been painfully apparent. A similarly jarring experience is in store for those who adopt a broad definition of cultural wealth while leaving intact the present false equation between education and schooling and the antiquated narrow definition of the latter's function.

In the United States, at least, the reduction of education to schooling is a relatively recent phenomenon. According to Bernard Bailyn (1960, 16ff.), the family was the main agency of education in the forming of U.S. society, and whatever it did not accomplish, the local community and the church undertook. Schools existed in the early colonial period, but they played a relatively small role. Indeed, even when, in the mid-nineteenth century, a system of free, universal, public schooling was under construction in the United States, most people took school to be a minor part of education. Lawrence Cremin tells us that the generation that instituted "the common school" is also the one that established public libraries, lyceums, mechanics' institutes, agricultural societies, and penny newspapers (Cremin 1965, 6–7). And the next generation introduced still more educative agencies, among them the social settlement.

It was only in the twentieth century that school came to be seen as the sum total of education. And at the millennium, it is still so perceived. True, religious leaders present themselves as educators, museums house education departments, and television networks label some programs "educational." Nevertheless, the conflation of education and schooling to which Ivan Illich so dramatically drew attention (Illich 1970) continues to govern this culture's educational thought. You open a newspaper or magazine to its education section expecting to read about school and universities. The government appoints a new commissioner of education and everyone assumes that his or her domain is the nation's schools. And, perhaps most telling of all, those people who describe themselves as education's critics and reformers and are labelled as such by others are, from first to last, school's critics and reformers.

Education is not the sole medium for transmitting cultural wealth, yet it is so central to the preservation and transmission of cultural assets that it is quite imprudent to reduce it to one of its institutional forms. A broad definition of cultural wealth requires a broad conception of *educational agency* so that large quantities of stock are not lost to posterity. When school is considered to be "the" educating agent, it is only natural to see it as "the" one true or legitimate transmitter of the heritage. But then, even if the assets in school's custody are assured safe passage, whatever is in the keep of other custodians is all too easily overlooked.

As it happens—indeed, as befits school's history—the assets that our culture has placed in school's keep represent one small portion of the wealth. For with the world of the private home culturally identified as women's realm and the world of work, politics, and the professions as men's, it stands to reason that school would not be expected to bother with wealth that, having been accumulated by women, was marked by the imprints of femininity; that, indeed, school would have its hands full trying to pass down to future generations the wealth that had been amassed by men and carried the imprints of masculinity.

The historic division between school and home of responsibilities for transmitting our culture's heritage effectively made school the guardian of a fraction of the wealth. That portion was then considerably reduced by the assimilationist policies to which our nation has subscribed. Full-fledged members of the world of work, politics, and the professions were—and to a great extent still are—expected to shed whatever minority religious, ethnic, and racial identities their families might have and to take on those of the dominant White, Protestant, middle-class, male tribe. As the institution charged with preparing young people for membership in that world, school's role was thus further circumscribed. The wealth placed in its keep was, in turn, limited to those assets that, when handed down, would meet the dominant group's needs and perpetuate its interests.

In view of the disruption of the old gendered-division of labor and the fact that school is now generally thought to be the predominant—nay, the one and only—educational agent in the United States, the gendered-division of educational functions makes no sense. In consequence, the present division of responsibilities for transmitting our culture's wealth loses whatever plausibility it once had. As if this were not enough to demonstrate how imperative it is to redefine both school's function and its custodial duties, one need only consider the great shifts in the composition of this nation's population. Casting doubt on the assimilationist model of schooling that has for so long been held up as an ideal, they, too, throw into question the limited conception of what wealth belongs in school's hands.

School clearly stands in need of radical reconceptualization. With the rejection of the false equation between education and schooling, one can see, however, that the process of rethinking must be part of a new theory of educational agency, one in which the whole range of custodians of cultural wealth are considered bona fide educational agents with practices and policies of their own. In Bailyn's narrative, the community cooperated with home and family by elaborating on their teachings. Now the tables have been turned and home tends to be regarded simply as school's helper in the educational process, and a very minor one at that.[11] I do not for a moment mean to suggest that with a redefined function and a new list of custodial responsibilities, school will need no more help. My point is, rather, that when school itself is seen as one among many educational agents, it will no longer be in a position to treat the aims and procedures of other institutions as automatically subordinate to its own.

School stands to gain from the radical reconceptualization I propose. True, when the whole range of cultural custodians is acknowledged to be educational agents, school will not be able to reduce home's educative function to that of proctoring children's homework— or, for that matter, reduce industry's educational function to that of providing expensive equipment. It will, however, be able to count on the collaboration and cooperation of genuine partners in the educational process.

One of the worst byproducts of the false equation of education and schooling is that no unacknowledged educational agent can, in good logic, be charged with *mis*educating our youth. Yet in bombarding young people with unwholesome, antisocial models of living and in making these appear fatally attractive, the print and electronic media are guilty of doing precisely this. By beginning to hold them accountable for the damage they are doing in preserving and transmitting our culture's liabilities rather than its wealth is to make public their actual status as educational agents.

Conclusion

Would that it were enough to democratize the definition of cultural wealth and broaden our conception of what counts as an educational agent! Would that we could redefine school's function and leave it at that! These measures enable one to see just how much cultural wealth there is and to breathe a sigh of relief that the tasks of preservation and transmission are not school's alone. But more is required, and that more involves the education of the whole range of cultural custodians themselves in accepting their educational responsibilities, in working together with other educational agents, and above all in bringing private gain into line with the public good. John Stuart Mill once wrote that education should make sure that "a direct impulse to promote the general good may be in every individual one of the habitual motives of action, and the sentiments connected therewith may fill a large and prominent place in every human being's sentient existence" (Mill 1962, 269). To this sentiment I add my wish that the actions of the whole range of cultural custodians and educational agents be similarly inspired.

With this caveat in mind, I look forward to a century that redefines school and ushers in a new era of cooperation across the *entire range* of society's educational agents—a category that definitely includes the electronic and print media. I cannot stress enough, however, the importance of keeping sight of the women in the educational landscape as we move ahead. For not only is there still much to do to improve the quality of girls' education. If there is one thing I have learned from my own research it is this: To make education rich and rewarding for every girl and boy and also as beneficial as possible for society as a whole, it is absolutely necessary to keep looking with clear and steady eyes on the girls and women in the educational landscape and on the cultural assets that have traditionally been placed in our keep.

Notes

[1]See also Martin (1984) and (1994a).

[2]See also Martin (1995a) and (1995b).

[3]For that discussion I will draw heavily on Martin (1996).

[4]I construe these broadly so as to include not just biological reproduction but childcare and rearing, running a household, serving the needs and purposes of family members, and so on.

[5]Here I read a concept introduced in Martin (1996) back onto my earlier work.

[6]Catharine Macaulay in her book, *Letters on Education,* entered this conversation a few years before Wollstonecraft with a scathing retort to Rousseau. See Chapter 2.

[7]Later, I will argue that home does indeed have a curriculum. My point here is simply that, tacitly, our culture both assumes and denies the existence of such.

[8]The material in this paragraph is drawn from Martin (1994b).

[9]There is an implicit value judgment in the notion of heritage, as I use it. In the broad sense of the term, murder, rape, etc. are part of our heritage. I speak here, however, only of that portion that is worthwhile.

[10]I should point out that it needs to be broad enough to encompass even those domestic processes and practices that transform human infants into creatures of culture and are often perceived, therefore, as standing closer to nature than to culture (cf Ortner 1974).

[11]Viz. the silent treatment accorded home in the reports of the 1980s on the condition of American education.

References

Bailyn, B. 1960. *Education in the Forming of American Society.* New York: Vintage.

Beattie, J. 1964. *Other Cultures.* New York: The Free Press.

Berry, W. 1987. *Home Economics.* Reprint. San Francisco: North Point Press.

Cremin, L. 1965. *The Genius of American Education.* New York: Vintage.

Dewey, J. 1956. *The School and Society.* Reprint. Chicago: University of Chicago Press.

_____ . 1961. *Democracy and Education.* Reprint New York: The Macmillan Co.

Eck, D. n.d. Responses to Pluralism: Worldviews in an Interdependent World. *Working Papers Series* 4: 20, Project on Interdependence, Radcliffe College. Cambridge, MA.

Gilligan, C. 1982. *In a Different Voice.* Cambridge: Harvard University Press.

Heilbroner, R. 1953. *The Wordly Philosophers.* New York: Simon and Schuster.

Herskovits, M. 1952. *Economic Anthropology.* New York: Alfred A. Knopf.

Illich, I. 1970. *Deschooling Society.* New York: Harper & Row.

James, W. [1910] 1970. A Moral Equivalent of War. In *War and Morality,* of R. A. Wasserstrom. Belmont, CA: Wadsworth Publishing Company.

Lane, H. 1979. *The Wild Boy of Aveyron.* Cambridge, MA: Harvard University Press.

Martin, J. R. 1976. What Should We Do With a Hidden Curriculum When We Find One? *Curriculum Inquiry* 6: 135–51.

_____ . 1981a. Needed: A New Paradigm for Liberal Education. In *Philosophy and Education 1981,* ed. J. P. Soltis. Chicago: The National Society for the Study of Education.

_____ . 1981b. Sophie and Émile: A Case Study of Sex Bias in the History of Educational Thought. *Harvard Educational Review* 51(3): 357–72.

_____ . 1981c. The Ideal of the EducatedPerson. *Educational Theory* 31(2): 97–110.

_____ . 1982. Excluding Women from the Educational Realm. *Harvard Educational Review* 52(2): 133–48.

_____ . 1984. Philosophy, Gender, and Education. In *Women and Education: World Yearbook of Education 1984,* ed. S. Acker. London: Kogan Page.

———. 1985. *Reclaiming a Conversation: The Ideal of the Educated Woman.* New Haven: Yale University Press.

_____ . 1992. *The Schoolhome: Rethinking Schools for Changing Families.* Cambridge, MA: Harvard University Press.

_____ . 1994a. *Changing the Educational Landscape.* New York: Routledge.

_____ . 1994b. Fatal Inaction: Overcoming School's Reluctance to Become a Moral Equivalent of Home. Lecture presented at American Montessori Society Seminar, Detroit, MI.

_____ . 1995a. A Philosophy of Education for the Year 2000. *Phi Delta Kappan* (January): 355–59.

_____ . 1995b. Education for Domestic Tranquillity. In *Critical Conversations in Philosophy of Education,* ed. W. Kohli. New York: Routledge.

_____ . 1996. There's Too Much to Teach: Cultural Wealth in an Age of Scarcity. *Educational Researcher* 25(2): 4–10, 16.

Mill, J. S. 1962. *Utilitarianism, on Liberty, Essay on Bentham.* Reprint. New York: New American Library.

Noddings, N. 1984. *Caring.* Berkeley: University of California Press.

Ortner, S. B. 1974. Is Female to Male as Nature is to Culture? In *Women, Culture, & Society,* ed. M. Z. Rosaldo and L. Lamphere. Stanford: University of Stanford Press.

Plato, 1974. *The Republic.* Trans. G. M. A. Grube. Indianapolis: Hackett Publishing Company.

Rodriguez, R. 1982. *Hunger of Memory.* Boston: David Godine.

Rousseau, J. [1762] 1979. *Émile.* Trans. A. Bloom. Reprint. New York: Basic Books.

Smith, A. [1776] 1976. *An Inquiry into the Nature and Causes of the Wealth of Nations.* ed. E. Cannan. Reprint. Chicago: University of Chicago Press.

Wollstonecraft, M. [1792] 1967. *A Vindication of the Rights of Woman.* Ed. C. W. Hagelman, Jr. Reprint. New York: Norton.

Woolf, V. 1938. *Three Guineas.* New York: Harcourt Brace Jovanovich.

Chapter 8

bell hooks

Excerpts from
Teaching to Transgress

Introduction

In the weeks before the English Department at Oberlin College was about to decide whether or not I would be granted tenure, I was haunted by dreams of running away—of disappearing—yes, even of dying. These dreams were not a response to fear that I would not be granted tenure. They were a response to the reality that I *would* be granted tenure. I was afraid that I *would* be trapped in the academy forever.

Instead of feeling elated when I received tenure, I fell into a deep, life-threatening depression. Since everyone around me believed that I should be relieved, thrilled, proud, I felt "guilty" about my "real" feelings and could not share them with anyone. The lecture circuit took me to sunny California and the New Age world of my sister's house in Laguna Beach where I was able to chill out for a month. When I shared my feelings with my sister (she's a therapist), she reassured me that they were entirely appropriate because, she said, "You never wanted to be a teacher. Since we were little, all you ever wanted to was write." She was right. It was always assumed by everyone else that I would become a teacher. In the apartheid South, black girls from working-class backgrounds had three career choices. We could marry. We could work as maids. We could become school teachers. And since, according to the sexist thinking of the time, men did not really desire

bell hooks
_____

"smart" women, it was assumed that signs of intelligence sealed one's fate. From grade school on, I was destined to become a teacher.

But the dream of becoming a writer was always present within me. From childhood, I believed that I would teach *and* write. Writing would be the serious work, teaching would be the not-so-serious-I-need-to-make-a-living "job." Writing, I believed then, was all about private longing and pesonal glory, but teaching was about service, giving back to one's community. For black folks teaching—educating—was fundamentally political because it was rooted in antiracist struggle. Indeed, my all-black grade schools became the location where I experienced learning as revolution.

Almost all our teachers at Booker T. Washington were black women. They were committed to nurturing intellect so that we could become scholars, thinkers, and cultural workers—black folks who used our "minds." We learned early that our devotion to learning, to a life of the mind, was a counter-hegemonic act, a fundamental way to resist every strategy of white racist colonization. Though they did not define or articulate these practices in theoretical terms, my teachers were enacting a revolutionary pedagogy of resistance that was profoundly anticolonial. Within these segregated schools, black children who were deemed exceptional, gifted, were given special care. Teachers worked with and for us to ensure that we would fulfill our intellectual destiny and by so doing uplift the race. My teachers were on a mission.

To fulfill that mission, my teachers made sure they "knew" us. They knew our parents, our economic status, where we worshipped, what our homes were like, and how we were treated in the family. I went to school at a historical moment where I was being taught by the same teachers who had taught my mother, her sisters, and brothers. My effort and ability to learn was always contextualized within the framework of generational family experience. Certain behaviors, gestures, habits of being were traced back.

Attending school then was sheer joy. I loved being a student. I loved learning. School was the place of ecstasy—pleasure and danger. To be changed by ideas was pure pleasure. But to learn ideas that ran counter to values and beliefs learned at home was to place oneself at risk, to enter the danger zone. Home was the place where I was forced to conform to someone else's image of who and what I should be. School was the place where I could forget that self and, through ideas, reinvent myself.

School changed utterly with racial integration. Gone was the messianic zeal to transform our minds and beings that had characterized teachers and their pedagogical practices in our all-black schools. Knowledge was suddenly about information only. It had no relation to how one lived, behaved. It was no longer connected to antiracist struggle. Bussed to white schools, we soon learned that obedience, and not a zealous will to learn, was what was expected of us. Too much eagerness to learn could easily be seen as a threat to white authority.

When we entered racist, desegregated, white schools we left a world where teachers believed that to educate black children rightly would require a political commitment. Now, we were mainly taught by white teachers whose lessons reinforced racist stereotypes. For black children, education was no longer about the practice of freedom. Realizing this, I lost my love of school. The classroom was no longer a place of pleasure or ecstasy. School was still a political place, since we were always having to counter white racist assumptions that we were genetically inferior, never as capable as white peers, even unable to learn. Yet, the politics were no longer counter-hegemonic. We were always and only responding and reacting to white folks.

That shift from beloved, all-black schools to white schools where black students were seen as interlopers, as not really belonging, taught me the difference between education as the practice of freedom and education that merely strives to reinforce domination. The rare white teacher who dared to resist, who would not allow racist biases to determine how we were taught, sustained the belief that learning at its most powerful could indeed liberate. A few black teachers had joined us in the desegregation process. And, although it was more difficult, they continued to nurture black students even as their efforts were constrained by the suspicion they were favoring their own race.

Despite intensely negative experiences, I graduated from school still believing that education was enabling, that it enhanced our capacity to be free. When I began undergraduate work at Stanford University, I was enthralled with the process of becoming an insurgent black intellectual. It surprised and shocked me to sit in classes where professors were not excited about teaching, where they did not seem to have a clue that education was about the practice of freedom. During college, the primary lesson was reinforced: we were to learn obedience to authority.

In graduate school the classroom became a place I hated, yet a place where I struggled to claim and maintain the right to be an independent thinker. The university and the classroom began to feel more like a prison, a place of punishment and confinement rather than a place of promise and possibility. I wrote my first book during those undergraduate years, even though it was not published until years later. I was writing; but more importantly I was preparing to become a teacher.

Accepting the teaching profession as my destiny, I was tormented by the classroom reality I had known both as an undergraduate and a graduate student. The vast majority of our professors lacked basic communication skills, they were not self-actualized, and they often used the classroom to enact rituals of control that were about domination and the unjust exercise of power. In these settings I learned a lot about the kind of teacher I did not want to become.

In graduate school I found that I was often bored in classes. The banking system of education (based on the assumption that memorizing information and regurgitating it represented gaining knowledge that could be deposited, stored and used at a later date) did not interest me. I wanted to become a critical thinker. Yet that longing was often seen as a threat to authority. Individual white male students who were seen as "exceptional," were often allowed to chart their intellectual journeys, but the rest of us (and particularly those from marginal groups) were always expected to conform. Nonconformity on our part was viewed with suspicion, as empty gestures of defiance aimed at masking inferiority or substandard work. In those days, those of us from marginal groups who were allowed to enter prestigious, predominantly white colleges were made to feel that we were not there to learn but to prove that we were the equal of whites. We were there to prove this by showing how well we could become clones of our peers. As we constantly confronted biases, an undercurrent of stress diminished our learning experience.

My reaction to this stress and to the ever-present boredom and apathy that pervaded my classes was to imagine ways that teaching and the learning experience could be different. When I discovered the work of the Brazilian thinker Paulo Freire, my first introduction to critical pedagogy, I found a mentor and a guide, someone who understood that learning could be liberatory. With his teachings and my growing understanding of the ways in which the education I had received in all-black Southern schools had been empowering, I began to develop a blueprint for my own pedagogical practice. Already deeply engaged with feminist thinking, I had no difficulty bringing that critique to Freire's work. Significantly, I felt that this mentor and guide, whom I had never seen in the flesh, would encourage and support my challenge to his ideas if he was truly committed to education as the practice of freedom. At the same time, I used his pedagogical paradigms to critique the limitations of feminist classrooms.

During my undergraduate and graduate school years, only white women professors were involved in developing Women's Studies programs. And even though I taught my first class as a graduate student on black women writers from a feminist perspective, it was in the context of a Black Studies program. At that time, I found, white women professors were not eager to nurture any interest in feminist thinking and scholarship on the part of black female students if that interest included critical challenge. Yet their lack of interest did not discourage me from involvement with feminist ideas or participation in the feminist classroom. Those classrooms were the one space where pedagogical practices were interrogated, where it was assumed that the knowledge offered students would empower them to be better scholars, to live more fully in the world beyond academe. The feminist classroom was the one space where students could raise critical questions about pedagogical process. These critiques were not always encouraged or well received, but they were allowed. That small acceptance of critical interrogation was a crucial challenge inviting us as students to think seriously about pedagogy in relation to the practice of freedom.

When I entered my first undergraduate classroom to teach, I relied on the example of those inspired black women teachers in my grade school, on Freire's work, and on feminist thinking about radical pedagogy. I longed passionately to teach differently from the way I had been taught since high school. The first paradigm that shaped my pedagogy was the idea that the classroom should be an exciting place, never boring. And if boredom should prevail, then pedagogical strategies were needed that would intervene, alter, even disrupt the atmosphere. Neither Freire's work nor feminist pedagogy examined the notion of pleasure in the classroom. The idea that learning should be exciting, sometimes even "fun," was the subject of critical discussion by educators writing about pedagogical practices in grade schools, and sometimes even high schools. But there seemed to be no interest among either traditional or radical educators in discussing the role of excitement in higher education.

Excitement in higher education was viewed as potentially disruptive of the atmosphere of seriousness assumed to be essential to the learning process. To enter classroom settings in colleges and universities with the will to share the desire to encourage excitement, was to transgress. Not only did it require movement beyond accepted boundaries, but excitement could not be generated without a full recognition of the fact that there could never be an absolute set of agenda governing teaching practices. Agendas had to be flexible, had to allow for spontaneous shifts in direction. Students had to be seen in their particularity as individuals (I drew on the strategies my grade school teachers used to get to know us) and interacted with according to their needs (here Freire was useful). Critical reflection on my experience as a student in unexciting classrooms enabled me not only to imagine that the classroom could be exciting but that this excitement could co-exist with and even stimulate serious intellectual and/or academic engagement.

But excitement about ideas was not sufficient to create an exciting learning process. As a classroom community, our capacity to generate excitement is deeply affected by our interest in one another, in hearing one another's voices, in recognizing one another's presence. Since the vast majority of students learn through conservative, traditional educational practices and concern themselves only with the presence of the professor, any radical pedagogy must insist that everyone's presence is acknowledged. That insistence cannot be simply stated. It has to be demonstrated through pedagogical practices. To begin, the professor must genuinely *value* everyone's presence. There must be an ongoing recognition that everyone influences the classroom dynamic, that everyone contributes. These contributions are resources. Used constructively they enhance the capacity of any class to create an open learning community. Often before this process can begin there has to be some deconstruction of the traditional notion that only the professor is responsible for classroom dynamics. That responsibility is relative to status. Indeed, the professor will always be more responsible because the larger institutional structures will always ensure that accountability for what happens in the classroom rests with the teacher. It is rare that any professor, no matter how eloquent a lecturer, can generate through his or her actions enough excitement to create an exciting classroom. Excitement is generated through collective effort.

Seeing the classroom always as a communal place enhances the likelihood of collective effort in creating and sustaining a learning community. One semester, I had a very difficult class, one that completely failed on the communal level. Throughout the term, I thought that the major drawback inhibiting the development of a learning community was that the class was scheduled in the early morning, before nine. Almost always between a third and a half of the class was not fully awake. This, coupled with the tensions of "differences," was impossible to overcome. Every now and then we had an exciting session, but mostly it was a dull class. I came to hate this class so much that I had a tremendous fear that I would not awaken to attend it; the night before (despite alarm clocks, wake-up calls, and the experiential knowledge that I had never forgotten to attend class) I still could not sleep. Rather than making me arrive sleepy, I tended to arrive wired, full of an energy few students mirrored.

Time was just one of the factors that prevented this class from becoming a learning community. For reasons I cannot explain it was also full of "resisting" students who did not want to learn new pedagogical processes, who did not want to be in a classroom that differed in any way from the norm. To these students, transgressing boundaries was frightening. And though they were not in the majority, their spirit of rigid resistance seemed always to be more powerful than any will to intellectual openness and pleasure in learning. More than any other class I had taught, this one compelled me to abandon the sense that the professor could, by sheer strength of will and desire, make the classroom an exciting, learning community.

Before this class, I considered that *Teaching to Transgress: Education as the Practice of Freedom* would be a book of essays mostly directed to teachers. After the class ended, I began writing with the understanding that I was speaking to and with both students and professors. The scholarly field of writing on critical pedagogy and/or feminist pedagogy continues to be primarily a discourse engaged by white women and men. Freire, too, in conversation with me, as in much of his written work, has always acknowledged that he occupies the location of white maleness, particularly in this country. But the work of various thinkers on radical pedagogy (I use this term to include critical and/or feminist perspectives) has in recent years truly included a recognition of differences—those determined by class, race, sexual practice, nationality, and so on. Yet this movement forward does not seem to coincide with any significant increase in black or other nonwhite voices joining discussions about radical pedagogical practices.

My pedagogical practices have emerged from the mutually illuminating interplay of anticolonial, critical, and feminist pedagogies. This complex and unique blending of multiple perspectives has been an engaging and powerful standpoint from which to work. Expanding beyond boundaries, it has made it possible for me to imagine and enact pedagogical practices that engage directly both the concern for interrogating biases in curricula that reinscribe systems of domination (such as racism and sexism) while simultaneously providing new ways to teach diverse groups of students.

In this book I want to share insights, strategies, and critical reflections on pedagogical practice. I intend these essays to be an intervention—countering the devaluation of teaching even as they address the urgent need for changes in teaching practices. They are meant to serve as constructive commentary. Hopeful and exuberant, they convey the pleasure and joy I experience teaching; these essays are celebratory! To emphasize that the pleasure of teaching is an act of resistance countering the overwhelming boredom, uninterest, and apathy that so often characterize the way professors and students feel about teaching and learning, about the classroom experience.

Each essay addresses common themes that surface again and again in discussions of pedagogy, offering ways to rethink teaching practices and constructive strategies to enhance learning. Written separately for a variety of contexts there is unavoidably some degree of overlap; ideas are repeated, key phrases used again and again. Even though I share strategies, these works do not offer blueprints for ways to make the classroom an exciting place for learning. To do so would undermine the insistence that engaged pedagogy recognize each classroom as different, that strategies must constantly be changed, invented, reconceptualized to address each new teaching experience.

Teaching is a performative act. And it is that aspect of our work that offers the space for change, invention, spontaneous shifts, that can serve as a catalyst drawing out the unique elements in each classroom. To embrace the performative aspect of teaching we are compelled to engage "audiences," to consider issues of reciprocity. Teachers are not performers in the traditional sense of the word in that our work is not meant to be a spectacle. Yet it is meant to serve as a catalyst that calls everyone to become more and more engaged, to become active participants in learning.

Just as the way we perform changes, so should our sense of "voice." In our everyday lives we speak differently to diverse audiences. We communicate best by choosing that way of speaking that is informed by the particularity and uniqueness of whom we are speaking to and with. In keeping with this spirit, these essays do not all sound alike. They reflect my effort to use language in ways that speak to specific contexts, as well as my desire to communicate with a diverse audience. To teach in varied communities not only our paradigms must shift but also the way we think, write, speak. The engaged voice must never be fixed and absolute but always changing, always evolving in dialogue with a world beyond itself.

These essays reflect my experience of critical discussions with teachers, students, and individuals who have entered my classes to observe. Multilayered, then, these essays are meant to stand as testimony, bearing witness to education as the practice of freedom. Long before a public ever recognized me as a thinker or writer, I was recognized in the classroom by students—seen by them as a teacher who worked hard to create a dynamic learning experience for all of us. Nowadays, I am recognized more for insurgent intellectual practice. Indeed, the academic public that I encounter at my lectures always shows surprise when I speak intimately and deeply about the classroom. That public seemed particularly surprised when I said that I was working on a collection of essays about teaching. This surprise is a sad reminder of the way teaching is seen as a duller, less valuable aspect of the academic profession. This perspective on teaching is a common one. Yet it must be challenged if we are to meet the needs of our students, if we are to restore to education and the classroom excitement about ideas and the will to learn.

There is a serious crisis in education. Students often do not want to learn and teachers do not want to teach. More than ever before in the recent history of this nation, educators are compelled to confront the biases that have shaped teaching practices in our society and to create new ways of knowing, different strategies for the sharing of knowledge. We cannot address this crisis if progressive critical thinkers and social critics act as though teaching is not a subject worthy of our regard.

The classroom remains the most radical space of possibility in the academy. For years it has been a place where education has been undermined by teachers and students alike who seek to use it as a platform for opportunistic concerns rather than as a place to learn. With these essays, I add my voice to the collective call for renewal and rejuvenation in our teaching practices. Urging all of us to open our minds and hearts so that we can know beyond the boundaries of what is acceptable, so that we can think and rethink, so that we can create new visions, I celebrate teaching that enables transgressions—a movement against and beyond boundaries. It is that movement which makes education the practice of freedom.

Engaged Pedagogy

To educate as the practice of freedom is a way of teaching that anyone can learn. That learning process comes easiest to those of us who teach who also believe that there is an aspect of our vocation that is sacred; who believe that our work is not merely to share information but to share in the intellectual and spiritual growth of our students. To teach in a manner that respects and cares for the souls our students is essential if we are to provide the necessary conditions where learning can most deeply and intimately begin.

Throughout my years as student and professor, I have been most inspired by those teachers who have had the courage to transgress those boundaries that would confine each pupil to a rote, assembly-line approach to learning. Such teachers approach students with the will and desire to respond to our unique beings, even if the situation does not allow the full emergence of a relationship based on mutual recognition. Yet the possibility of such recognition is always present.

Paulo Freire and the Vietnamese Buddhist monk Thich Nhat Hanh are two of the "teachers" who have touched me deeply with their work. When I first began college, Freire's thought gave me the support I needed to challenge the "banking system" of education, that approach to learning that is rooted in the notion that all students need to do is consume information fed to them by a professor and be able to memorize and store it. Early on, it was Freire's insistence that education could be the practice of freedom that encouraged me to create strategies for what he called "conscientization" in the classroom. Translating that term to critical awareness and engagement, I entered the classrooms with the conviction that it was crucial for me and every other student to be an active participant, not a passive consumer. Education as the practice of freedom was continually undermined by professors who were actively hostile to the notion of student participation. Freire's work affirmed that education can only be liberatory when everyone claims knowledge as a field in which we all labor. That notion of mutual labor was affirmed the Thich Nhat Hanh's philosophy of engaged Buddhism, the focus on practice in conjunction with contemplation. His philosophy was similar to Freire's emphasis on "praxis"—action and reflection upon the world in order to change it.

In his work Thich Nhat Hanh always speaks of the teacher as a healer. Like Freire, his approach to knowledge called on students to be active participants, to link awareness with practice. Whereas Freire was primarily concerned with the mind, Thich Nhat Hanh offered a way of thinking about pedagogy which emphasized wholeness, a union of mind, body, and spirit. His focus on a holistic approach to learning and spiritual practice enabled me to overcome years of socialization that had taught me to believe a classroom was diminished if students and professors regarded one another as "whole" human beings, striving not just for knowledge in books, but knowledge about how to live in the world.

During my twenty years of teaching, I have witnessed a grave sense of dis-ease among professors (irrespective of their politics) when students want us to see them as whole human beings with complex lives and experiences rather than simply as seekers after compartmentalized bits of knowledge. When I was an undergraduate, Women's Studies was just finding a place in the academy. Those classrooms were the one space where teachers were willing to acknowledge a connection between ideas learned in university settings and those learned in life practices. And, despite those times when students abused that freedom in the classroom by only wanting to dwell on personal experience, feminist classrooms were, on the whole, one location where I witnessed professors striving to create participatory spaces for the sharing of knowledge. Nowadays, most women's studies professors are not as committed to exploring new pedagogical strategies. Despite this shift, many students still seek to enter feminist classrooms because they continue to believe that there, more than in any other place in the academy, they will have an opportunity to experience education as the practice of freedom.

Progressive, holistic education, "engaged pedagogy" is more demanding than conventional critical or feminist pedagogy. For, unlike these two teaching practices, it emphasizes well-being. That means that teachers must be actively committed to a process of self-actualization that promotes their own well-being if they are to teach in a manner that empowers students. Thich Nhat Hanh emphasized that "the practice of a healer, therapist, teacher or any helping professional should be directed toward his or herself first, because if the helper is unhappy, he or she cannot help many people." In the United States it is rare that anyone talks about teachers in university settings as healers. And it is even more rare to hear anyone suggest that teachers have any responsibility to be self-actualized individuals.

Learning about the work of intellectuals and academics primarily from nineteenth-century fiction and nonfiction during my pre-college years, I was certain that the task for those of us who chose this vocation was to be holistically questing for self-actualization. It was the actual experience of college that disrupted this image. It was there that I was made to feel as though I was terribly naive about "the profession." I learned that far from being self-actualized, the university was seen more as a haven for those who are smart in book knowledge but who might be otherwise unfit for social interaction. Luckily, during my undergraduate years I began to make a distinction between the practice of being an intellectual/teacher and one's role as a member of the academic profession.

It was difficult to maintain fidelity to the idea of the intellectual as someone who sought to be whole—well-grounded in a context where there was little emphasis on spiritual well-being, on care of the soul. Indeed, the objectification of the teacher within bourgeois educational structures seemed to denigrate notions of wholeness and uphold the idea of a mind/body split, one that promotes and supports compartmentalization.

This support reinforces the dualistic separation of public and private, encouraging teachers and students to see no connection between life practices, habits of being, and the roles of professors. The idea of the intellectual questing for a union of mind, body, and spirit had been replaced with notions that being smart meant that one was inherently emotionally unstable and that the best in oneself emerged in one's academic work. This meant that whether academics were drug addicts, alcoholics, batterers, or sexual abusers, the only important aspect of our identity was whether or not our minds functioned, whether we were able to do our jobs in the classroom. The self was presumably emptied out the moment the threshold was crossed, leaving in place only an objective mind—free of experiences and biases. There was fear that the conditions of that self would interfere with the teaching process. Part of the luxury and privilege of the role of teacher/professor today is the absence of any requirement that we be self-actualized. Not surprisingly, professors who are not concerned with inner well-being are the most threatened by the demand on the part of students for liberatory education, for pedagogical processes that will aid them in their own struggle for self-actualization.

Certainly it was naive for me to imagine during high school that I would find spiritual and intellectual guidance in university settings from writers, thinkers, scholars. To have found this would have been to stumble across a rare treasure. I learned, along with other students, to consider myself fortunate if I found an interesting professor who talked in a compelling way. Most of my professors were not the slightest bit interested in enlightenment. More than anything they seemed enthralled by the exercise of power and authority within their mini-kingdom, the classroom.

This is not to say that there were not compelling, benevolent dictators, but it is true to my memory that it was rare—absolutely, astonishingly rare—to encounter professors who were deeply committed to progressive pedagogical practices. I was dismayed by this; most of my professors were not individuals whose teaching styles I wanted to emulate.

My commitment to learning kept me attending classes. Yet, even so, because I did not conform—would not be an unquestioning, passive student—some professors treated me with contempt. I was slowly becoming estranged from education. Finding Freire in the midst of that estrangement was crucial to my survival as a student. His work offered both a way for me to understand the limitations of the type of education I was receiving and to discover alternative strategies for learning and teaching. It was particularly disappointing to encounter white male professors who claimed to follow Freire's model even as their pedagogical practices were mired in structures of domination, mirroring the styles of conservative professors even as they approached subjects from a more progressive standpoint.

When I first encountered Paulo Freire, I was eager to see if his style of teaching would embody the pedagogical practices he described so eloquently in his work. During the short time I studied with him, I was deeply moved by his presence, by the way in which his manner of teaching exemplified his pedagogical theory. (Not all students interested in Freire have had a similar experience.) My experience with him restored my faith in liberatory education. I had never wanted to surrender the conviction that one could teach without reinforcing existing systems of domination. I needed to know that professors did not have to be dictators in the classroom.

While I wanted teaching to be my career, I believed that personal success was intimately linked with self-actualization. My passion for this quest led me to interrogate constantly the mind/body split that was so often taken to be a given. Most professors were often deeply antagonistic toward, even scornful of, any approach to learning emerging from a philosophical standpoint emphasizing the union of mind, body, and spirit, rather than the separation of these elements. Like many of the students I now teach, I was often told by powerful academics that I was misguided to seek such a perspective in the academy. Throughout my student years I felt deep inner anguish. Memory of that pain returns as I listen to students express the concern that they will not succeed in academic professions if they want to be well, if they eschew dysfunctional behavior or participation in coercive hierarchies. These students are often fearful, as I was, that there are no spaces in the academy where the self-actualized can be affirmed.

This fear is present because many professors have intensely hostile responses to the vision of liberatory education that connects the will to know with the will to become. Within professional circles, individuals often complain bitterly that students want classes to be "encounter groups." While it is utterly unreasonable for students to expect classrooms to be therapy sessions, it is appropriate for them to hope that the knowledge received in these settings will enrich and enhance them.

Currently, the students I encounter seem far more uncertain about the project of self-actualization than my peers and I were twenty years ago. They feel that there are no clear ethical guidelines shaping actions. Yet, while they despair, they are also adamant that education should be liberatory. They want and demand more from professors than my generation did. There are times when I walk into classrooms overflowing with students who feel terribly wounded in their psyches (many of them see therapists), yet I do not think that they want therapy from me. They do want an education that is healing to the uninformed, unknowing spirit. They do want knowledge that is meaningful. They rightfully expect that my colleagues and I will not offer them information without addressing the connection between what they are learning and their overall life experiences.

This demand on the students' part does not mean that they will always accept our guidance. This is one of the joys of education as the practice of freedom, for it allows students to assume responsibility for their choices. Writing about our teacher/student relationship in a piece for the *Village Voice*, "How to Run the Yard: Off-Line and into the Margins at Yale," one of my students, Gary Dauphin, shares the joys of working with me as well as the tensions that surfaced between us as he began to devote his time to pledging a fraternity rather than cultivating his writing:

> People think academics like Gloria [my given name] are all about difference: but what I learned from her was mostly about sameness, about what I had in common as a black man to people of color; to women and gays and lesbians and the poor and anyone else who wanted in. I did some of this learning by reading but most of it came from hanging out on the fringes of her life. I lived like that for a while, shuttling between high points in my classes and low points outside. Gloria was a safe haven . . . Pledging a fraternity is about as far away as you can get from her classroom, from the yellow kitchen where she used to share her lunch with students in need of various forms of sustenance.

This is Gary writing about the joy. The tension arose as we discussed his reason for wanting to join a fraternity and my disdain for that decision. Gary comments, "They represented a vision of black manhood that she abhorred, one where violence and abuse were primary ciphers of bonding and identity." Describing his assertion of autonomy from my influence he writes, "But she must also have known the limits of even her influence on my life, the limits of books and teachers."

Ultimately, Gary felt that the decision he had made to join a fraternity was not constructive, that I "had taught him openness" where the fraternity had encouraged one-dimensional allegiance. Our interchange both during and after this experience was an example of engaged pedagogy.

Through critical thinking—a process he learned by reading theory and actively analyzing texts—Gary experienced education as the practice of freedom. His final comments about me: "Gloria had only mentioned the entire episode once after it was over, and this was to tell me simply that there are many kinds of choices, many kinds of logic. I could make those events mean whatever I wanted as long as I was honest." I have quoted his writing at length because it is testimony affirming engaged pedagogy. It means that my voice is not the only account of what happens in the classroom.

Engaged pedagogy necessarily values student expression. In her essay, "Interrupting the Calls for Student Voice in Liberatory Education: A Feminist

Poststructuralist Perspective," Mimi Orner employs a Foucauldian framework to suggest that

> Regulatory and punitive means and uses of the confession bring to mind curricular and pedagogical practices which call for students to publicly reveal, even confess, information about their lives and cultures in the presence of authority figures such as teachers.

When education is the practice of freedom, students are not the only ones who are asked to share, to confess. Engaged pedagogy does not seek simply to empower students. Any classroom that employs a holistic model of learning will also be a place where teachers grow, and are empowered by the process. That empowerment cannot happen if we refuse to be vulnerable while encouraging students to take risks. Professors who expect students to share confessional narratives but who are themselves unwilling to share are exercising power in a manner that could be coercive. In my classrooms, I do not expect students to take any risks that I would not take, to share in any way that I would not share. When professors bring narratives of their experiences into classroom discussions it eliminates the possibility that we can function as all-knowing, silent interrogators. It is often productive if professors take the first risk, linking confessional narratives to academic discussions so as to show how experience can illuminate and enhance our understanding of academic material. But most professors must practice being vulnerable in the classroom, being wholly present in mind, body, and spirit.

Progressive professors working to transform the curriculum so that it does not reflect biases or reinforce systems of domination are most often the individuals willing to take the risks that engaged pedagogy requires and to make their teaching practices a site of resistance. In her essay, "On Race and Voice: Challenges for Liberation Education in the 1990s," Chandra Mohanty writes that

> resistance lies in self-conscious engagement with dominant, normative discourses and representations and in the active creation of oppositional analytic and cultural spaces. Resistance that is random and isolated is clearly not as effective as that which is mobilized through systemic politicized practices of teaching and learning. Uncovering and reclaiming subjugated knowledge is one way to lay claims to alternative histories. But these knowledges need to be understood and defined pedagogically, as questions of strategy and practice as well as of scholarship, in order to transform educational institutions radically.

Professors who embrace the challenge of self-actualization will be better able to create pedagogical practices that engage students, providing them with ways of knowing that enhance their capacity to live fully and deeply.

Chapter 9

SETTING DOWN THE TRADITION

By Connie Titone and Karen E. Maloney

We began this book with a quote from Virginia Woolf about the daunting challenge that faced nineteenth-century women writers: "when they came to set their thoughts on paper . . . they had no tradition behind them, or one so short and partial that it was of little help. For we think back through our mothers if we are women" (Woolf 1929/1981, 76). Our work in this book contributes to the setting down of the very long tradition of women's ideas on education. We welcome these women with whom we share a concern for improving women's status, building a better society than the ones in which we live, and doing this in part by elevating the importance of women's traditional interests and concerns in educational settings. That tradition is actually already behind us and with us—present but often inaccessible—extant but too short and too partial in its presentation to give interested persons a clear understanding of the past and its connection to the present.

As we think through the mothers presented in this book, and begin to imagine how many more we have yet to meet, our minds can't help but race with excitement and wonder. The ideas in this volume are complex and rich; the women's ways of voicing their views, passionate, and well reasoned. How many more foremothers who had wonderful ideas about education are yet to be uncovered? Our knowledge is still so incomplete.

The Tradition

In the last two decades, scholars from several disciplines have published theories on women and their various ways of approaching life and work. Although many write within disciplines other than the philosophy of education, their insights have implications for what counts as knowledge, for how knowledge is constructed, and for understanding the long tradition of women who have argued about what is worth knowing and by whom. Carol Gilligan, Mary Belenky, Jean Baker Miller, Mary Ellen Waithe, and Gerda Lerner, to name only a few scholars, have all produced groundbreaking research and theory on women in psychology, history of philosophy, and history of intellectual thought. They have focused on issues, questions, and the value of qualities and dispositions that have traditionally been associated with the female in our societies: intuition, relational connection, tenderness, concern for the equitable education of girls and women, and mothering. They have traced these topics throughout historical periods—as in the case of Mary Ellen Waithe and Gerda Lerner—and also within the context of the individual lives of girls and women—as in the case of Carol Gilligan and Mary Belenky. Jean Baker Miller presents an opus on psychological theory growing out of her own work as a clinician. Her work shows the connection between the emotional lives of women and how they reflect the social and political system of the context in which they live.

Taken all together, these theoretical works tell an honorable and powerful story of the consistent presence of women and their realities existing concomitantly alongside the traditionally male-defined paradigms of reason and rationality. Macaulay, Gilman, and Cooper are part of this two hundred-year old tradition of naming and honoring those dispositions traditionally associated with the female, but they make a significant move in recommending that these dispositions be cherished, taught to, and demonstrated by men as well as women. Jane Roland Martin maintains this tradition today. Regardless of the telling of this story, however, and regardless of this repeated recommendation, many women's ideas and works have been minimized and/or erased from our collective memory. There have been, and clearly are, potent cultural forces working in opposition to transformation.

In the educational arena, feminist pedagogy is one creation in which theorists and practitioners attempt to delineate the reasons for, and the methods of, politicizing classroom practice for the purpose of guiding all students to develop the aforementioned qualities. Institutional controls are slow to relax and often individuals lack the skills or motivation to change. Frances Maher and Mary Kay Thompson Tetreault in *The Feminist Classroom* and Carmen Luke and Jennifer Gore in *Feminisms and Critical Pedagogy* illustrate pedagogical situations that can nurture "uneasy," tension-filled interactions in order to challenge students' assumptions and unconscious habits of thought. bell hooks understands the psychological implications of these types of interactions. In *Teaching to Transgress,* she describes her "engaged pedagogy" where "there is an aspect of our work that is sacred . . . our work is not merely to share information but to share in the intellectual and spiritual growth of our students. To teach in a manner that respects and cares for the soul of our students is essential if we are to provide the necessary conditions where learning can most deeply and intimately begin" (hooks, see Chapter 8 p.186).

Organization of the Chapter

The aim of this chapter is to point out and discuss the continuities and discontinuities among the educational theories of the seven women analyzed in this book: Catharine Macaulay, Ana Roqué de Duprey, Anna Julia Cooper, Charlotte Perkins

Gilman, Mabel McKay, Jane Roland Martin, and bell hooks. When we brought together into one volume the theories of these women, so different in time, place, race, religion, age, ethnicity, and class, we expected to see many discontinuities. We were not expecting to find, however, so many significant continuities among their thought.

Also in this chapter, we explore how each woman's position in her society might have enabled her to see dimensions and aspects of social issues or problems that had gone unrecognized as salient. We present a discussion focusing on the women's beliefs about human nature, their recommendations on pedagogy and learning, and the roles of women and education in society. The next four sections will each focus on one of the previously mentioned philosophical topics as treated in the individual woman's thought.

Beliefs about Human Nature

The work of Catharine Macaulay fits into the long tradition of philosophical inquiry but surpasses and refigures those male-defined traditions by taking a critical approach to its key concepts. For her, human nature is separate and distinct from the exhibited set of properties of women and men as observed in society. She intimates that the "essential man"—both male and female—has been created in the image of one deity that is neither male nor female, but encompasses both. This holistic deity integrates both masculine and feminine characteristics, and this wholeness was mirrored for her in the nature of the human being who had been created in the deity's image. Therefore, both men and women had the innate potential to be complete and, thus, more divine. Because her ideas were grounded on this whole, perfect base, she believed that it was possible for both the female and the male in society to transcend the bonds of social custom and the prejudice of gender limitation. Indeed, this transcendence was not only possible but required in order for the individual to attain the salvation of the soul—that which Macaulay believed to be the purpose of life.

Anna Julia Cooper's conception of human nature was also based on a Christian God, "the one ideal of perfect manhood and womanhood." By nature, the human being aspired to reach this ideal. She believed that humanity followed a "universal law of development" toward a potential of perfection and that this was the same for every Black person as had been accepted for every White person regardless of the socially constructed limitations or expectations society placed on groups of individuals. She said: "The universal law of development is onward and upward. It is God-given and inviolable. From the unfolding of the germ in the acorn to reach the sturdy oak, to the growth of a human soul into the full knowledge and likeness of its Creator, the breadth and scope of the movement in each and all are too grand, too mysterious, too like God himself, to be incompassed [sic] and locked down in human molds" (Cooper 1892/1988, 39). And specifying desires of human nature in human experience, she explains: "There is the hunger of the eye for beauty, the hunger of the ear for concords, the hungering of the mind for development and growth, of the soul for communication and love . . ." (Cooper 1892/1988, 257). Thus, Black and White, female and male, share the same essential nature. So, whereas one hundred years before, Macaulay had envisioned one human nature regardless of sex, Cooper made the same argument of one human nature regardless of race. Cooper dedicated her life to teaching and inspiring children and adults to work toward achieving their highest potential, within her overarching commitment to uplift the Black race.

Ana Roqué de Duprey shared with Positivism the view that human beings and their societies are governed by natural laws and immutable scientific principles. She believed, however, that these scientific principles and laws are created by God, and "contain in them a moral order to which all human beings are subordinate" (Padilla, see Chapter 3 p. 51). Human consciousness had to be developed. She believed that it was the human being's nature and duty to understand these laws governing individual and social progress through observation and reason, and that this understanding should naturally lead them to take action when appropriate. Like Auguste Comte, the founder of Positivism, whose work influenced her, Roqué believed that society must develop in a positive direction. The momentum behind the development was an inevitable and irreversible force moving the human being and society toward perfection. Roqué stressed the importance of moral education to direct the human being's natural forces and to reform human conduct. Her own experience and these beliefs led her to conclude that through education, individuals could learn to be free in thought and action.

Charlotte Perkins Gilman, like Roqué, believed in the possibility of human progress according to discernible natural laws. But Gilman, an atheist, did not believe these laws were God-given. She spent her life discovering the natural laws by which society evolves and convincing people to follow them. Like Macaulay, she thought that society's gender socialization had sacrificed the essence of humanness for the purposes of excessive sex-distinction. To Gilman, the natural laws of progress involved the "humanization" of society by allowing both masculine and feminine qualities into social institutions such as education. She saw this as a first step in developing both masculine and feminine qualities in each individual.

Mabel McKay saw an essential tie between humans and the sacred. For her, human beings are communal, responsible to the community, to the earth, and to each other. Rituals and ceremony provide access and reminders of the sacred, but each individual must develop his or her own relationship with, and understanding of, the sacred. In her storytelling, one of her purposes was to focus on the individual and overturn his or her implicit, often unspoken, assumptions about oneself and the world.

Though Jane Roland Martin does not speak explicitly about her concept of human nature, it is clear that for her it does encompass traditional masculine and feminine qualities. Like Macaulay, Gilman, and Cooper, Martin has a holistic perspective on human essence. She believes that the good of society is based on every individual valuing and acquiring the traits, qualities, skills, and knowledge traditionally associated with women and the home, and on school as an institution valuing and teaching these things to all children. Speaking of Jean Jacques Rousseau's two characters in his book *Émile,* she says: "Indeed it must be acknowledged that if men and women are to be complete people, regardless of their gender, they must acquire Sophie's virtues as well as Émile's—or some appropriate transformation thereof" (Martin, see Chapter 7 p. 155). She promotes the general good, remapping the public world to include all types of human knowledge and skill, including those values we honor in all cultures and in the domestic sphere. She links care, concern, and connection to the happiness of each boy and girl as well as society as a whole. She sees the nation and the world as a home, extending the concept of "domesticity" into the public world and worldwide.

bell hooks believes that the innate inclination of the human being is to be free and to become more fully human. She brings people of African ancestry from the margins of U.S. society to the center, presenting them as a vital part of our whole. She sees education as having the potential to inspire major changes in individuals through her concept of education as the practice of freedom, naming teaching as a sacred work of caring for the souls of students as the teacher aims toward their intellectual and spiritual growth.

A discontinuity among these women's ideas lies in the basis on which they build their claims about human nature. Macaulay, Roqué, Cooper, and McKay all have a spiritual basis for their beliefs, whereas Gilman, Martin, and hooks do not make such beliefs explicit in their writings. While Macaulay, Roqué, and Cooper all based their beliefs on their own version of a Christian God, McKay was led by the Spirit's voice, which spoke to her in her dreams, grounded in a Native American spirituality.

Pedagogy and Learning

Having considered the women's metaphysical beliefs and touched upon the political contexts in which they lived, it is interesting to turn directly to their views on pedagogy and learning and to notice the links between them. Each woman gives careful attention to the creation of the learning environment—whether this be a physical, public space or a student/teacher relationship.

hooks has the most detailed descriptions of a pedagogical practice that aims to encourage and support learners to engage in their own education as a practice of freedom. In her book *Teaching to Transgress* (1994), she situates her own teaching in a fundamentally political context, rooted in an historically vibrant antiracist struggle. From this philosophical commitment, hooks' work brings with it a recognition of, as well as a deep and experienced understanding of, the psychological implications of learning and teaching. She argues for the need for both teacher self-actualization and collective student engagement. She also believes that the classroom should be an exciting, never boring, place where pleasure in learning is a daily occurrence. She argues that fun and excitement in the classroom can coexist with and actually stimulate serious intellectual involvement. She stresses the need for teachers and students to act responsibly and respectfully together and to create a learning environment in which they engage critically with the subject matter, their own personal histories and experiences, and with each other to learn and grow.

Martin says that traditionally "the function of education is to transform children who have heretofore lived their lives in one place into members of another" (See Chapter 7 p. 157). She argues that education's ideology and practices are predicated on a gender-coded dichotomy of the public world and the home. Because of this she calls for a radical reconceptualization of "school." Like hooks, she focuses on the classroom climate and the teaching pedagogy for making changes. Her vision includes an environment in which school routines, rituals, and pedagogies are guided by a spirit of family-like affection, and she envisions the ideal relationship between students and teachers and among the students themselves as guided the same way. Concerning curriculum, she maintains that honoring diversity is not enough; curriculum must alsopresent the knowledge and cultural wealth of all cultures in our society. The curriculum should reveal the disciplines of knowledge as merely one part of the person's education. She urges educators to view the child as a *whole* child and implement a curriculum and pedagogy that integrates thought and action, reason and emotion, and education and life. This kind of teaching and learning would not divorce persons from their social and natural contexts. She asks all of society to bring "home" and its traditionally honored values of care, concern, and connection into schooling in a substantial and meaningful way in order to preserve domestic cultural wealth.

Gilman, whose personal aim was to change the world, focused her pedagogical suggestions on teaching and learning for the youngest children. This youth most needed what she called social nourishment in order to grow and develop. She socialized human motherhood (most notably demonstrated in her book *Herland* [1915]) and connected mothering to a rational activity in the public domain. She advocated that educators design the external environment of young children in what she called baby-gardens in order to nurture proper learning and education. In this environment, the stress would be on experience connecting knowledge and activity. She advocated a natural, "unconscious education" driven by the interests of the child and tailored to each child's abilities and needs.

Cooper experienced and advocated a rigorously classical academic education for any Black student who desired it, but she also understood that for teachers something more than book learning was required. Cooper's vision required that the Black teachers themselves be "keen about the enigma of the Universe, or even about the enigma of Mississippi and Texas" so that this "flaming torch" might light the minds and hearts of their students (Cooper 1930, 393). She bemoaned the "dry-as-dust abstractions and mental gymnastics embalmed in an outworn college curriculum that have no discoverable connection with the practical life interest of the student" (Cooper 1930, 387).

McKay's method of teaching is traditional "Pomo" oral storytelling. From the voice she hears in her dreams, McKay gains access to the sacred. McKay shares her knowledge by telling stories whose purpose it is to serve as a catalyst for listeners to gain their own insight and understanding. By overturning people's implicit, unspoken assumptions, she forces the listener's mind to rethink and to question his or her own thought processes. Storytelling creates a relationship, and the good listener "will change the story, co-create the story as they listen and then innovate for the next listeners". From this expectation, we see a "tribal understanding of knowledge as contextual, inseparable from experience, and implicit in sacred/everyday life" (Bredin, see Chapter 6 p. 139). Shared reality becomes visible, and critical and creative thinking are fostered. All of this is embedded in what Bredin calls the "affective elements" of life, which include artistic and mythical dimensions, ritual and ceremony, sacred ecology, and spiritual orientations.

Macaulay advocates a coeducational education that not only opens to girls the education that boys had been receiving but also would alter boys' education to include domestic skills such as learning to sew and to express traditionally "feminine" qualities such as sympathy and benevolence. A rigorous academic education was stressed for both, with formal education to begin at the age of twelve. Reading the Bible would not commence until the student reached the age of twenty-one, to allow the student to judge the text with precision. Throughout the period of formal education, discipline was to be applied (even corporal punishment) with kindness and tenderness. The qualities of the teacher were extremely critical for the successful implementation of Macaulay's ideas. Her ideal teacher would be expected to demonstrate a combination of virtues of understanding and learning with virtues of the heart. She criticized the practice of giving each child a material reward as motivation for being virtuous. For Macaulay, the mere act of being virtuous should, and indeed did, carry its own reward.

A second discontinuity in their ideas of pedagogy and learning is apparent in our discussion of their pedagogies. Macaulay, Cooper, and Roqué all assume a traditional, classical form of education centered around the disciplines, taking the form of lectures, readings, and so forth. Gilman, McKay, Martin, and hooks do not share completely in this traditional image of pedagogy. McKay espouses indigenous tribal educational practices, which she modeled throughout her life. Her idea of pedagogy is centered around the individual in the storyteller/listener relationship, with the listener responsible to make meaning out of the stories as they apply to his or her life. Gilman advocates a child-centered, experiential pedagogy that is individualized for each child according to that child's own interests and abilities. hooks and Martin both have a pedagogical vision that synthesizes traditional discipline-based education with an experiential, individualized curriculum. Both Martin and hooks advocate a holistic type of education. Martin writes:

> I . . . ask that we educate all our children in our whole heritage so that they will learn to live in the world together. Because that whole heritage includes ways of living as well as forms of knowing, societal activities and practices as well as literary and artistic achievement, we need more than a curriculum that honors diversity. We need a new curricular paradigm: one that does not ignore the disciplines of knowledge, but reveals their proper place in the general scheme of things as but one part of a person's education; one that integrates thought and action, reason and emotion, education and life; one that does not divorce persons from their social and natural contexts; one that embraces individual autonomy as but one of many values. (See Chapter 7 p. 163)

hooks says that her pedagogical practices "emerged from the mutually illuminating interplay of anticolonial, critical, and feminist pedagogies" (see Chapter 8 p. 184).

hooks calls these practices "engaged pedagogy" and describes it as "holistic," aiming toward the well-being of the individual student. In her teaching, hooks aims at "integrating theory and practice, ways of knowing with habits of being" (hooks 1994, 43).

The Role of Women in Society and the Education of Girls and Women

Many of the women in this book thought deeply and carefully about the difference between masculine and feminine qualities and virtues and what this meant for the social and intellectual education of girls and boys. Macaulay recognized that what seemed to be essential differences between men and women were actually social products. She believed that the character of our species is formed from the influence of education. Although Macaulay did not maintain that any traits belonged naturally to either men or women, she acknowledged throughout her work that girls and boys were socialized differently by the world around them, which restricted their abilities to express all of their natural qualities. She argued for girls and boys to be taught together and to be given an education that would enable both males and females to develop all their natural qualities.

Gilman also understood that what society viewed as naturally male and female traits were actually products of socialization. Gilman wanted to see both the masculine and the feminine influence in all social institutions, from the public world of business and commerce to the private world of raising children and housework. She believed that masculine and feminine qualities must be balanced in social institutions such as education at the same time that education is developing these qualities in each person. This is why she called herself a "humanist" rather than a feminist—because she wanted education to develop the full range of human qualities in both men and women so that all of us would be more fully human as individuals and as a society. She argued for equal education for women so that they could develop all human qualities, just as she argued that men be educated to develop all human qualities, including those traditionally associated with women.

Martin goes much further in her understanding of masculine and feminine traits and what is needed to develop them in all of us. By the time Martin writes in the late 1980s, scholars have developed and elaborated the concept of gender and gender socialization, the kernel of which is found in the works of Macaulay and Gilman. Martin recognizes that it is not enough to bring the feminine qualities into education, we must deal with the reality that these qualities are genderized in that they are "evaluated positively in females but negatively in males" (see Chapter 7 p. 155). Thus, it is not enough to teach them equally when we live in a world that values them differently. Instead, she argues for a "gender-sensitive ideal" in education that would address the differential valuing of genderized traits in both males and females. Whereas Gilman wanted to bring the traditionally masculine traits of rationality and technical skill to bear on the traditionally feminine sphere of home and family, and move its duties out of the private world into the public world, Martin wants to bring the domestic sphere, with its emotional knowledge, skills, character traits, and "cultural wealth" into the school as an essential part of education. She wants to explode the distinction between public and private in terms of the cultural wealth that the home has traditionally been entrusted with maintaining and transmitting to the next generation.

bell hooks adds a race and class analysis of the differential valuing of traits and behaviors to Martin's understanding of the differential valuing based on gender. From hooks' work we see that among women, traits and behaviors are differentially valued according to the woman's race and class. This adds another layer of complexity to our understanding of the ways in which gender, race, and class relations structure our concepts and our actions. hooks adds a sophisticated analysis of power differentials and a deep understanding of the resistance by students and social institutions to attempts to equalize power among groups and individuals in our society. The psychological impact that these changes have on both students and teachers is a central consideration in her work.

By following the development of these women's ideas in this way we see that our understanding of gender and genderized traits has progressed in the past two hundred years. Macaulay saw how wrong and negative such gender socialization was, and she wanted to use a transformed education to eradicate the effects of society's false beliefs about gender in the individual. Gilman saw that masculine and feminine traits needed to be equally present in social institutions such as education as well as developed in each individual. Martin adds the dimension of the differential valuing of traits according to gender and argues that this dimension must be addressed as well before it will be possible to make traditionally masculine and feminine traits equally valued and equally present in society and each individual. hooks adds an analysis of race, class, and power differentials to further complexify and clarify the problem of this transformation of society.

Roqué and Cooper have a different view on masculine and feminine qualities and the role of women in society. Roqué based her argument for women's right to vote and be involved in politics in Puerto Rico on a particular aspect of their femaleness: their role as mothers. She generalized the maternal role from being a mother in private to being a mother in the public world; from being responsible for her private home to being responsible for her homeland (see Chapter 3 p. 60). As Garcia Padilla states, "Although she did not question the common assumption that women are naturally inclined toward motherhood . . . she redefined and broadened that role" (see Chapter 3 p. 61). According to Gerda Lerner, this move of authorizing women's involvement in politics by basing it on women's common experience as mothers was typically used in Europe and the United States well into the twentieth century (1993, 137). Roqué wanted all women to assume their responsibility for being mothers to all children and for the extended homeland of Puerto Rico (see Chapter 3 p. 62). In this sense she was much more of a traditionalist than her predecessor Macaulay and her contemporary Gilman in her ideas of women's role in society, because she based it, at least in part, on their role and duties as mothers.

Cooper's writings indicate that she, too, based many of her arguments for educating women—particularly Black women, the subject of her writings—on their traditional role of wife and mother. Cooper often referred to the common view of her day that women and men were complementary—the very view that Macaulay had argued against one hundred fifty years earlier. Cooper maintained that the world had been dominated by the masculine influence and that "women's educated voice and unique influence" was necessary to give "symmetry" to society. She writes: "the civilized world has been like a child brought up by his father. It has needed the great mother heart to teach it to be pitiful, to love mercy, to succor the weak and care for the lowly" (Cooper 1892/1988, 51). Each sex must be educated to exert its influence on the world, she wrote, "related not as inferior and superior . . . but as complements in one necessary and symmetric whole" (Cooper 1892/1988, 60). In fact, Cooper uses the metaphor of a chord of music, describing how the chord is incomplete without the "soprano obligato" that the Black woman brings to the music of our country (Cooper 1892/1988, i). But Cooper consistently argues that it is the *educated* Black woman whose voice needs to be heard, whose influence must be felt in order to achieve the regeneration of the Black race after the devastations of slavery, which was her ultimate goal. In this way she argued that Black women's uplift was essential to the uplift of the entire race. Cooper adds an understanding of the convergence of racism and sexism that affected Black women. In her own life experience, Cooper not only received no support but actually encountered active discouragement in her pursuit of higher education—because she was a woman. She understood how Black women had an even greater struggle than White women because they had to convince White women that, as women, the education of Black women was just as imperative as the education of White women to the progress of women. At the same time, Black women had to convince Black men that, as Blacks, the education of Black women was just as imperative as the education of Black men to the social progress of the Black race.

McKay lived a life that indicates her freedom from traditional Western, White conceptions of gender roles. She was a great Pomo healer and Dreamer, a gift that gave her access to the sacred. She used this gift, and the authority it conferred on her, in her tribal communities as she felt was best. She was a daughter, wife, and mother, but her life did not seem to be prescribed by these roles. She was able to expand within them and around them as she discerned what the Spirit wanted.

A third discontinuity emerges in how these women understand or acknowledge race, gender, and class differences. Although Macaulay mentioned her disbelief that any race was innately superior or inferior, she focused on gender differences almost exclusively in *Letters on Education*; Roqué saw class differences in the lack of autonomy and colonization that Puerto Rico experienced under both Spanish and U.S. rule; Cooper saw clearly both race and gender as fundamental points of discrimination. In terms of class, her writings indicate that she was very aware of class distinctions, both within White and Black societies in her time. However, she did not challenge such distinctions, although she did argue that the individual—in terms of talent, potential, and interest—should be a primary factor in developing educational programs for Blacks of different classes. Gilman was aware of class differences but seemed to believe that her educational theory would eliminate them as all occupations became valued because they contributed to the betterment of society. However, she had the same flaws as other White, upper-class women of her day in holding the classist, racist, and xenophobic beliefs of her social group. Gilman saw so clearly the damaging effects of uncritical adherence to social mores and beliefs when it came to men and women; sadly, she was not able to extend this formidable insight to other beliefs that were just as mistaken. McKay never explicitly refers to class issues as such, but she does have a very well-developed sense of the different life chances open to her people, other working people, and more privileged Whites. She understood how racist assumptions played a role in different communities in which she lived during her long life. Martin explicitly identifies the ability to live constructively in a truly multicultural world as a primary goal of her educational philosophy. The integrative activities she advocates in her pedagogical theory, she believes, will "weave young people of different races, classes, ethnicities, physical abilities, sexual orientations into their own web of connection" (Martin, see Chapter 7 p. 164). In this collection, hooks has by far the clearest, deepest, and sharpest analysis of race, class, and gender relations, and their structural and personal intersections. She has spent a good part of her writing life analyzing and discussing these issues, and she also shares with us how she deals with these complex issues in the classroom.

The Role of Education in Society

These women viewed education as an essential means of social change. Macaulay identified the educational arena—rather than the family, legal system, or church—as the critical context for addressing and changing beliefs and behaviors. She describes how it is the formal educational process that shapes the human being. In Macaulay's time, education was carried out by individual parents. There was no compulsory schooling for either boys or girls, and no standardized curriculum. Macaulay thought that the education of all children was much too important to be left to individual parents who had varying interests in the task and varying resources to accomplish it. She believed that the government should become involved in standardizing the process of educating children so that all children would benefit from a similar curriculum and instruction in knowledge, skills, and morals, which would ultimately benefit society. Macaulay had spent many years of her life studying the social and political history of England and publishing her multi-volume *History of England.* Later in her life, when she wrote *Letters on Education,* she understood how important education was to any project to change society.

Roqué's primary goal was what she called her "civilization project" for Puerto Rico. She was passionately devoted to the progress of her home island. She believed that schools, and education in general, were the main avenues of her civilization project for three reasons: education disseminates knowledge, cultivates reason, and initiates children from all social classes into what they need to know in life. Roqué believed that cultivating reason was especially important, since her thought was shaped within the Positivist tradition, which held that society developed according to natural laws that could be discerned by reason. Roqué saw schools as the central loci for civilization, and teachers as the primary civilization agents. So teacher education was a main concern of hers.

Gilman also saw education as the central force for social progress. Like Roqué, Gilman believed that society was governed by natural laws that could be discerned by reason and that society would progress once people were helped to understand these laws and to follow them. McKay's view of education is rather different in that she did not think of education as an isolated social institution in the same way. Rather, she saw education as a learning about life that happened every day and all day. She herself learned in various ways—from the Spirit in her dreams, from her grandmother, from her neighbors, the Sulphur Bank women. She shared what she learned through her stories, her healings, and her life. Her stories show that she saw learning about oneself and one's place in life as a central task of life.

Martin sees education as the means of "remapping the public world." Her vision of the schoolhome integrates thought and feeling, traits and skills genderized as masculine and feminine, mind and body, public and private, reason and emotion, education and life—many of the primary dualisms of Western thought. She believes that this type of curriculum is essential for creating a better world, a truly inclusive, multidimensional, multicultural world, in which children are helped to develop into "constructive, contributing members of culture and society, into individuals who want to live in a world composed of people very different from themselves and who have practiced doing so" (Martin, see Chapter 7 p. 165).

hooks comes from a background in which education was understood to be fundamentally political and rooted in antiracist struggle. Like Paulo Freire, noted Brazilian philosopher and educator, whose work strongly influenced hooks' ideas, she understands how central education is to changing society. hooks' conception of education as the practice of freedom means that each student is actively engaged in learning, along with the "teacher," and that every individual is respected and valued. She develops her idea of the classroom as a community that can have radical transformative potential. It emphasizes wholeness and well-being. It requires that teachers be actively committed to a process of self-actualization that promotes their own well-being so that they are able to create the classroom climate necessary to empower their students. It joins mind and body, thought and feeling, reason and emotion, individual history and theory.

Conclusion

Thinking Through Our Mothers

Catharine Macaulay, Ana Roqué de Duprey, Anna Julia Cooper, Charlotte Perkins Gilman, Mabel McKay, Jane Roland Martin, and bell hooks were all driven to challenge the existing paradigms about education and to develop new understandings about education. In this sense, they were pioneers. What propelled these women? Certainly it was not society, role models, teachers, or social expectations. In fact, in most cases these actively discouraged these women from developing their ideas. In our opinion, they all had a commitment to a great value in their life that pushed them to develop their theories and advocate changes in education. Macaulay was committed to her spiritual beliefs in the Divine as holistic and in human nature as progressing toward the Divine. Her educational theory makes the connection between that belief and her theory explicit. Roqué's lifelong commitment was to the progress of Puerto Rico toward self-governance and autonomy. She believed that Puerto Rican women had an essential role to play in this progress and that education was the central social institution through which such progress could be made. Cooper's deep commitment was to the uplift of the Black race, and she saw the education of Black women as essential to this goal. At seventeen Gilman set for herself the goal "to help humanity," from which she never wavered. Her insights into women's place in society and the damage that the Victorian notion of separate spheres produces in society led her to argue for the necessity of bringing the traits and qualities traditionally associated with women into all social institutions in order to enable both sexes to develop "masculine" and "feminine" qualities and thus become more fully human. McKay led her life deeply committed to be true to the Spirit within her and to communicating to others what it taught her through indigenous educational practices such as storytelling. Martin's commitment grows out of her realization that bringing women and the traits and qualities traditionally associated with them into the educational realm has the power to transform not only our concepts about education, but also society as a whole. hooks is committed to transforming society to heal the divisions along gender, race, and class lines. She sees education as the practice of freedom as the way she can personally work toward this goal as a teacher, creating, with her students, communities of respect and critical engagement with the subject matter.

In her essay, "Theory as Liberatory Practice," hooks describes the pain of what it is like to live in a world that you believe is wrong, unjust, and unfair. She found theory to be the way to heal that pain:

> I came to theory because I was hurting. . . . I came to theory desperate, wanting to comprehend—to grasp what was happening around and within me . . .
>
> I found a place of sanctuary in "theorizing," in making sense out of what was happening. I found a place where I could imagine possible futures, a place where life could be lived differently. This "lived" experience of critical thinking, of reflection and analysis, [became] a place where I worked at explaining the hurt and making it go away. Fundamentally, I learned from this experience that theory could be a healing place. (hooks 1994, 59–61)

It seems to us that each of the "intellectual mothers" portrayed in this book came to theory in much the same way. They lived in worlds that they experienced as unjust in very significant ways, and they sought remedies through education. Each used her experience, background, and the historical moment in which she lived. Each sought a deeper sense of being human in order to liberate herself and others from oppressive social restrictions.

In trying to understand and correct our injustices, it helps to think through these mothers. Yes, it may complicate our responses, but it surely adds a richness to our thoughts that we lacked before. It gives us a more accurate, more inclusive picture of the world. As we engage with the ideas and stories of these "intellectual mothers," we become part of the story, and their stories become a living thing, a storytelling that lives on in each of us. We shouldn't be the same people after engaging with these stories. We might even recognize our own internal paradigm shift as to how we perceive education and women's place in education. This is a sort of "pedagogical gift to be unpacked" as we use their thoughts to inform our thoughts about contemporary issues in education, making their thoughts our own. In this way, thinking through our mothers broadens and extends our collective educational lineage.

In her concluding chapter to *Reclaiming a Conversation*, Martin shows us how the traditional Western idea of cumulative theory development is false. Rather than thinking of successive theorists as each seeing farther than those before under some sort of model of linear progress, Martin explains, educational theorists over the centuries have seen differently from one another. This collection of women's philosophies of education most certainly illustrates this point. The intellectual mothers with whom we have engaged in this volume have seen different aspects of education and various roles of women in society. Partly due to their own histories and backgrounds, they have studied the educational landscape and observed different features. Macaulay saw the potential for developing integrated people with both masculine and feminine qualities who would better represent the Divine in the world; Roqué saw the possibility of advancing Puerto Rico toward self-governance; Cooper saw the place that both race and sex discrimination played in hindering the advancement of Blacks after the Civil War; Gilman saw how women and young children were treated so unfairly because they were seen in individualistic terms rather than in social terms as groups; Martin saw how the entire educational landscape, and the social world itself, can be transformed by including women and the knowledge and skills traditionally associated with them; hooks saw how education as the practice of freedom can transform our understandings and behavior and enable us to develop authentic communities of mutual respect across class, gender, and racial lines.

Just as these "intellectual mothers" observed different features in the educational landscape, they used different lenses as well. Roqué, Cooper, and Gilman all use a wide focus, placing more emphasis on the social nature of education and change than on the individual. Macaulay, Martin, and hooks use a double lens, looking both at the social and the individual dimensions of this type of educational change. McKay focuses more on the individual and that person's growth and development. Through storytelling, McKay invites her listeners to join with her in understanding themselves, their world, her, and their place in their world. The listeners (read: students) must actively engage in this process, they must derive the meaning of these stories for themselves, and from themselves. As Greg Sarris describes his growing understanding of McKay's pedagogy after years of listening to her stories, asking questions, and repeating stories:

> I sat back in my chair. I felt my feet on the ground. I saw clearly. Things came together. It wasn't just her story she had wanted me to know. While trying to help her, while trying to trace her story, I traced my own. . . . Her story, the story, our story. Like the tiny basket

in my shirt pocket, different threads, sedge and redbud, woven over
one willow rod into a design that went round and round, endless.
(Sarris 1994, 164–65)

These women all represent different threads, reaching across time, culture, class, and place, all woven round and round, endless. We know that there are many more women, many more threads, yet to be discovered. Our purpose in this book was to inform readers about the existence of a number of women, of various times, cultures, and classes, who over the course of U.S. history have thought systematically about U.S. education and have had important things to say about its purposes, its theories, and its practices. With access to this broader range and depth of information, we hope that students of the philosophy of education and women's studies will embrace this more inclusive view of the scope of thought on educational issues as they begin to form their own answers to the essential questions about education. Now that we can "think through these mothers," we can decide exactly what they mean to us individually and collectively, personally and professionally. Their stories, our story, the story—these stories are about us all.

References

Cooper, A. J. [1892] 1988. *A Voice from the South.* Reprint. New York: Oxford University Press.
_____ . 1930. Humor of Teaching. *The Crisis* (November): 387–94.
hooks, b. 1994. *Teaching to Transgress: Education as the Practice of Freedom.* New York: Routledge, Inc.
Lerner, G. 1993. *The Creation of Feminist Consciousness: From the Middle Ages to 1870.* Oxford: Oxford University Press.
Martin, J. R. 1995. *Reclaiming a Conversation: The Ideal of the Educated Woman.* New Haven, CT: Yale University Press.
Sarris, G. 1994. *Mabel McKay: Weaving the Dream.* Berkeley: University of California Press.
Woolf, V. [1929] 1981. *A Room of One's Own.* Reprint. New York: Harcourt Brace & Company.

INDEX